The Adventure Guide
to the

DOMINICAN REPUBLIC

The Adventure Guide
to the

DOMINICAN REPUBLIC

Harry S. Pariser

HUNTER
PUBLISHING INC

Hunter Publishing, Inc.
300 Raritan Center Parkway
Edison NJ 08818
(908) 225 1900
Fax (908) 417 0482

ISBN 1-55650-629-5

2nd Edition © 1995 Hunter Publishing, Inc.

Maps pages 3, 5, 102, 107, 180, 198 by Joyce Huber
All others by Kim André

Cover: *Punta Cana* (Superstock)
All other photographs by author, except where indicated.

Books by Harry S. Pariser from Hunter Publishing:

Jamaica: A Visitor's Guide (ISBN 1-55650-536-1)
Adventure Guide to Barbados (ISBN 1-55650-277-X)
Adventure Guide to Costa Rica (ISBN 1-55650-598-1)
Adventure Guide to Puerto Rico (ISBN 1-55650-628-7)
Adventure Guide to the Virgin Islands (ISBN 1-55650-597-3)
Adventure Guide to Belize (ISBN 1-55650-647-3)
Adventure Guide to the Dominican Republic (ISBN 1-55650-629-5)

Acknowledgments

Thanks go out to Michael Hunter and his staff, mapmakers Joyce Huber and Kim André, and a very special thanks to Angie Jimenez, and J.J. O'Connell for their suggestions on the manuscript. Thanks also to Marisol Ortiz, Jim Buehler, Joanne Peterson, Ramon Ortiz, informative Michael Ruge, Michael Reyes, Sjaiak Broers, Marie-Antoinette Piguet, Marlene Fretz, Sonia de Ginebra, Lise Pineau, Dr. Leonel Fernández, Pamela Graham, and to all of the Dominicans who were so friendly and open despite their adverse circumstances. A final thank you goes out to my mother who always worries about me.

Abbreviations

Av – avenida (avenue)
D$ – Dominican *peso* (US$1=D$12.50)
C – centigrade
C. – century or *calle* (street)
d – double
E – east, eastern
ha – hectare
Hwy. – highway
Km, km – kilometer (s)
L – left
m – meter
mi – miles
min. – minutes
N – north, northern
no. – number
OAS – Organization of American States
OW – one way
pp – per person
pn – per night
R – right
RT – round trip
s – single
S – south, southern
W – west, western

Contents

INTRODUCTION 1
The Land 1
Climate 6
Flora 8
Fauna 9
History 18
Government 37
Economy 39
Agriculture 45
The People 48
  Los Dominicanos/The Dominicans 49
Religion 55
  Catholicism 56
  Other Denominations 58
Language 58
Arts And Crafts 59
  Music And Dance 60
Festivals And Events 61
Food 67
  Fruit 70
  Drinks 71
  Dining Practicalities 72
Sports And Recreation 74
  Water Sports 74
  Other Sports 76
Practicalities 77
  Arrival 78
  Internal Transport 80
  Accommodations 83
  Visas, Services, and Health 85
  Money and Shopping 89
  Conduct 93
Other Practicalities 97
  What to Take 98
SANTO DOMINGO 101
  Old Santo Domingo Sights 105
  Metropolitan Santo Domingo Sights 113
Citywide Practicalities 121
  Santo Domingo Hotels 121
  Santo Domingo Dining and Food 125
  Santo Domingo Entertainment 130

Santo Domingo Shopping	134
From Santo Domingo	141
THE SOUTHWEST	**145**
San Cristóbal	145
Baní	147
Azua	147
Barahona	149
Parks of the Southwest	151
Reserva Científica Natural Laguna De Rincón	151
Parque Nacional Sierra De Bahoruco	151
Laguna Enriquillo Y Parque Nacional Isla Cabritos	152
Parque Nacional Jaragua	153
Onward to Haiti	154
THE CORDILLERA CENTRAL REGION	**155**
Bonao	155
La Vega	156
Jarabacoa	157
Constanza	159
Aguas Blancas	161
Reserva Científica Valle Nuevo	161
Parque Nacional Armando Bermúdez & Parque Nacional José del Carmen Ramírez	162
Pico Duarte	163
THE CIBAO	**165**
Santiago de los Treinta Caballeros	165
Vicinity of Santiago	171
PUERTO PLATA AND THE NORTH	**173**
Puerto Plata	173
Puerto Plata Accommodations	176
Food	183
Heading West From Puerto Plata	188
Sosúa	191
Vicinity of Sosúa	199
SAMANA PENINSULA	**207**
Santa Bárbara de Samaná	209
Vicinity of Santa Bárbara de Samaná	212
Las Terrenas	214
THE SOUTHEAST	**221**
Parque Nacional Los Haitises	221
Higüey	223
Costa Del Coco	224
The Rest of the South	225

THE EAST   **227**
La Romana   227
  Vicinity of La Romana   228
  Altos de Chavón   228
Boca de Yuma   229
Isla de Catalina   230
Bayahibe   230
Parque Nacional Del Este   230
San Pedro De Macorís   231
The Costa Caribe   233
  Boca Chica   233
  Juan Dolio   237
  Parque Nacional Submarino La Caleta   238
Spanish Vocabulary   239
Booklist   245

List of Maps

The Caribbean   2
Hispaniola Land Features   4
The Dominican Republic   5
Parks and Reserves   7
Metropolitan Santo Domingo   102
Old Santo Domingo   107
La Fortaleza   109
Cultural Plaza   114
Southwestern Dominican Republic   148
Central Santiago   166
North Coast   173
Puerto Plata   180
Sosúa   192
Río San Juan   203
Samaná Peninsula   207
Santa Barbara de Samaná   208
Las Terrenas   213
Southeastern Dominican Republic   222
Boca Chica   234

About the Author

Harry S. Pariser was born in Pittsburgh and grew up in a small town in southwestern Pennsylvania. After graduating from Boston University in 1975, Harry hitched and camped his way through Europe, traveled down the Nile by steamer, and by train through Sudan. After visiting Uganda, Rwanda, and Tanzania, he traveled by passenger ship from Mombasa to Bombay, and then on through Asia before settling down in Kyoto, Japan, where he studied Japanese and ceramics. Using Japan as a base, he trekked to the vicinity of Mt. Everest in Nepal, taking tramp steamers to remote Indonesian islands like Adonara, Timor, Sulawesi, and Ternate, and visiting rural parts of China. He returned to the US in 1984, via the Caribbean, where he researched two travel guides: *Guide to Jamaica* and *Guide to Puerto Rico and the Virgin Islands*, the first editions of which were published in 1986. Returning to Japan in 1986, he lived in the city of Kagoshima at the southern tip of Kyushu. During that year and part of the next, he taught English and wrote for *The Japan Times*. He currently lives in San Francisco. Besides traveling and writing, his other pursuits include printmaking, painting, cooking, backpacking, and listening to music – especially jazz, salsa, and African pop.

A Note on Prices

For the reader's convenience, room rates are listed in US dollars (generally inclusive of 23% tax and 10% service where applicable). Throughout the text, unless otherwise indicated, $ prices refer to US dollars.

Hotel rates are subject to fluctuation and should be used only as a guideline. Wherever you go, there are likely to be one or more newer places not listed in this guide. Local hotels usually charge on a per-room basis. Tourist-oriented hotels normally price singles at the same rate or only slightly less than doubles. Establishments for which no prices are listed are classified as follows: **low budget** ($2-10), **inexpensive** ($11-30), **moderate** ($31-50), **expensive** ($51-80), and **luxury** (over $80). Listing of a hotel does not necessarily constitute a recommendation.

We Love to Get Mail!

In today's world, things change so rapidly that it's impossible to keep up with everything that's happening in any one place. Travel books are like automobiles: they require fine tuning and frequent overhauls if they are to stay in top condition. We need input from readers so that we can continue to provide the best, most current information available. Please write to let us know about any inaccuracies, new information, or misleading suggestions. Although we try to make our maps as accurate as possible, errors can occur. If you have suggestions for improvement or places that should be included, please let us know.

We especially appreciate letters from female travelers, local residents, and hikers and outdoor enthusiasts. We also like hearing from experts in the field as well as from local hotel owners and individuals wishing to accommodate visitors from abroad. Send your comments to Harry S. Pariser, c/o Hunter Publishing, 300 Raritan Center Parkway, Edison NJ 08818. Fax 908 417 0482.

Reader's Response Form

The Adventure Guide to Dominican Republic

I found your book:

Your book could be improved by:

The best places I stayed in were (explain why):

I found the best food at:

Some good and bad experiences I had were:

Will you return to the Dominican Republic?   If so, where do
you plan to go?

If not, why not?

I purchased this book at:

Please include any other comments on a separate sheet and mail
completed form to Harry S. Pariser c/o Hunter Publishing, 300
Raritan Center Parkway, Edison, NJ 08818 USA.

Oldest known illustration of the discovery of Hispaniola.

Introduction

Known for its old Spanish ruins, palm-lined beaches, and baseball players, the Dominican Republic is the second largest nation (after Cuba) in the Caribbean Sea. Only slightly larger than Vermont and New Hampshire combined, the country is divided into three diverse regions by its five mountain ranges. Still, it is small enough that nearly every point is readily accessible by vehicle. Although parts of the country have been developed for the mass tourist market, much remains untouched, unspoiled, and virtually unvisited. The Dominican Republic offers the highest mountain in the Caribbean, the authentic Spanish atmosphere of Old Santo Domingo, the vast plains of sugarcane surrounding La Romana, deserted coasts and white sand beaches, and a very Latin lifestyle.

The Land

Because the Dominican Republic's location has served as a "gateway" to Central America and the Panama Canal as well as to the northernmost nations of South America, it has been a center of conflict from the time when the Spanish, French, and English fought to control Hispaniola through to the American economic and military interventions of the 20th C.

GEOGRAPHY: Covering the eastern two-thirds of Hispaniola, the island it shares with Haiti, the Dominican Republic lies 600 miles (1,000 km) SE of Florida and is separated from Puerto Rico to the E by the 68-mile-wide (110 km) Mona Passage. One of the world's most geographically diverse nations for its size, its 19,386 sq miles (50,210 sq km) comprise more than 20 distinct geographic regions with a remarkable variety of scenery: everything from lush tropical jungle to semi-arid deserts to some of the most agriculturally-productive land in the entire Caribbean.

LOWLANDS AND VALLEYS: Agriculture and animal husbandry flourish in the fertile alluvial soils of the country's lowlands. The Valle de Cibao, which covers 2,000 sq miles or 10% of the national territory, is the most fertile and extensive. It stretches some 140 miles from Samaná Bay to the Haitian frontier, then continues in

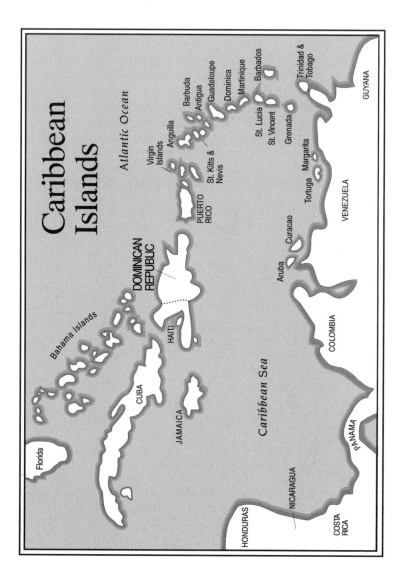

Caribbean Islands

Atlantic Ocean

Florida

Bahama Islands

CUBA

JAMAICA

HAITI

DOMINICAN REPUBLIC

PUERTO RICO

Virgin Islands

Anguilla

St. Kitts & Nevis

Barbuda

Antigua

Guadeloupe

Dominica

Martinique

St. Lucia

Barbados

St. Vincent

Grenada

Margarita

Tortuga

Trinidad & Tobago

GUYANA

VENEZUELA

Curaçao

Aruba

COLOMBIA

Caribbean Sea

PANAMA

COSTA RICA

NICARAGUA

HONDURAS

Haiti as the Northern Plain. Its E portion is known as the Vega Real (Royal Plain), appropriately named because it contains some of the most productive agricultural land. The 650-sq-mile (1,800 sq km) Valle de San Juan lies to the S. It extends into Haiti as the Central Plateau. The other major valley, the Neiba or Hoya de Enriquillo, comprises 710 sq miles (1,839 sq km) of semi-arid to arid land at below sea level elevations. Largest of the other lowland regions is the Llanura Costera del Caribe (Caribbean Coastal Plain) to the N which covers more than 1,100 sq miles (2,900 sq km) and is the center of cattle-raising and sugar production. There are also a number of other small valleys and basins including the Los Haitises, a national park.

RIVERS AND LAKES: For the most part the rivers are shallow. The Valle de Cibao contains the 399-km Yaque del Norte, the longest river, as well as the 185-km Yuna. The Valle de San Juan, S of the Cordillera Central, is drained by a tributary of the Artibonito and, to the SE, by the Yaque del Sur. Among the numerous rivers to the E are the 87-km Río Ozama, which cuts through Santo Domingo, as well as the Río Macorís to the E. Lago Enriquillo, in the Valle de Neiba, is the largest natural lake and has the lowest elevation of any point in the Caribbean islands; there are a number of smaller lagoons. Artificial lakes have been created by the construction of dams on the Río Yaque del Norte at Tavera and on the Nizao at Valdesia. Of the many islands located off the coast, only three are inhabited: Isla Saona, the largest, off the SE tip; Isla Beata, off Península de Pedernales near the Haitian border; and tiny Isla Catalina, a few miles SW of La Romana.

MOUNTAINS: Four parallel mountain ranges dominate the nation's rough terrain, traversing it from the NW to the E where they are crossed by a single range of low mountains. These largely unpopulated ranges divide the country and separate the capital city of Santo Domingo from the rich agricultural Valle de Cibao and the N coast. The main range is the Cordillera Central, extending from Santo Domingo NW into Haiti, where it becomes the Massif du Nord. Its ridges crest at 4,921-8,202 ft (1,500-2,500 m) and contain Pico Duarte (10,417 ft, 3,175 m), and Pico La Pelona (10,393 ft, 3,168 m) the Caribbean's highest peaks. Taken together with its Haitian extension, the range makes up a third of the Hispaniolan landmass. Flanked along the N coast by the Cordillera Septentrional – a range rising from the W near Monte Cristi, the Cordillera Central is bordered on the S by the Sierra de Neiba. The E portion of the latter is separated from the similar range of Sierra de Martin

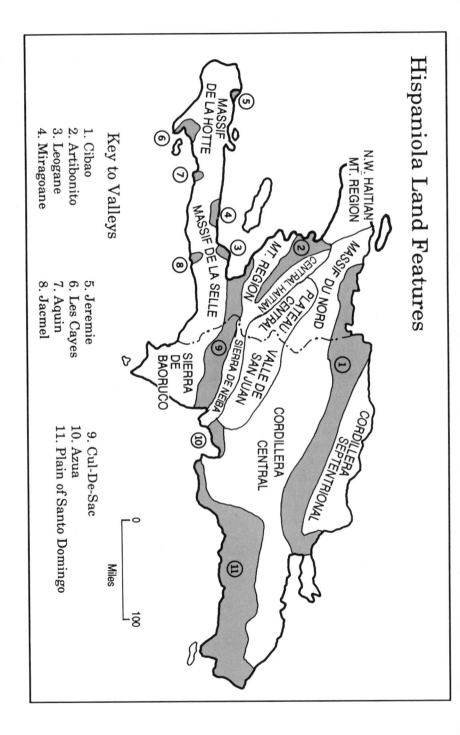

Hispaniola Land Features

Key to Valleys

1. Cibao
2. Artibonito
3. Leogane
4. Miragoane

5. Jeremie
6. Les Cayes
7. Aquin
8. Jacmel

9. Cul-De-Sac
10. Azua
11. Plain of Santo Domingo

N.W. HAITIAN MT. REGION

MASSIF DE LA HOTTE

MASSIF DE LA SELLE

MT. REGION

CENTRAL HAITIAN MT. REGION

PLATEAU CENTRAL

MASSIF DU NORD

CORDILLERA SEPTENTRIONAL

VALLE DE SAN JUAN

CORDILLERA CENTRAL

SIERRA DE NEIBA

SIERRA DE BAORUCO

Miles

0   100

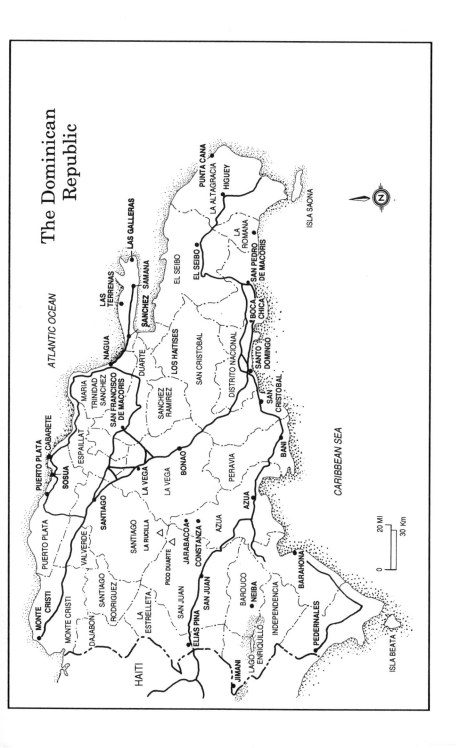

The Dominican Republic

Garcia on Samaná Peninsula by the swamps surrounding the mouth of the Río Yuna. Still farther S, the Sierra de Baoruco extends from Haiti while the Cordillera Oriental forms a minor chain to the E. The latter is more of a narrow band of hills extending from the Cordillera Central than a proper mountain range.

Climate

As holds true for the rest of the Caribbean, the Dominican Republic has a delightful climate. Its mild, subtropical weather varies little throughout the year with most of the variation in temperatures coming from differences in elevation. The coolest spots are in the Cordillera Central while the coastal extremities are warmest. There is little seasonal change, and temperatures vary from 64° to 90°F (18° to 32°C). The temperature falls to 68°F (20°C) only in Dec. Humidity is frequently stiflingly high.

RAINFALL: The rainy season runs from May to Nov. Rainfall is heaviest in the N and E and much less in the S and W where the mountains remove much of the moisture from the NE trade winds. While areas such as Barahona and Monte Cristi are extremely arid, the town of Samaná near the tip of Samaná Peninsula may receive 100 in. (2,500 mm) or more annually; average rainfall is about 55 in. (139.7 cm). Much rain falls at night. The Republic averages 245 days of sunshine.

HURRICANES: You should be aware of one severe drawback: the infrequent hurricanes. These low-pressure zones are serious business and should not be taken lightly. Where the majority of structures are poorly constructed, property damage from hurricanes may run into the hundreds of millions of dollars. A hurricane begins as a relatively small tropical storm, known as a cyclone when its winds reach a velocity of 39 mph (62 kph). At 74 mph (118 kph) it is upgraded to hurricane status, with winds of up to 200 mph (320 kph) and ranging in size from 60-1,000 miles (100-1,600 km) in diameter. A small hurricane releases energy equivalent to the explosions of six atomic bombs per second. A hurricane may be compared to an enormous hovering engine that uses the moist air and water of the tropics as fuel, carried hither and thither by prevailing air currents – generally eastern trade winds which intensify as they move across warm ocean waters. When cooler, drier air infiltrates it as it heads N, the hurricane begins to die, cut off

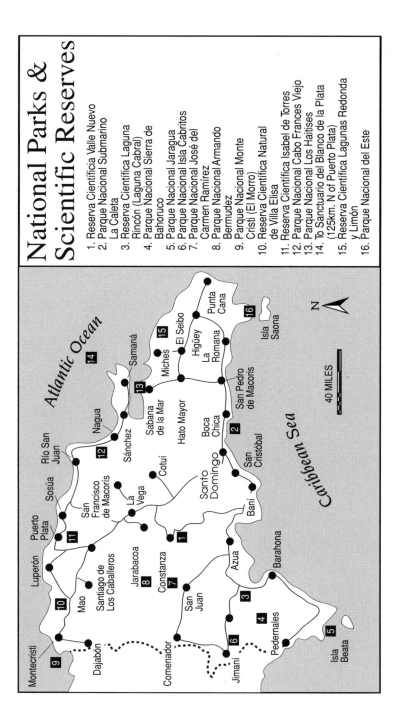

National Parks & Scientific Reserves

1. Reserva Cientificia Valle Nuevo
2. Parque Nacional Submarino La Caleta
3. Reserva Científica Laguna Rincón (Laguna Cabral)
4. Parque Nacional Sierra de Bahoruco
5. Parque Nacional Jaragua
6. Parque Nacional Isla Cabritos
7. Parque Nacional José del Carmen Ramírez
8. Parque Nacional Armando Bermudez
9. Parque Nacional Monte Cristi (El Morro)
10. Reserva Científica Natural de Villa Elisa
11. Reserva Científica Isabel de Torres
12. Parque Nacional Cabo Frances Viejo
13. Parque Nacional Los Haitises
14. To Sanctuario del Blanco de la Plata (125km. N of Puerto Plata)
15. Reserva Científica Lagunas Redonda y Limón
16. Parque Nacional del Este

the life-sustaining ocean currents that have nourished it from in-
fancy. Routes and patterns are unpredictable. As for their fre-
quency: "June – too soon; July – stand by; August – it must;
September – remember." So goes the old rhyme. Unfortunately,
hurricanes are not confined to July and August. Those forming in
Aug. and Sept. typically last for two weeks while the ones that form
in June, July, Oct., and Nov. (many of which originate in the
Caribbean and the Gulf of Mexico) generally last only seven days.
Approximately 70% of all hurricanes (known as Cabo Verde types)
originate as embryonic storms coming from the W coast of Africa.
Since record-keeping began, a number of hurricanes have wreaked
havoc here. In 1930 a massive hurricane hit, killing 2,000 and
changing the nation's history by allowing Trujillo to consolidate
his power. The most recent, Hurricane David, struck in Aug. 1979.
It caused a billion dollars in damage, leaving more than 1,000 dead
and as many as 10,000 homeless. Hurricane Frederick followed
shortly thereafter.

Flora

Despite the nation's relatively small size, the Dominican Republic
has climatic zones ranging from the coniferous forest lining the
slopes of towering Pico Duarte and Pico La Pelona, the Caribbean's
highest points, to the desertlike environment surrounding below-
sea-level Lago Enriquillo. All in all, there are nine basic and seven
transitional vegetation zones. Covering nearly half of the nation's
territory, subtropical moist forest predominates. Occurring princi-
pally on the slopes of mountain ranges, subtropical wet and lower
montane forest covers most of the remainder. Sadly, less than 5%
of the nation remains covered with pine. Much of the old growth
forest has vanished, removed for agriculture or charcoal-making.
There are some 5,500 flowering plants and ferns.

TREES: Mahogany, *capá* (used in shipbuilding), and royal palm
predominate in the subtropical moist forest. The last is present
almost everywhere but abounds in the Vega Real. Its trunk may be
used for soft lumber, its fronds (known as *yagua*) for thatch, and its
nuts are fed to hogs. Secondary growth trees found in pastures and
along streams include the lancewood, cashew, yellowood, log-
wood, and the *jagua* palm. Ground oak and *malphigia* are among
the trees found in pastures.

MANGROVES: Mangrove forests are found along the coasts; these water-rooted trees serve as a marine habitat which shelters sponges, corals, oysters, and other members of the marine community around its roots – organisms which, in turn, attract a variety of other sealife. Some species live out their lives in the shelter of the mangroves, and many fish use it as a shelter or feeding ground. Above the water level, they shelter seabirds and are important nesting sites. Their organic detritus, exported to the reef by the tides, is consumed by its inhabitants, providing the base of an extensive food web. Mangroves also dampen high waves and winds generated by tropical storms. By trapping silt in their roots and catching leaves and other detritus which decompose to form soil, the red mangroves act as land builders. Eventually, the red mangroves kill themselves off, by building up enough soil for the black and white mangroves take over. Meanwhile, the red mangroves have sent out progeny in the form of floating seedlings – bottom-heavy youngsters that grow on the tree until they reach six inches to a foot in length. If they drop in shallow water, the seeds touch bottom and implant themselves. In deeper water they stay afloat and, crossing a shoal, drag until they lodge.

Fauna

The Dominican Republic hosts some 5,600 animal species, of which 36% are indigenous. As holds true elsewhere in the Caribbean, there are few indigenous mammals. The cattle, goats, pigs, chickens, and horses you will see are all imports.

REPTILES: *Caiman* (alligators) are found only around Lake Enriquillo in the SW. Other lizards include the rhino iguana and Rocard's iguana.

BIRDS: Declared the national bird in 1967, the Hispaniolan palmchat or palmthrush (*cigua palmera*) flocks in open areas, especially near royal palms. It builds its six ft multi-compartmented nests high on their trunks at low elevations. The cotorra (nicknamed *cotica* – "little parrot" and *cuca*), the local parrot, began its path to extinction when the Tainos gave them as presents to arriving Spaniards. Flamingos are found in the Río Yuna delta and in Lake Enriquillo. Originally an African import, the Madam Sagá or village weaver builds unique nests.

THE SOLENODON: A relative of Madagascar's tenrec, the solenodon (*solenodonte*) is found only on Hispaniola and in Cuba. It is the Caribbean's only surviving insectivore. The brown, ratlike mammal has a rather strange way of walking called "unglitude" in which it places only the edge of its foot on the ground. Asleep by day in small caves and dry tree trunks, it prowls at night, preying on insects, worms, mollusks, and small vertebrates. Standing on hind legs and tail, it tears its quarry apart with its claws before dining. Despite its multimillion-year history, the destruction of its natural environment, combined with the advent of the mongoose, have greatly decreased its numbers, and many fear it may already be extinct.

Hutias

THE HUTIA (*JUTÍA*): This endangered endemic rodent, measuring some 12 in (30 cm) in length, resides in tree trunks and in caves; a skillful climber, it hunts at night.

Marine Life

MANATEE (*MANATÍ*): Popularly known as the sea cow, this ungainly creature is elusive but sometimes is spotted offshore. Once ranging from S America up to N Carolina, its numbers have dwindled dramatically – threatened by hunting, propellor blades of motor boats, and the careless use of herbicides. Currently inhabiting the coastal waters from Florida to N Brazil, manatees move along the ocean floor (at a maximum pace of six mph) searching for food and surfacing every four or five minutes to breathe. Surprisingly, especially in light of the fact that the manatee's nearest living relative is the elephant, the creature was thought to be the model for the legend of the mermaid – perhaps because of the mother's habit of sheltering her offspring with her flipper as the infant feeds. Weighing 400-1,300 lbs., the pudgy creature is covered with finely wrinkled grey or brown skin decorated with barnacles and algae; it may reach 12 ft in length. Although to you they may appear ugly with their small eyes, thick lips, bristly muzzles, and wrinkled necks, they are affectionate with each other, kissing and sometimes swimming flipper-to-flipper. Dwelling in lagoons and in brackish water, they may eat as much as 100 lbs. of aquatic vegetables per day. Strictly vegetarian, their only enemy is man who has hunted them for their hides, oil, and meat.

HUMPBACK WHALES: Migrating every fall from the polar waters through the passage between Puerto Rico and the Virgin Islands where they breed, these marine mammals may be sighted offshore near Puerto Plata. The Dominican Republic is the only nation which has established an offshore wildlife refuge specifically designed to protect them. Overhunting during the early to mid-19th C. has endangered them; they have been internationally protected since the mid-1960s. Thickset, they range in length from 30-40 ft (12-15 m). You may see them leap belly-up from the water, turn a somersault, and arch backwards – plunging headfirst back into the watery depths with a loud snapping noise. When making deep dives, these whales hump their backs forward and bring their tails out of the water. In addition to diving, they love vocalizing. Their moans, cries, groans, and snores are expressed in "songs" that can last five to 35 minutes. They feed on small fish, plankton, and shrimp-like crustaceans – all of which they strain of water with their baleen. Distinguished by their very long pectoral fins, which are scalloped on their forward edges, as well as by large knobs on their jaws and head, humpbacks are black-bodied with a varying amount of white on their underbelly.

SEA TURTLES: All four types of sea turtle are found here. Medium-sized with a total length of about three ft and weighing around 400 lbs., the large-finned, herbiverous green turtle (*tortuga blanca* or *tortuga verde*) lays eggs every two to three years, storming the beaches in massive groups termed *barricadas*. It is readily identifiable by its short rounded head. One of the smallest sea turtles at 35 in. or less in length, the hawksbill (*tortuga carey*) has a spindle-shaped shell and weighs around 220 lbs. Because of its tortoise shell (a brown translucent layer of corneous gelatin that covers it and peels off the shell when processed) it has been pursued and slaughtered throughout the world. The hawksbill dines largely on sponges and seaweed. Worldwide demand for its shell, which sells for a fortune in Japan, appears to have condemned it to extinction. Owing to its large, narrow, and bird-jawed head, twice the size of the green turtle's, the short-finned loggerhead turtle (*tortuga cabezona*) rarely exceeds four ft. It dines on sea urchins, jellyfish, starfish, and crabs. The loggerhead is threatened with extinction by coastal development, egg gathering, and from hunting by raccoons. Black with very narrow fins, the leatherback's name comes from the leathery hide which covers its back in lieu of a shell. Reaching up to six ft in length and weighing as much as 1,500 lbs., the leatherback's chief predator has always been the poacher.

REEF FISH: Common reef fish here include the sargeant major, the blue tang, the blue chromis, the blue headed wrasse, the yellowtail snapper, the trumpet fish, and the French angelfish. There are also a wide variety of fish, hermit crabs, spiny lobster, and other species.

ECHINODERMATA: Combining the Greek words for *echinos* (spiny) and *derma* (skin), this large division of the animal kingdom includes sea urchins, sea cucumbers, and starfish or sea stars. All share the ability to propel themselves with the help of tube "feet" or spines. Known by the scientific name *Astrospecten*, **starfish** (*estrellas de mar*) are five-footed carnivores which use their modified "tube-feet" to burrow into the sea. Sluggish **sea cucumbers** ingest large quantities of sand, extract the organic matter, and excrete the rest. Crustaceans and fish reside in the larger specimens.

Avoid trampling on that armed knight of the underwater sand dunes, the **sea urchin**. Consisting of a semi-circular calcareous (calcium carbonate) shell, the sea urchin is protected by its brown, jointed barbs. It uses its mouth, situated and protected on its underside, to graze by scraping algae from rocks. Surprisingly to those uninitiated in its lore, sea urchins are considered a gastronomic delicacy in many countries. The ancient Greeks believed they held aphrodisiacal and other properties beneficial to health. They are prized by the French and fetch four times the price of oysters in Paris. The Spanish consume them raw, boiled, in *gratinés*, or in soups. In Barbados they are called "sea eggs," and the Japanese eat their guts raw as sushi. Although a disease in recent years has devastated the sea urchin population, they are making a comeback. **contact:** If a sea urchin spine breaks off inside your finger or back. **contact:** If a sea urchin spine breaks off inside your finger or toe, don't try to remove it. It's impossible! You might try the cure people use in New Guinea. Use a blunt object to mash up the spine inside your skin so that it will be absorbed naturally. Then dip your finger in urine; the ammonia helps to trigger the process of disintegration. More safely, apply triple-antibiotic salve. Best of all, avoid contact. Sea urchins often hide underneath corals, and wounds occur when you lose your footing and scrape against one.

SPONGES: Found in the ocean depths, reddish or brown sponges are among the simplest forms of multicellular life and have been around for more than a half-billion years. They pump large amounts of water through their internal filters to extract plankton. There are numerous sizes, shapes, and colors, but they all can be recognized by their large, distinctive excurrent openings. Unlike other animals, they exhibit no reaction when disturbed.

CNIDARIANS: The members of this group – hydroids, anemones, corals, and jellyfish – are distingushed by their simple structure: a cup-shaped body terminating in a combination mouth-anus encircled by tentacles. While hydroids and corals (covered later in this section) are colonial, jellyfish and anemones are individual. This phylum's name comes from the Greek word for another identifying characteristic: stinging capsules (or nematocysts) used for defense and capturing prey. Hydroids ("water forms" in Greek) spend their youth as solitary medusas before settling down in colonies which resemble groups of ferns or feathers. Some will sting, and the best known hydroid is undoubtedly the floating Portuguese Man-Of-War; its stinging tentacles can be extended or retracted. There have been reports of trailing tentacles reaching 50 feet! It belongs to the family of *siphonophores*, free-floating hydroid colonies which control their depth by means of a gas-filled float. The true jellyfish are identifiable by their domes which vary in shape. Nematocysts are found in both the feeding tube and in their tentacles. Also known as sea wasps, box jellies can be identifed by their cube-shaped dome. From each corner a single tentacle extends. Many of them have a fierce sting; keep well away. If you should get stung by any of the above, get out of the water and peel off any tentacles. Avoid rubbing the injured area. Wash it with alcohol and apply meat tenderizer for five to 10 minutes. The jellyfish season is Aug. to Oct. Solitary bottom-dwellers, sea anemones are polyps with no skeleton; they use their tentacles to stun prey and force it to their mouth. Shrimp and crabs, immune to their sting, often live nearby for protection. Their tentacles may retract when disturbed. One type of anemone lives in tubes buried in the muck or sand. Their tentacles only come out to play at night.

CRUSTACEANS: A class of arthropods, crustaceans are distinguished by their jointed legs and complex skeleton. The decapods (named for their five pairs of legs) are the largest order of crustaceans. These include shrimp, crabs, and lobsters. The ghost crab (*ocypode*) abounds on the beaches, tunneling down beneath the sand and emerging to feed at night. Although it can survive for 48 hrs. without contacting water, it must return to the sea to moisten its gill chambers as well as to lay its eggs which hatch into planktonic larvae. The hermit crab carries a discarded mollusc shell in order to protect its vulnerable abdomen. As it grows, it must find a larger home, and you may see two struggling over the same shell.

OTHER UNDERWATER HAZARDS AND CURES: Not a true coral, **firecoral** mimics its appearance; it takes many forms and has the ability to encrust nearly any object, taking on its host's shape. Generally colored mustard yellow to brown, firecoral often has white finger-like tips. Its sting is quite painful. As with coral wounds, you should wash the affected area with soap and fresh water, then apply a triple-antibiotic salve. Found on rocky or coral bottoms, the **spotted scorpionfish** is well camouflaged so it's easy to step on them Although the Caribbean species is non-lethal, its bite can be painful. Another cleverly camouflaged denizen of the deep, the **stingray** will whip its tail if stepped on – driving the serrated venomous spine into the offender. If this happens, see a doctor. Fuzzy creatures, **bristle worms** have glass-like bristles which may break off in the skin and are very painful. Apply tape to the skin and attempt to pull the bristles out; reduce the pain with rubbing alcohol. **Moray eels** have a tendency to bite at things thrust at them; they have a tight grip and can be difficult to dislodge. Once again, preventing bites is best. Always exercise caution before reaching into a crevice!

The Coral Reef Ecosystem

One of the least appreciated of the world's innumerable wonders is the coral reef. This is in part because little has been known about it until recent decades. This wondrous environment in many ways goes beyond the limits of any wild fantasy conjured up in a science fiction novel. It is a delicate environment: the only geological feature fashioned by living creatures. Many of the world's reefs –

which took millions of years to form – have already suffered devastation at the hand of man.

Corals produce the calcium carbonate (limestone) responsible for most of the island's offlying cays and islets as well as most of the sand on the beaches. Bearing the brunt of waves, they also conserve the shoreline. Although reefs began forming millenia ago, they are in a constant state of flux. Seemingly solid, they actually depend upon a delicate ecological balance to survive. Deforestation, dredging, temperature change, an increase or decrease in salinity, silt, or sewage discharge may kill them Because temperature ranges must remain between 68° and 95°F, they are only found in the tropics and – because they require light to grow – only in shallow water. They are also intolerant of fresh water, and reefs can not survive where rivers empty into the sea.

THE CORAL POLYP: While corals are actually animals, botanists view them as being mostly plant, and geologists dub them "honorary" rocks. Acting more like plants than animals, corals survive through photosynthesis: the algae inside the coral polyps do the work while the polyps themselves secrete calcium carbonate and stick together for protection from waves and boring sponges.

Bearing a close structural resemblance to its relative the anemone, a polyp feeds at night by using the ring or rings of tentacles surrounding its mouth to capture prey (such as plankton) with nematocysts, small stinging darts.

The coral polyps appear able to survive in such packed surroundings through their symbiotic relationship with the algae present in their tissues: Coral polyps exhale carbon dioxide and the algae consume it, producing needed oxygen. Although only half of the world's coral species possess such a symbiotic relationship with these single-celled captive species of dinoflagellates (*Gymnodinium microdriaticum*), these species – called hermatypic corals – are the ones that build the reef. The nutritional benefits gained from their relationship with the algae enable them to grow a larger skeleton and to do so more rapidly than would otherwise be possible. Polyps have the ability to regulate the density of these cells in their tissues and can expel some of them in a spew of mucus should they multiply too quickly. Looking at coral, you will see that the brownish colored algal cells show through transparent tissues. When you see a coral garden through your mask, you are actually viewing a field of captive single-celled algae.

An added and vital but invisible component of the reef ecosystem is bacteria, micro-organisms which decompose and recycle all matter on which everything from worms to coral polyps feed.

Inhabitants of the reef range from crabs to barnacles, sea squirts to multicolored tropical fish. Remarkably, the polyps themselves are consumed by only a small percentage of the reef's inhabitants. They often contain high levels of toxic substances and are also thought to sting fish and other animals that attempt to consume them Corals also retract their polyps during daylight hours when the fish can see them. Reefs originate as the polyps develop; the calcium secretions form a base as they grow. One polyp can have a 1,000-year lifespan.

CORAL TYPES: Corals can be divided into three groups. The hard or **stony corals** (such as staghorn, brain, star, or rose) secrete a limey skeleton. The **horny corals** (for example sea plumes, sea whips, sea fans, and gorgonians) have a supporting skeleton-like structure known as a gorgonin (after the head of Medusa). The shapes of these corals result from the fashion in which the polyps and their connecting tissues excrete calcium carbonate; there are over a thousand different patterns – one specific to each species. Each also has its own method of budding. Found in the Caribbean, giant elk-horn corals may contain over a million polyps and live for several hundred years or longer. The last category consists of the **soft corals**. While these too are colonies of polyps, their skeletons are composed of soft organic material, and their polyps always have eight tentacles instead of the six or multiples of six found in the stony corals. Unlike the hard corals, soft corals disintegrate after death and do not add to the reef's stony structure. Instead of depositing limestone crystals, they excrete a jelly-like matrix which is imbued with spicules (diminutive spikes) of stony material; the jelly-like substance gives these corals their flexibility. Sea fans and sea whips exhibit similar patterns. There are also false corals. A type of soft coral is the precious **black coral**. Prized by jewelers because its branches may be cleaned and polished to high gloss ebony-black, it resembles bushes of fine grey-black twigs. Don't buy products made with this coral, however, because doing so contributes to and encourages reef destruction.

COMPETITION: To the snorkeler, the reef appears to be a peaceful haven. The reality is that because the reef is a comparatively benign environment, the fiercest competition has developed here. Although the corals appear static to the onlooker, they are continually competing with each other for space. Some have developed sweeper tentacles which have an especially high concentration of stinging cells. Reaching out to a competing coral, they stick and execute it. Other species dispatch digestive filaments which eat the prey. Soft corals appear to leach out toxic chemicals called terpines which kill nearby organisms. Because predation is such a problem, two-thirds of reef species are toxic. Others hide in stony outcrops or have formed protective relationships with other organisms such as the classic case of the banded clown fish which lives among the sea anemones whose stingers protect it. The cleaner fish protect themselves from larger fish by setting up stations at which they pick parasites off their carnivorous customers. Mimicking the coloration and shape of the feeder fish, the sabre-toothed blenny is a false cleaner fish which takes a chunk out of the larger fish and runs off!

CORAL LOVE AFFAIRS: Not prone to celibacy or sexual prudery, coral polyps reproduce sexually and asexually through budding, and a polyp joins together with thousands and even millions of its neighbors to form a coral. (In a few cases, only one polyp forms a single coral). During sexual reproduction polyps release millions of their spermatozoa into the water. Many species are dimorphic – with both male and female coral. Some species have internal, others external fertilization. Still others have both male and female polyps. As larvae develop, their "mother" expels them and they float off to found a new coral colony.

EXPLORING REEFS: As is mentioned under "environmental conduct" in the Practicalities section later in the book, coral reefs are extremely fragile environments. Much damage has been done to reefs worldwide through human carelessness. Despite their size, reefs grow very slowly and it can take decades or even hundreds of years to repair the effects of a few moments. Do nothing to provoke moray eels which may retaliate when threatened. Watch out for fire corals, recognizable by the white tips on their branches, which can inflict stings. In general, look but don't touch is the maxim to follow.

UNDERWATER FLORA: Most of the plants you see underwater are algae, primitive plants that can survive only underwater because they do not have the mechanisms to prevent themselves from drying out. Lacking roots, algae draw their minerals and water directly from the sea. Another type of algae, calcareous red algae, are very important for reef formation. Resembling rounded stones, they are 95% rock and only 5% living tissue. Plants returned to live in the sea, sea grasses are found in relatively shallow water in sandy and muddy bays and flats; they have roots and small flowers. One species, dubbed "turtle grass," provides food for turtles. In addition, seagrasses help to stabilize the sea floor, maintain water clarity by trapping fine sediments from upland soil erosion, stave off beach erosion, and provide living space for numerous fish, crustaceans, and shellfish.

History

PRECOLUMBIAN DOMINICANA: Little is known of the island's original inhabitants. They were dominated by the Taino, who spoke a dialect of Arawak (the word means meal- or cassava-eater). Although yucca was their staple food, they also grew corn, sweet potatoes, chilis, and peanuts. They ate fish, turtles, shellfish, and manatee. The Indians called their island Quisqueya ("Greatness") or Haiti ("Rugged Mountain"). The island was divided into five *caciazgos* each ruled over by a *cacique* with names like Higüey and Jaragua. Land was owned and cultivated communally,

Native hut or bohio preferred by the Taino chiefs

and there was little armed conflict. Gifted artists and craftsmen, the Taino carved sculptures, wove baskets, and produced pottery. Masks and necklaces were fashioned from gold, a practice that was to have unfortunate consequences later on. Also on the island were a group of Caribs settled around the Samaná peninsula.

ENTER COLUMBUS: Modern Dominican history began in 1492 with the arrival of Columbus and the Spanish. The admiral ran the *Santa Maria* aground at Navidad (present-day Cap Haitian in Haiti) on Christmas Day, 1492 and received a friendly reception. In his logbook Columbus described the Taino as "open hearted" and

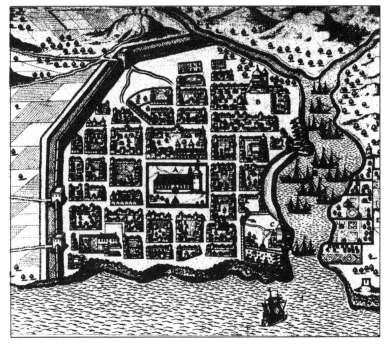

Early view of Santo Domingo

"fit to be ordered and made to work." On his return the next year, he found the colony of 39 men left there had been killed after they had pillaged for gold and kidnapped some local lasses. Because the Taino told them there was gold in the area, a second settlement was established at Isabela, where the pioneers supplemented agricultural activities with pursuits such as stealing gold ornaments, raping women, and capturing slaves for shipment to Spain.

GENOCIDE: After the Isabela settlement ran into trouble, Bartolomew Columbus moved along with most of the settlers to the site of present day Santo Domingo in 1496. It had some 300 inhabitants in 1498. Subsequently, Spain, the first great colonial power in the Americas, established Santo Domingo as its New World headquarters. Francisco Bobadilla, appointed by the Crown as chief justice and commissioner, took power and sent Columbus back in chains. Bobadilla was replaced by Nicolás de Ovando who became governor and supreme justice. Because of his success in instituting the system of *ecomienda* (see below), he was made "Founder of Spain's Empire in the Indies." Under the system of *repartimiento* ("distribution") established by Columbus, the Taino had been ac-

Taino cacique

costed and set to work in construction and in the mines or fields. Under the similar system of Crown control instituted in 1503, termed *ecomienda* ("commandery"), they were forcibly extracted from villages and set to labor for a *pátron* on his estate. Although, in return, the Indians were supposed to receive protection and learn about the wonders of Catholicism, this system was a thinly disguised form of slavery; the number of Taino shrank from an estimated one to three million in 1492 to approximately 500 in 1548. Along the way they left some legendary martyrs who are still known today. Among these is the valiant *cacique* Caonabo who died while being shipped to Spain. Considered to be the most beautiful woman of the island, Anacaona, his widow, was among the many murdered by Hitlerian-style humanist Gov. Nicolás de Ovando. Another famous Indian was Enriquillo. The son of a *cacique* murdered at Jaragua by de Ovando's forces, he was educated by monks and, after being faced with re-enslavement under *repartimiento* became the leader of an insurrection from 1520-33 which ended with him and his followers being resettled on a reserve. His legend is recorded in Manuel de Jesús Galván's classic novel *Enriquillo*, published in 1882. Begun in 1503 as another de Ovando brainstorm, the importation of slaves put in place a race-regulated hierarchy which survives to this day.

THE AUDENCIA: In an attempt to put checks on Diego Columbus, who was appointed governor in 1509, the crown devised the *audencia* in 1511, a three-judge tribunal whose authority extended all over the West Indies. The highest court of appeals, its influence expanded and it became the Royal Audencia in 1524, commanding jurisdiction over the Caribbean, Mexico, and the N coast of S America, including all of Venezuela and portions of Colombia. In 1526, a separate *audencia* for Mexico was established in an attempt to curb the power of Cortés. Along with the government came the church. The first missionaries had arrived with Columbus on his second voyage in 1493, and the hemisphere's first bishopric was established in 1511; it was made the first archbishopric in 1547.

DECLINE OF IMPORTANCE: With the discovery of gold and silver in Mexico and Peru and the depletion of gold deposits in 1520 as well as the extermination of the island's indigenous people, Santo Domingo began to lose luster in the first part of the 16th C. In 1564, Santiago and Concepción de la Vega were destroyed by an earthquake, and Santo Domingo was sacked by Sir Francis Drake in 1586. Although the town repelled a British invasion in 1655, the Spaniards torched their settlements on the island's N coast in order to stave off smuggling and keep them from falling under French control. Under the Treaty of Ryswick in 1697, Spain ceded the western third of the island to France. This area, then known as "Hayti," became the most prosperous colony in the world while Santo Domingo slipped into a 250-year slump. The Spanish colony grew to 150,000 by 1785. Approximately 40,000 were of Spanish ancestry, 40,000 were African slaves, and the rest were black or mulatto freedmen.

THE HAITIAN OCCUPATION: Haitian slaves, led by Toussaint L'Ouverture, revolted in 1791, sparking a confused civil war. Toussaint's forces fought with the Spanish against the French, until they heard of the emancipation of the slaves by the French. Shifting his allegiance, Toussaint helped the French drive the Spanish from Saint-Dominique, the French name for Haiti. Appointed governor of the French colony of Saint-Dominique by the French Convention, Toussaint marched into Santo Domingo in 1801. His new constitution freed slaves, causing the Spanish colony to lose one-third of its white elite, who migrated to Puerto Rico, Cuba, and Venezuela. In 1802, French forces under the command of General Le Clerc (Napoleon's brother in law) drove the Haitians back to the W, capturing Toussaint in the process. Toussaint was replaced by the despotic duo of Henri Christophe and Jean Jacques Dessalines. The latter declared Haiti's independence on Jan. 1, 1804. The French controlled Santo Domingo until 1809, when the Spanish drove them out with British assistance. In 1821 colonial treasurer José Nuñez de Caceres declared independence, but he and other leaders made the mistake of looking for support from Haitian leader General Jean Pierre Boyer, who invaded. Meeting little resistance – Nuñez de Caceres handed over the keys to Santo Domingo on a silver platter – the Haitians stayed until 1844. The Haitian occupation remains a bitter memory. Although the slaves were emancipated, emigration increased, sugar and tobacco production were paralyzed, all church properties were seized, and the economy staggered under the weight of a tyrannical bureaucracy and plundering by Haitian soldiers. An independence underground flourished under the leadership of Juan Pablo Duarte and his secret society La Trinitaria. On Feb. 27, 1844, the Dominican rebels siezed Ozama fortress in Santo Domingo. Caught by surprise, the Haitians hastily exited, and a provisional government took control.

INDEPENDENCE: Duarte, however, was reluctant to take command of the presidency, and he soon found himself usurped and exiled by two self-appointed generals, Buenaventura Báez and Pedro Santana, a rancher with his own private army. Alternating as president over the next 45 years, these two dictators helped to fill their own pockets more than they helped anyone else. Taking control of the presidency in Nov. 1844, Santana began a quest to sell the country to the highest bidder. In particular, he held out as crown jewel the Samaná peninsula, which has a superb natural harbor. From 1848 to 1855, the nation was repeatedly threatened by Haitian dictator Faustin I. By 1861 the country was bankrupt and, now in his third term as president, Santana announced that the República Dominicana would again become a Spanish colony. By midsummer, Santo Domingo was once more swarming with Spaniards and, by mid-fall, the Dominicans were revolting again. This War of Restoration had begun to drive the Spanish back by 1863. Independence was not re-established until 1865 when Báez took his third crack at the presidency. He was, however, forced to leave the country five months later because of a revolt led by Gen. Gregorio Luperón. Soon called back from exile, Báez convinced the Grant administration to sign a treaty annexing the country to the US. All Dominicans were to become US citizens and his government would be compensated to the tune of $1.5 billion. However, coming under stiff opposition led by Sen. Charles Sumner, the treaty failed to pass the US Senate by only 10 votes in 1870. Not to be outdone, in 1872 Báez negotiated a 99-year lease of Samaná Bay to a New York Company, and he was once again driven from office after the plebiscite called to ratify the contract was revealed to have been rigged. Báez was replaced from 1874-79 by reformist Ulises Espillat, who began issuing paper currency without backing. Unable to control the situation, he fell from power and Báez returned for his final fling at the presidency. But after only two months, he took $300,000 and fled to Puerto Rico – leaving his country in shambles behind him.

ULISES HEUREUX: Following Báez, General Luperón took another turn at the presidency and was replaced by his lieutenant, Ulises Heureux who was popularly known as "Lilís." Although he increased a large foreign debt tenfold, Heureux achieved political stability and modernized the economy during his 17 dictatorial years at the helm. All of this came at a high price. Despite a semblance of elections and a facade of constitutional government, he destroyed the party system, ruthlessly persecuted any opposition, and established a national and international network of spies and informers. As he became more ruthless and authoritarian, his unpopularity grew. It was finally greed that brought him down. Heureux negotiated an agreement loaning Samaná Bay to a Dutch Bank, giving preferential treatment to the Americans. European criticism caused the agreement's collapse but led to the nation's bankruptcy in the late 1890s. The last of five coup attempts was successful when in July

1899 Heureux was shot and killed at a public gathering by Ramon Cáceres, an opposition leader.

POLITICAL FACTIONALISM: Between 1899 and 1906, the country polarized into two competing factions: "Horacistas," followers of Horacio Vásquez, and the "Jimenistas," followers of Juan Isidro Jiménez. These were nicknamed *bolos* and *rabudos* after two types of fighting cocks. The ensuing conflict further reduced the economy. With the dawning of the 20th C, a new era of relations with the US began. In 1904 President Theodore "big stick" Roosevelt had pronounced a new order of relations with the Caribbean. The Roosevelt Corollary to the Monroe Doctrine set up the US as an "international police power." In 1907, the entire country was placed under receivership by Theodore Roosevelt who, sensing an opportunity to expand US influence, negotiated an agreement whereby the US would administer the now $40 million Dominican debt by collecting and distributing customs duties. Under its terms, the US would collect the export customs duties (the principal source of government revenue) and deliver 45% of them to the Dominican government while using the remainder to pay off the external debt. The 1905 agreement, signed by then-president Carlos Morales, was followed by a 1907 treaty which required the US to approve any decision to expand the debt. Heureux's assassin, Ramón Cáceres, became president in 1908, bringing with him a brief era of reform and modernization. Following tradition, he too was assassinated in 1911. During the course of the ensuing civil war, Juan Isidro Jiménez became president.

THE US INVADES: Given the continued degeneration of the Dominican political system, coupled with the spread of German influence in Haiti, the Wilson administration was watching events carefully. On May 16, 1916, Jiménez was impeached by the Dominican Congress and a rebellion followed. That same year American troops landed and began an eight-year occupation under martial law. Divided, the Dominican politicians continued their fratricidal conflicts rather than banding together to oppose the invasion. Press freedom was restricted, and US publications with articles about the nation were banned. Although bands of patriots rebelled, they were forcibly put down. Marines engaged in rape, murder, and torture on numerous occasions. Many of the officers were from the South and faced an opposition largely black and mulatto. US private investors supplied funds for schools and sanitation systems. A highway system was built. The Tariff act of 1920 reduced tariffs dramatically, flooding the nation with US imports and losing the government badly needed revenue. Baseball was introduced, and social reforms were instituted, but most measures were short-lived. One legacy which was to have unfortunate consequences was the institution of a Marine-trained *Guardia Nacional Dominicana* (Dominican National Guard), the first formally trained and organized military force in the nation's history. In 1921, Harding's Secretary of State Charles Evans Hughes negotiated the Hughes-Peynado agreement which permitted US departure and the accession of sugar king Juan Batista Vicini to the head of a provisional government. In 1924, after elections which left newly elected but aging General Horacio Vásquez in charge, the Marines exited.

THE RISE OF TRUJILLO: For six years everything went relatively smoothly. Vásquez prolonged his term from four to six years, then repealed the ban on re-election. But, in 1930, a revolt was spearheaded from Santiago. With the tacit support of the head of the new National Guard – a young but ruthlessly clever fellow named Rafael Trujillo – the rebels toppled Vásquez. Trujillo first encouraged rebel leader Rafael Estrella Ureña to run for president and then "convinced" him to run for vice-president. Winning the 1930 elections with more votes than there were eligible voters, Trujillo began his metamorphosis into the persona of Generalissimo Doctor Rafael Leonidas Trujillo Molina, Benefactor de la Patria y Padre de la Patria Nueva. Born in the little village of San Cristóbal in 1891, Trujillo worked as a telegraph operator with a gang of hoods nicknamed "the 44," and as a weigher at sugar estates before entering the National Guard in 1918. He had been promoted to Lieutenant Colonel and Chief of Staff by Vásquez in 1924, and he was further elevated to Brigadier General and Chief of the National Army – the successor to the National Guard – in 1927.

THE TRUJILLO ERA: After taking power, Trujillo went on to establish a reputation that has made his name synonymous with totalitarianism. In the history of the Western Hemisphere there has never been a dictator more ruthless or bloodthirsty than Trujillo; it is estimated that more than half a million people were executed during his rule. One night in 1937, under Trujillo's orders, his troops massacred 12-25,000 Haitians whom he had invited in to work on his sugar plantations. More than any other leader in the history of the Dominican Republic, Trujillo shaped and, through his lasting legacy, continues to shape the nation's political, economic, and social fabric. Dominating the nation from 1930-61 and turning it into his personal fiefdom, Trujillo amassed a fortune estimated at $300 million to one billion dollars. Together with his family and friends, he came to control nearly 60% of the country's assets, including the majority of the sugar industry (80% of the mills), 50-60% of its arable lands, shipping lines, airlines, the national lottery, and dozens of other concerns. Approximately 60% of the labor force worked for Trujillo either directly or indirectly. One of the two or three richest men in the world at the time of his death, he has been said to have resembled Croesus more than Caesar, and a common joke was that if something lost money it belonged to the government, but if it made money it was Trujillo's. One tragic aspect of his wealth was that the bulk of his profits were exported to Swiss banks, impoverishing the nation in the process. Although other Latin American dictators – such as Argentina's Juan Perón and Castro's Batista – have become incredibly wealthy and sent hundreds of millions out of the country, none were able to institutionalize fraud and monopolize economic control to the extent of Trujillo. An incredible cult of adulation grew up around the man. Santo Domingo was renamed Ciudad Trujillo, the highest mountain was named Pico Trujillo, and the dictator became the godfather of scores of children brought to mass baptisms. *El jefe*'s figure – in the form of busts, statues, and photos – became the regime's symbol, and time was measured in the "Era of Trujillo." All buildings were engraved with his name on their cornerstone and excerpts from his speeches were engraved on their walls. Signs at village pumps read "Only Trujillo Gives Us Drink" and those at hospitals informed visitors that "Only Trujillo Cures Us." A neon sign proclaiming "God and Trujillo" hung at the entrance to the capital's harbor. In retrospective appreciation of his megalomania, it appears surprising that God's name was placed first! An equally famous sign, displayed over the lunatic asylum at Nigua, read "We owe everything to Trujillo."

TRUJILLO'S MODUS OPERANDI: The massive hurricane of 1930 allowed Trujillo to buy up property from impoverished landowners and eliminate constitutional guarantees by claiming the need for strong centralized rule. Instituting a series of austere policies – re-negotiating foreign debt, raising taxes, and cutting the budget – Trujillo channeled money into service and industrial enterprises that were controlled by him or his relatives. The Dominican Republic produced nearly a million tons of sugarcane for export to the US during the 1950s, placing it just behind number-one exporter, Cuba. In order to sustain the nation's sugar quota Trujillo lobbied and bribed US officials. During his regime, he met with Franklin Delano Roosevelt at the White House, and was praised by businessmen, a cardinal, supreme court justices, and congressmen – one of whom asserted that Latin America could use 20 men like him! Secretary of State Cordell Hull even proclaimed Trujillo "a splendid President, who is outstanding among all those in the American nations." Pan American World Airways even took out full page newspaper ads in his honor. He hired lobbyists, PR firms, and law firms to propagandize for him, and even paid the Mutual Broadcasting System $750,000 to broadcast his propoganda as news; the story came out only when he sued because he was unhappy with the services he was receiving! Ironically in retrospect, this totalitarian tyrant also promoted himself as the world's "Number One Anticommunist." And, to Trujillo, all those who disagreed with his concept of "democracy" were "communists." The Mutual Security Act of 1951 permitted his regime to purchase US military equipment and weapons: the Dominican Republic received over $6 million in arms from 1952-61. In 1953, the nation became the first in Latin America to sign a bilateral Mutual Defense Assistance Agreement with the US.

SOCIAL CONTROL: A genius of manipulation, Trujillo stacked the armed forces, like the goverment, with his friends and relatives. His son Ramfis (Rafael Trujillo Martinez), for example, became a brigadier general at the mature age of nine and later served as chief of staff of the air force. Over a hundred of his relatives served in the armed forces. Informants were everywhere, mail was censored, and phone tapping was commonplace. Santo Domingo featured armed traffic cops on nearly every streetcorner despite a paucity of traffic, forts were built in each town of 15,000 or over, and checkpoints were established every 20 miles throughout the country. In addition to carrying a *cedula* (identification card) without which one could not drive, work, travel, marry, or vote, citizens had to carry a certificate of good conduct from the secret police. Anyone standing in opposition to his regime was branded a "Communist," and even those neutral or apathetic towards the regime were also persecuted as subversives. Arrested on the flimsiest of premises, political prisoners were harshly treated, and a common method of discipline was to deny a prisoner any drink save his own urine. Torture techniques included electric shocks, nail extraction, castration, and immolation. No one knows how many were murdered. In order to keep the armed forces in line, firearms were kept under lock and key, and many soldiers used only clubs and machetes. The serfs on *el jefe's* sugarcane plantations were kept in line through membership in the Trujillo-created labor union *Confedración Dominicano del Trabajo* (CDT). "Freedom" only existed under Trujillo's eclectic definition of the word which called for "private discernment" (i.e., restraint) under "norms of general convenience." To Trujillo, a society in which individuals were subordinated to the "common good" was one in which individuals were "truly free." Under the credo *trujillismo*, all loyalty was placed in *Dominicanismo*, a new political and social myth which identified nationalism with Trujillo. Under the "Dominican Revolution" Trujillo avowed that "all progress, to be effective, must be harmonious" – which meant stifling all dissent. These concepts gained legitimacy because Dominicans were kept isolated and indoctrinated from youth. Startlingly salutary in its praise of the regime, the elementary school primer was authored by Trujillo himself. It even encouraged children to turn in their parents: "If you should find in your home a man who wishes to disturb order, see that he is handed over to the police." Presented to the children as a great work of moral philosophy, Señora Trujillo's book *Moral Meditations*, a compilation of newspaper columns of the Norman Vincent Peal genre, was compulsory reading. The entire news media was brought under Trujillo's ownership, unsympathetic radio broadcasts from foreign shores were jammed, and the foreign news media was manipulated at times as well. Art too was subordinated, and artists willingly prostituted themselves. Poets, musicians, and painters represented Trujillo as God, Pegasus, the eagle, the sun, volcanic lava, and Plato. His infallibility was proclaimed in *merengues*, and in a 10-part symphonic program (featuring movements titled "Public Works" and "Struggle Against Communism").

GOVERNMENTAL STRUCTURE: Often termed a "parody," the constitution was amended and laws were passed to suit Trujillo's needs – even to expedite his desires for a divorce, to disown daughter Flor de Oro, and to legally enfranchise two of his bastard but beloved children. Subject to extensive investigation by a "purification" commission prior to employment, Government personnel were continually shuffled and reshuffled; any appointed government employees, along with all judges, were forced to submit a signed but undated resignation letter upon their appointment. Similarly, few legislators were permitted to serve their full term without finding themselves "resigning." Voting was mandatory, and nonvoting was viewed as a subversive act. Established in 1931, Trujillo's *Partido Dominicano* was partially funded through automatic 10% deductions from the paychecks of government employees. In 1941, after Trujillo had joined the US as an ally in the fight against Axis fascism, he created an opposition party, the Trujillo

Party. He then ran as its head, and when its ballots were tallied together with those of the *Partido Dominicano*, he again garnered 100% of the votes! Most of Trujillo's selected candidates were unanimously elected as well.

TRUJILLO'S OVERTHROW: Nothing resting under God's heaven lasts forever, not even dictators, and Trujillo's regime began to sag during the late 1950s. In 1956, Trujillo made a major mistake – killing Jesús de Galindez, an expatriate in exile, a brilliant social critic and Columbia University professor. Several months later, Oregonian Gerald Murphy, who had flown Galindez to the US, was also killed mysteriously. The ensuing scandal made front page headlines all over the world. Tourism plummeted and attempts at PR damage control backfired. Plummeting sugar prices and his three unsuccessful plots to assassinate President Betancourt of Venezuela (which resulted in a trade and arms embargo by the OAS) increased the opposition's clout. Another incident which sealed his demise was the slaughter of the three Mirabel sisters, wives of three prominent dissidents. They were murdered after they spurned Trujillo's advances. The US, perhaps recognizing that it could not oppose Castro and still support Trujillo, began to move against Trujillo. Hypocritically, OAS sanctions were complied with while the sugar quota was quadrupled. Responding to criticism, the Eisenhower administration later levied a sugar excise tax which cost Trujillo $30 million in revenues. In order to arm himself against invasion, Trujillo had to hock the country to Canadian banks to the tune of $40 million – the first foreign indebtedness the nation's "Financial Emancipator" had incurred since 1947. A group of younger air force officers, who had been trained in the Canal Zone where they came into contact with new ideas and officers from democratically governed Latin American nations, privately opposed Trujillo. New clerics in the heretofore sycophantic church, turned against him, breaking all ties in a pastoral letter dated Jan. 25, 1960. On May 30, 1961, Trujillo was assassinated by a seven-man hit team coached and armed by the CIA. The middle-class assassins, comprised of businessmen, politicians, and former generals, missed their opportunity to seize power, and all but two of the two dozen conspirators were eventually murdered in retribution; several were slowly tortured to death. Trujillo's iron fist was inherited by his son Ramfis, along with puppet president Joaquin Balaguer.

FREE ELECTIONS: Under American pressure, Ramfis and Balaguer allowed exiles to return and permitted the growth of opposition parties. Instituting a series of cosmetic "democratiza-tion" reforms, Ramfis created more opposition and incurred the wrath of Trujillo's brothers, his "wicked uncles" Héctor and Aris-mendi, who returned from exile in Bermuda and attempted to supplant him. Taking $90 million, Ramfis and the rest of the family fled the country in Nov. 1961. A seven-man Council of State, which included Balaguer as well as two of Trujillo's assassins, was formed on Jan 1, 1962, but was overturned by a military coup. Two days later, a counter-coup restored the Council but forced Balaguer into exile in New York City. During this period, the US poured in millions of dollars in aid and technical assistance, more per capita than to any other Latin American nation at the time. However, the Council was criticized for failing to rid the nation of Trujillo-era bureaucrats, and neglecting social welfare programs, social in-equalities, and agrarian reform. A new spirit of democracy reigned and one of its chief beneficiaries was Juan Bosch, the fiery head of the social democratic *Partido Revolucionario Dominicano* (PRD, Do-minican Revolutionary Party). Becoming the first democratically elected president in the nation's history on Dec. 20, 1962, his two-to-one victory over Virato Fiallo's National Civic Union repre-sented a victory of the people over the traditional ruling elites. It all seemed to be too good to be true and it was. Promising democratic, economic, and social reforms, his administration quickly ran into difficulties trying to fulfill its pledge. The Catholic Church and the Army felt threatened by his administration, in particular by its promise to extend participation in the political process to Marxist groups. The Church was further alienated by his refusal to declare Catholicism as the state religion, and he also refused to snuggle up with the US Embassy. His parceling out of Trujillo's former estates to peasants enraged large landowners who worried that they might be next. He also offended some US officials by seeking investment and aid in Europe in an effort to liberate the nation from its slavish dependence on the US. In Sept. 1963, after only seven months in office, Bosch was overthrown in a bloodless military coup led by Col. Elias Wessín y Wessín. The military replaced Bosch with a three-man civilian junta dominated by Donald Reid Cabral, a local CIA agent nicknamed *El Americanito* ("the little American"). Reportedly, US President John. F. Kennedy dis-patched his confidant, a Colonel Reed, to the Dominican Republic to scout out prospects for a counter-coup. To his credit, Kennedy refused to recognize the "Triumvirate," withdrew his ambassador, and cut off aid. But Kennedy was assassinated only two months after the coup and his successor, Lyndon Johnson, restored aid and recognition. In exchange he received a promise of elections that would never take place.

THE SECOND AMERICAN INTERVENTION: On April 24, 1965, Bosch's supporters, the PRD and its allies – known as Constitutionalists – staged a rebellion. As the military prepared to counterattack, Constitutionalist leader Col. Francisco Caamaño Deñó sought to arrrange a cease fire with US ambassador William Tapley Bennett. Bennett, a staunch anti-communist, believed that the Constitutionalists were attempting to create a "second Cuba." With US encouragement, the military led by General Elías Wessín y Wessín counterattacked, but on April 28 they were routed from Santo Domingo. Following the precedent set by Wilson 50 years before him, President Johnson – concerned with prevention at all costs of "another Cuba" and with sending a message to the North Vietnamese – ordered troops in that same day. Altogether, 23,000 American troops occupied the nation. The invasion was justified to the American public by the need to protect American lives and, when that explanation didn't wash, the administration pulled from a hat a contrived list of 58 "communists" maintained to be hiding in the Constitutionalists' ranks. The US pressured OAS members into sending token units to comprise an Inter-American Peace Force but compromised the OAS's integrity in the process by gerrymandering the vote tally through inclusion of a representative of the Dominican junta. With the exception of Costa Rica, only totalitarian OAS members such as Nicaragua and Paraguay agreed to send troops. Despite the US claim that the invasion was to protect and evacuate US citizens, its real intent was to prevent the return of Juan Bosch and the Constitutionalists. On Aug. 31, 1965, after several thousand deaths, the war was halted when the US pressed Constitutionalist and conservative forces to sign an OAS-crafted Institutional Act and an Act of Reconciliation, which led to the appointment of Hector Garcia-Godoy as interim president. The US government showed the world how a strong nation can control the destiny of a weaker one, a heavy hand which continues right up to the present day.

BALAGUER RETURNS: Although Bosch was permitted to return from exile and run for the presidency, threats to his life forced him to keep a low profile. Heading his *Partido Reformista* (PR, Reformist Party) Balaguer won 57% of the vote to Bosch's 39%, but he also spent $13 million on the campaign; the Americans – who had arrived to *prevent* Bosch from regaining power – were still occupying the nation, and there were widespread reports of fraud and intimidation. Officially, 25% more votes were cast in this election than the one previous, a statistic which curiously corresponded directly with Balaguer's margin of victory. Ruling from 1966 to '78, the former Trujillo puppet president, often seen as a civilian *caudillo* (general), proved himself a shrewd administrator. His administration was characterized by graft and abuse, and he turned a blind eye to the mysterious right-wing death squad known as *La Banda*, whose 2,000 victims included three newsmen. The group, believed to have been partially composed of police and military officers in civilian garb, was allegedly controlled by National Police commander Gen. Pérez y Pérez and disbanded after national and international pressures forced Balaguer to replace him. Re-elected twice in farcical elections, Balaguer presented a hyperbolic image of prosperity which in no way accorded with the underlying realities of a socially and economically devastated nation. The US gave the nation over $132 million during Balaguer's first two years in office, and its sugar quota was upped as well. During the mid to late 70s, he spent hundreds of millions of dollars on public works projects such as dams, roads, and tourist facilities, creating a "Miracle," which benefited the middle and upper class while denying pay increases to government workers, raising taxes, and stunting social welfare programs. Multinationals were given red carpet treatment – and gold mining, ferronickel, and bauxite production bloomed along with tourism – but unemployment remained at an abysmal 20-25%. Peasants were forced to subsidize the "boom" through government-imposed price controls on agricultural products. On Feb. 3, 1973, former Constitutionalist force commander Francisco Caamaño Deñó, in the company of nine companions, staged an unsuccessful invasion attempt. At the commencement of the invasion, Balaguer declared a state of emergency, closing newspapers and radio and TV stations, sending troops onto streets and campuses, and detaining some 1,400 labor, political, and student leaders. Later that year, defeated for his party's nomination, Juan Bosch formed his *Partido Liberacion Dominicano* (PLD, Dominican Liberation Party). The PRD, headed by Peña Gomez, nominated prosperous rancher Antonio Guzmán in both the 1974 elections – during which soldiers sported *Partido Reformista* flags from the ends of their bayonets – and again in 1978.

THE GUZMÁN PRESIDENCY: In the 1978 elections Balaguer and his clique pressured government workers to vote for him and instituted a massive PR campaign. When early returns showed Guzmán leading by 180,000 votes, military units seized the ballot boxes for the National District from the Central Electoral headquarters in Santo Domingo. Captain America, personified this time by the Carter Administration, came to the rescue. Secretary of State Cyrus Vance, together with the head of the Canal Zone-based US Southern Military Command, flew to Santo Domingo. Under US pressure and with the threat of a general strike hanging over his head, Balaguer had no choice but to compel the military to return the ballot boxes. After granting considerable concessions to the Balaguer camp, Guzmán became president. The Guzmán years were undistinguished, and he was faced with rising oil prices and falling sugar revenues. Although he doubled the minimum wage – which had been frozen during the Balaguer years – the increase failed to compensate for inflation. After he doubled gas prices in July 1979, a protest by taxi drivers ended with several deaths. Guzmán then nationalized the public transportation system. In Aug. 1979 Hurricane David struck, causing a billion dollars in damage and leaving over 1,000 dead and as many as 10,000 homeless. Hurricane Frederick followed close on its heels. In Oct. 1979, the government purchased Rosario Dominicano, S.A., a gold mine.

THE JORGE BLANCO PRESIDENCY: Choosing not to run again, Guzmán was replaced by moderate-left lawyer Salvador Jorge Blanco. Running against Blanco were Joaquín Balaguer and Juan Bosch. Receiving 47% of the popular vote, the PRD victory was marred by Guzmán's suicide in the National Palace just a month before Blanco's inauguration. Through his death, he staved off investigation of a corruption scandal involving his daughter Sonia who served as his personal secretary. Unfortunately, he also missed the opportunity to become the first president in Dominican history to have been elected, to have completed his office without attempting to extend it, and to have turned over his office to a properly elected successor. After sugar prices plunged to four cents a pound and the public debt skyrocketed to $4 billion, the IMF agreed to loan the nation $599 million, contingent upon currency devaluation, import restrictions, and budget cuts. After the government raised oil prices as dictated by the IMF in 1984, riots erupted in Santo Domingo in April, quickly spreading to 20 cities and towns. In three days of fighting, 7,000 were arrested, 500 were injured, and 100 died. Notably, the government employed the US-trained crack troops, the *Cazadores de la Montaña* to shoot protesters. The administration disputed guidelines with the IMF for a year while an emergency $50 million loan from the US prevented the nation from defaulting on a number of major foreign loans. In 1985 the IMF agreed to loosen its hangman's noose and loaned $79 million, only a quarter of the $300 million which would have been given had the austerity measures been complied with. In that same year judges walked out on a three-month strike in protest against the administration's failure to increase salaries and depoliticize the courtroom. On Feb. 11, in reaction to staggering price increases for food and gas, a general strike virtually shut down Santo Domingo as well as at least five other cities. Rollbacks followed. During Blanco's tenure, despite his reputation as a defender of human rights and liberties, the government arrested and detained important labor leaders, attempted the licensing of journalists, and allegedly repressed left-wing activists. Unfortunately, despite pledges to the contrary, he failed to prune the government bureaucracy, and the number of employees shot up 40% to 250,000. Although Blanco did not use it as a tool as Balaguer had allegedly done before him, corruption reached dizzily dismaying levels. Positive points of his administration were a low-income housing program and a literacy campaign. As a footnote, the final verdict on his administration is not in. On Aug. 8, 1991, Blanco was convicted of embezzling $5 million through inflating the price of equipment purchased by the military and national police force during his last two years in office. Along with his chief of armed forces, he has been sentenced to 20 years in jail. The sentences are under appeal, and Blanco maintains that he is being persecuted by the Balaguer administration.

BALAGUER RETURNS: For the 1986 elections, the PRD selected Jacobo Majluta, former interim president after Guzmán's suicide. Leftists within the party disputed the choice, charging that Majluta was but a carbon copy of Guzmán. Heading the Reformist Social Christian party ticket, Balaguer brought reminiscences of the good old days to the minds of voters. Early returns showed Balaguer and Majluta running neck-and-neck, with Balaguer commanding a slim lead. Claiming victory, Majluta demanded a recount. An independent commission headed by the Catholic archbishop of Santo Domingo verified Balaguer's victory and persuaded Majluta that it would be in the nation's best interests to accept it. In the final count Balaguer had won by less than 50,000 votes, and Bosch had gained 18% of the vote. Continuing to rule in his old clientelist, patrimonial fashion – dispensing land titles in the outback each weekend and ordering subsidized food dispensed from government trucks – the now nearly sightless 79-year-old Balaguer ran a "moralization campaign" which focused on the PRD opposition. The campaign forced ex-president Jorge Blanco into US exile. Tourists surpassed the one million mark in 1987 for the first time. New industrial duty-free zones opened, but as import-substitution industries were not expanded, basic goods became increasingly scarce and services deteriorated to the point where hundreds of people would stand in street corners to await transport, electric blackouts were frequent, and basic foodstuffs (eggs, flour, bread, sugar) were in short supply. Rioting began in early 1988, largely led by the nebulous *Coordinadora de Luchas Populares* (Coordinator of Popular Struggles). The organization lost support after the nation's major opposition parties and labor confederation criticized its violent approach. The Catholic Church stepped in and organized the Tripartite Dialogue; it forged a compromise which was ratified on May 28. However, business reneged on its promises and by mid-June labor confederations were again calling for a strike. The inflation rate soared to some 60% that year.

BALAGUER YET AGAIN: In May 1990, an 83-year-old Balaguer, garnering 35% of the vote, defeated 80-year-old Juan Bosch. Bosch cried foul and invoked a period of "national mourning." Combined with increases in fuel and food prices, the controversy over the election led to three strikes as well as rioting which shut down the nation for weeks. The same year saw inflation double from the year before and climb to over 100% for the first time in the nation's history, and the foreign debt climbed to more than $45 billion. Fuel became scarce and power blackouts frequent; basic foodstuffs such as beans, rice, bread and even sugar became either unavailable or for sale only at black market prices. In spite of it all, Balaguer has continued his classically *caudillo* form of rule, having spent some $3 billion on roads, housing, stadiums, and the Columbus Lighthouse since 1986. Millions have been spent on sharks and whales to populate the new aquarium. As pundits on the opposition put it, "If Balaguer cannot make the republic rich, at least he can make it beautiful." The question that remains unanswered has been whether beautiful will satisfy? Balaguer himself has remained a shadowy and iconoclastic figure. Always clad in a dark suit and fedora, he pays a visit to his mother's tomb every Sun.

THE 1994 ELECTIONS: The major candidates in this race were incumbent 86-year-old president Joaquin Balaguer, José Francisco Peña Gómez of the PRD, and another octogenarian, Juan Bosch of the PLD. Other candidates included Jacobo Majluta of the *Partido Revolucionario Independiente*, who served as president for a month after Guzmán's suicide, and controversial and outspoken priest Antonio Reynoso of the *Movimiento Nuevo Poder*, a grassroots coalition of minority parties. After making public his candidacy, the Catholic Church announced his suspension as Jarabacoa's parish priest. Balaguer took his time in formally announcing his candidacy. Donald Reid-Cabral – former Interim Government President after Juan Bosch's deposition, member of Reverend Sun Myung Moon's "International Host Committee" – led the *Movimiento Lo Que Diga Balaguer*, a cheerleading squad exhorting him to run during the course of near-daily televised rallies. Balaguer was re-elected in May 1994. Peña Gómez cried fraud and claimed that some 100,000 of his supporters were somehow omitted from the voting rolls. Independent observers also cited irregularities. Balaguer's re-election is bad news for the newly-announced total boycott of Haiti. Smuggling of oil and other goods is widespread, and it is alleged that the same military who are supposed to be policing the smuggling are in fact engaging in it.

Important Dates In Dominican History

1492:	Columbus lands on Hispaniola.
1564:	Santiago and Concepcíon de la Vega rocked by earthquake.
1586:	Santo Domingo sacked by Sir Francis Drake.
1655:	Santo Domingo repels another British invasion.
1697:	Under Treaty of Ryswick, Spain cedes the western third of the island to France.
1801:	Toussaint invades Santo Domingo.
1809:	The Spanish drive the French out.
1821:	Haitians occupy the nation.
1844:	Juan Pablo Duarte and La Trinitaria drive out the Haitians.
1861:	President Pedro Santana announces that the nation will again become a Spanish colony.
1865:	Dominican independence re-established.
1870:	Bill authorizing annexation of Samaná Peninsula fails to pass the US Senate.
1882:	Jesus Galván's classic novel *Enriquillo* published. Ulises Heureux becomes president.
1899	President Ulises Heureux assassinated.
1907	The nation is placed under receivership by Theodore Roosevelt.
1911:	President Ramón Cáceres assassinated.
1916:	US troops land and begin an eight-year occupation.
1930:	Trujillo wins the 1930 elections with more votes than there are eligible voters. Hurricane hits the nation hard.
1953:	The Dominican Republic becomes first Latin American nation to sign a bilateral Mutual Defense Assistance Agreement with the US.

1961:	Trujillo assassinated.
1962:	Juan Bosch becomes the first democratically elected president in the nation's history.
1963:	Juan Bosch overthrown.
1965:	Constitutionalists lead a rebellion; US invades.
1966:	Joaquin Balaguer elected president; he is re-elected in 1970 and 1974.
1978:	Antonio Gúzman elected president.
1979:	Hurricanes David and Frederick strike.
1982:	Jorge Blanco elected.
1986:	Joaquin Balaguer re-elected president; he is re-elected in 1990 and in 1994.

Government

Historically, as just described, the Dominican Republic has been plagued by self-serving, megalomaniacal, and corrupt dictators who have provided the role models for political leadership up to the present. Although he has been dead for nearly a quarter-century, the shadow of Trujillo still looms large over the Dominican political scene. This *caudillo* on horseback, though despicable, was nonetheless a brilliant showman who brought a degree of order and organization to the country. Like a woman who cannot decide between two suitors, the nation remains continually torn between authoritarianism and democracy. Today, Dominican political culture can best be characterized as a struggle between the authoritarian tradition of the *conquistadores* – typified by the *caudillo* and *personalismo* – and the US-influenced tradition of democratic legalism. Political parties remain dependent on a single leader and have failed to emerge as true institutions. Although no form of government has ever worked well in the Dominican Republic, with elections held since 1978, democracy is now better established than ever before.

POLITICAL STRUCTURE: The country is currently on its 25th constitution, one ratified in 1966. As in many other Latin American nations, the system of checks and balances and citizens' rights associated with democracies have been guaranteed by each constitution and cast aside as soon as the ink has dried. Elected to a four-year term by direct vote, the president heads the executive branch of government. He must not have been on active duty with the armed forces or the police within one year prior to the election. Because the people have come to expect a personal and paternalistic approach from their leader, an extraordinary amount of power is couched in the executive branch. Head of the public administration and supreme chief of the armed forces, the president also appoints cabinet members. The bicameral legislature, the National Assembly, is divided into the Senate and the Chamber of Deputies. One senator from each of the 26 provinces (and one from the National District of Santo Domingo) is elected by direct vote to four-year terms. Also serving four years, the 120 members of the Chamber of Deputies are apportioned in accordance with the population of each province. Congress meets for two 90-day sessions which begin on Feb. 27 and Aug. 16 respectively. The Congress commands broad legislative powers, including the ability to approve treaties, regulate the national debt, levy taxes, and to proclaim a state of national emergency. The President appoints a governor to head each of the 26 provinces (*provincias*), and provinces have no legislature nor much independence. The provinces are divided into 96 municipalities (*municipos*). The judicial branch is headed by the Supreme Court of Justice; its nine members are elected by the Senate. As all judges serve four-year terms, judicial independence is not maintained.

ELECTIONS: All citizens 18 yrs. or older or those who are under 18 but married are entitled to vote. Although voting is compulsory, the law is not enforced. Elections are held for both local and national offices once every four years in May. The three members of the Central Electoral Board, a supervising body responsible for printing ballots, are elected by the Senate.

POLITICAL PARTIES: Although there are some 20 parties, only three are of consequence. The *Partido Reformista Social Cristiano* (PRSC, Christian Social Reformist Party) represents a fusion of Joaquín Balaguer's *Partido Reformista* (PR, Reformist Party) and the Christian Social Revolutionary Party (PRSC), a merger which cemented his surprise victory in 1986. While the alliance gave the Christian Socialists an opportunity to play a major role in the political scene, Balaguer benefited from the legitimacy afforded by a party representing the Church and urban workers. It also helped that the party had ties with the Christian Democratic World Union and other organizations related to the international Christian democratic movement. The *Partido Revolucionario Dominicano* (PRD, Dominican Revolutionary Party) offers a center-left face: it is social democratic and a member of the Socialist International. Since Juan Bosch left in 1973, it has been driven by José Francisco Peña Gómez who headed his party's presidential ticket in 1990 and again in 1994. The nation's third major party is the *Partido Libera-cion Dominicano* (PLD, Dominican Liberation Party) which gained 18% of the votes in the 1986 election. Although Juan Bosch has smoothed over his rhetoric, he continues to champion the poor while attacking Balaguer's as well as the PRD's corruption. His 1986 campaign theme was "Neither a murderer or a thief." The extraordinary surge in Bosch's support during the 1990 campaign reflected the deep seated dissatisfaction many Dominicans felt with the current regime as well as the failure of a younger, capable leader to emerge in the nearly three decades since Bosch's over-throw. In any event, as twin titans Balaguer and Bosch pass on in the coming years, the nation's major parties appear headed for a shakeup. As both the PLD and PRSC spring from their *patrón's* support base, it is unlikely that either will survive intact in their present form

Economy

The Dominican Republic's export economy has historically re-volved around a single crop, sugarcane, and one foreign nation, the United States. Although attempts have been made to diversify the economy, the country has been traditionally so dependent upon sugar that price fluctuations, imposed from abroad, have managed to topple many administrations. Second only to Puerto Rico as a market for US goods in the Caribbean, the US also buys two-thirds of the country's exports. One factor that has worked against the nation in recent years has been the rising cost of oil. Wheras 1,000 lbs. of sugar purchased 12 barrels of oil in 1974, the same amount of sugar bought less than three by 1981. **persistent problems:** Despite the substantial sugar and import-export business, the Do-minicans have remained impoverished. This is because only the elite and foreigners have have benefited from the economy's largesse. Another problem has been that much of the nation's potential has been underdeveloped or undeveloped. Reasons for this include 300 years of colonial neglect under the Spanish, the political chaos of the 19th C which continued unabated into the 20th, the chilling effects of the Trujillo years, the lack of investment capital, and a small population. The infrastructure has remained poor until recently. **balance of payments:** Excluding the free trade zone transactions which exceed those of the rest of the nation combined, the Dominican Republic reported a $226 million current account deficit in 1990. Exports contracted 24% owing to the US recession and lower ferronickel prices; sugar exports also fell by 26%. Remittances by Dominicans living abroad rose to $315 million, and tourism contributed $900 million, a 10% increase. In 1992, the nation's export trade volume reached $2.5 billion and imports dropped to $660 million. A major underground source of income in the Dominican Republic comes from the transshipment of cocaine, which is first brought into Haiti from Colombia (to the tune of one metric ton per month) and then smuggled into the Dominican Republic where it goes to Puerto Rico and then into the US. The Colombian operators, who are thought to have ties with the Cali drug cartel, pose as Dominicans when crossing the border.

WAGES AND UNIONS: The minimum wage stands at D$1,450 a month. Only about 15% of some 200 workers belong to organized unions. Still in force since the Trujillo era, the Labor Code forbids public employees from striking. Lacking a strong financial base, unions are also divided, and many are often affiliated with political parties. The once-contentious situation at the Gulf & Western sugar refineries and tourist complex has been smoothed over since its takeover by Central Romana. At present an estimated 30% of Dominicans are unemployed and another 20% are underemployed. Over 40% of the population is between 18 and 29, and the lack of job opportunities has understandably led to social tension and instability.

THE PUBLIC SECTOR: An ironic inheritance of the Trujillo Era is the extensive involvement by the government in industry, agriculture, and commerce. Although the government originally confiscated Trujillo's properties in order to sell them and terminate his family's influence, the state has ended up holding on to the properties and practicing a form of mismanaged socialism. Today, government assets are divided into two major divisions. The *Consejo Estatal de Azúcar* (CEA – State Sugar Council) and the *Corporación de Fomento Industrial* (CFI – the State Enterprises Corporation). A deficit-laden white elephant, the *Corporación Dominicana de Electricidad* (CDE, Dominican Electricity Corporation) is legendary for its blackouts; it continues to be overstaffed with poorly maintained facilities. **employees:** Nearly half of all Dominicans are estimated to be government employees, for the most part in 23 state enterprises. Estimates in the late 1980s had the public sector generating nearly 20% of the GNP, 40% of all investment, and 40% of all financial activities. Much of the reason for the huge bureaucracy is that presidents have viewed the civil service as their private fiefdom and awarded posts galore to friends, family, and loyal party members. Despite rhetoric to the contrary, Guzmán increased the number of employees by 50-60% and Jorge Blanco upped the ante by 40%.

THE PRIVATE SECTOR: One reason for the nation's dire straits is the attitude taken by businessmen. With no annual land tax, no property tax, no taxes on wealth, no taxes on capital gains, and loophole-laden corporate taxes, the Dominican Republic has been unable to generate revenues adequate to keep pace with its growing economy. Despite their recognition of the pressing need for fiscal and other reform, members of the aristocratic business class, appearing to lack a sense of social responsibility, remain firmly opposed paying their fair share.

FOREIGN INVESTMENT: A growth in US investments has often followed US political/military intervention in the Dominican Republic. As a major source of investment capital, US firms operate some 414 subsidiaries in the country's 26 "free zones." Companies with substantial investments include Esso, Alcoa, 3M, Xerox, Gilette, Colgate, Palmolive, and Phillip Morris. Many fear that these multinationals are striving to take over the government. In an attempt to cope with this problem by taking matters into their own hands, the government purchased the Rosario Dominicana, the largest open-pit gold mine in the Western Hemisphere. In an about-face, the Balaguer administration has now put it on the market again. Under the Caribbean Basin Initiative's "twin-plant program," firms with operations in Puerto Rico are permitted to operate a second support facility. For example, Westinghouse employs some 800 Dominicans at exploitative wages (around US70¢ ph or less) to work on circuit boards, circuit breakers, and other devices which are then shipped to Puerto Rico for assembly and calibration. In 1994, Mickey Kantor, US trade representative, is scheduled to rule on a petition from the AFL-CIO to deny preferential access to Dominican goods because the 420 companies which operate in its 26 duty free zones allegedly are denied the right to organize. Although there are over 100 official trade unions in the zones, not one has ever negotiated a labor contract. The manufacturers claim that the Dominicans are happy with things as they are – low wages and poor working conditions. The AFL-CIO asserts that female employees are sexually harrassed, health and safety regulations are regularly violated, and clean drinking water and basic sanitary facilities are denied. An earlier petition in 1992 was turned down after the nation adopted a new labor code. It is generally agreed that this code is not being enforced. Although a commission (composed of government offi-cials, workers, and employers) was instituted in August 1993, it has been wracked by internal conflict and has yet to meet! **Gulf & Western:** Until it sold its holdings in 1985 to the Fanjul family of Palm Beach, Florida, the name of Gulf & Western was synonymous with the evils associated with foreign control. Gulf & Western, through such activities as union-busting and bribery, managed to antagonize both the left and the right; many, including the Domini-can Liberation Party, had called for its nationalization. Elements of its $200 million stake in the country ranged from sugar refineries to real estate and top hotels. Sometimes referred to as a "state within a state," its annual sales exceeded the nation's GNP. Acquir-ing the sugar plantations and refinery of South Puerto Rico Sugar Company in 1966, Gulf & Western moved to destroy the inde-pendent sugarcane workers' union; a company-controlled union was substituted. In a nation where only 14% of the land is arable and 75% of the population is either landless or cultivating subsis-tence plots, Gulf & Western owned a full 2% of the land area. Less than half of this was used for sugar; the rest was devoted to ranching and other export crops. The company also held a major share of the tourist industry, with its own multi-million dollar resort complexes (Casa del Campo and Altos de Chavon) in La Romana, as well as control of luxury hotels in Santo Domingo. In 1969, Gulf & Western set up an industrial free zone (in which goods are manufactured utilizing cheap Dominican labor) near La Ro-mana – the first company to do so – under a 30-yr. government contract. About half of the companies operating in the zone were Gulf & Western subsidiaries. **frankly Fanjul:** Purchasing Gulf & Western's Dominican and Florida holdings for an estimated $200-240 million, the new owners of the Gulf & Western properties have kept a lower profile. Cuban-born entrepreneurs Alfonso and José "Pepe" Fanjul have made a fortune in the sugar business in Florida and maintain many ties to right wing groups both in the US and in the Dominican Republic. In addition to having Carlos Morales, the nation's vice president, as a minority stockholder, they also have loaned their Lear jet to Balaguer on occasion. Pepe, who donated US$100,000 to Bush's election campaign, has dined at the White House. The Fanjuls have become notorious for their alleged under-payment of workers slaving in their Florida sugarcane plantations. While their conditions at their US plantations have been termed exploitative, their Dominican estates are said to provide the best working conditions in the country.   "Best," of course is relative compared to conditions on the government-run plantations which human rights group Americas Watch has likened to slavery.

genealogy: The Fanjul's family history reads like a Cuban "Dynasty." The lineage's founder, André Goméz Mena, arrived in Cuba as an impoverished teenager in the 1850s, built up a small fortune, became a prosperous landowner, and perished when he was shot by a cuckolded husband in 1917. One of his daughters married Alfonso Fanjul, Sr., a prosperous sugar broker. The Fanjul family had invested in New York City real estate and fled there after Batista's overthrow in 1959. Investing $165,000 to gain a 25% stake in a company, which moved a Louisiana sugar mill to 4,000 acres of remote Florida farmland just drained by the Corps of Engineers, they built up a new sugar empire. Today, their net worth has been estimated by *Forbes* to be in the $500 million range.

DUTY-FREE ZONES: First established in 1970, 300 firms operate in the nation's 25 duty-free zones. They are located in the vicinity of La Romana, San Pedro de Macorís, Puerto Plata, Santiago, Azua, Barahona, El Seibo, Higüey, San Francisco de Macorís, La Vega, Baní, and elsewhere. Foreign firms have been lured by attractive tax exemptions (75-100% on income), dirt cheap labor (37¢ per hour), the lack of unions, low to no customs duties, cheap rent (14¢ per sq ft per month) and other benefits. The multinational firms must pay for rent, salaries, and local supplies in US dollars through the Central Bank. Still, the duty-free zones contribute only slightly to reducing inflation and to the nation's balance of payments. Over 90% of exports go to the US; garments and textiles account for 60% of production, and footwear, leather goods, and electronic components are also manufactured. In 1990, they employed some 120,000 and exports came to $790 million.

TOURISM: Seen by some as the "new sugar," tourism has grown dramatically in recent decades, from near zero under Trujillo to 1.3 million visitors today, of whom 25% are returning Dominicans. The nation has some 25,000 hotel rooms and an additional 7,000 are under construction. Today, tourism has surpassed sugarcane in importance and now comprises some 13% of the GNP. Some leaders believe increased political stability is one of the benefits of tourism. Because civil strife or military coups scare away tourists, possibly plunging the economy into recession, politicians will be forced to negotiate rather than fight and the constitution will take on new importance.

MANUFACTURING: Sugar refining accounts for half of the nation's manufacturing sector. Other major products are cement and other non-metallic minerals, leather goods, clothing, footwear, textiles, food, and drink. About 20% of the labor force works in manufacturing. Shamefully, in 1993 US Customs discovered illegally transhipped textile goods from China in 15 of 23 factories they inspected. China has been taking advantage of Section 907 to export duty-free goods to the US illegally.

MINERALS AND MINING: Ferro-nickel and doré, a gold-silver alloy, are the most profitable minerals. Ferro-nickel is mined by Falconridge at Bonao. Panned since the early colonial days, gold is mined along with silver at a mine located near Pueblo Viejo. Established in 1973 as a joint US-Dominican venture and nationalized in 1979, the mine's reserves are rapidly being depleted. About 24 miles W of Barahona in the Valle de Neiba are the major salt deposits, including a million tons of almost pure gypsum and some 250 million tons of salt. The world's largest salt deposit is 10-mile-long Salt Mountain. Salt is also reclaimed from sea water along the coast between Santo Domingo and Barahona. Granite and marble are also mined in the Barahona region, and very high grade marble is found near Samaná. Other ornamental stones include travertine and onyx. Once a mainstay averaging half a million tons per year, bauxite production ceased in 1984 with the withdrawal of Alcoa. The government resumed mining in 1987; some 150,000-200,000 tons are now shipped to Surinam annually for refining. Although oil deposits have been located in the Barahona region in the SW, they are as yet untapped.

LIVESTOCK: The nation has over a million cattle, many of which are descended from the smaller varieties introduced by the Spanish. One recent crossbreed is the Romana Red developed by the La Romana sugar estate. Most of the dairy-produced milk is used to make cheese. Although there are only a few commercial farms, pork is an important form of meat. Pigs dine on refuse and on nuts from the royal palm. Small sheep herds are used for meat rather than wool because the climate precludes the production of high quality wool. A source of meat and milk, goats roam the farms and *barrios*.

FORESTRY AND FISHING: An example of what unregulated logging can do, the Dominican Republic no longer has a forestry industry. Fires and indiscriminate cutting by landless farmers and loggers led to the criminalization of tree felling in 1967. Fishing is only small scale. The major fishing areas are in the Samaná Bay and off Monte Cristi where red snapper, mackerel, kingfish, and shrimp are found.

Agriculture

THE FARMERS: Some 45% of the Dominican population are rural farmers who own small farms (*finquitas*) or sharecrop. Owing to unequal distribution of land – with the upper 10% of the rural farmers controlling 62.7% of the land – the majority must squat on private or government land. Per acre production is among the lowest in Latin America. Wages are extremely low, and plantations which hire less than 10 workers are exempt from labor regulation including minimum wage. Unemployment ranges upward from 70% in the outback, and average annual income is $700. As part of the lasting legacy imparted by 30 years of repressive Trujilloism, the farmers are fatalistic, but they have become more politically active in recent years.

SUGARCANE: Legend has it that sugarcane was introduced to the island by Christopher Columbus when he stopped off at Puerto Plata during his second visit. In fact, sugar has been grown since the 16th C, but only small quantities were grown until the end of the 19th C. Two events changed this. One was the Spanish reoccupation (1861-1865) which brought Spanish and Italian immigrants who moved into business and agriculture. Second and more important was Cuba's Ten Years War (1868-1878), which resulted in the migration of displaced sugar planters to the Dominican Republic. Well capitalized and possessing the needed technical skills, they instituted mass production in the 1870s. Sugar rapidly became the cornerstone of the national economy. In 1921, a banner year for production, sugar exports garnered $45 million, a figure 423% higher than all other exports combined! Sugar prices have always been susceptible to severe fluctuation. Between the late 1910s and the early 1920s the price dipped from 22¢ a pound to 2¢ a pound! The ups and downs in the market meant consolidation. By 1925, only 21 estates remained, and 12 of these were US-owned, controlling over 81% of the total acreage. All this development did not come without a price. Economic problems resulting included the transfer of the domestic economy into foreign ownership, a greatly increased dependance on the international commodity market, and decreasing capability to grow enough food for local consumption owing to the destruction of diversified agriculture in the cane-growing regions. Along with these other changes, the populace in these areas were transformed from independent farmers with small holdings into a rural proletariat totally dependent on the sugar companies. Politically disenfranchised and voiceless, the peasantry were powerless to prevent the takeover of their land and the destruction of their way of life. If the companies could not buy land, they could cheat or violently force peasants out of their tracts. Many did not have leases or held insufficient title; the land title system was chaotic and antiquated to say the least. The legal system and laws favored the large companies who could hire lawyers and pay surveyors' fees. In some cases, sugar companies obtained title to whole villages. The Central Romana estate burned El Caimoní and Higüeral, two such small villages, in 1921 leaving 150 families homeless without compensation. Even if a peasant consented to become an independent *colono* raising cane for the plantation, he would have to borrow from the sugar estate and put his land up as collateral in order to finance the transformation. One bad season and he could be ruined. Work conditions on the estates have always been bleak. The practice of importing labor (from Haiti and the Windwards) kept labor prices depressed and prevented workers from unionizing. Despite the high levels of unemployment and underemployment that have traditionally prevailed in the Dominican Republic, it has been cheaper for companies to import more desparate workers from abroad – who might be paid even lower wages than Dominican *braceros* – rather than raise wages to a level which might attract Dominicans. The government-owned and -operated *Consejo Estatal de Azúcar* (CEA – State Sugar Council), which owns 12 of the sugarcane plantations, was formed to run properties expropriated from Trujillo. After building up debts of $200 million by the late 1980s, it has launched a diversification program. The 1985 quota cutback strained relations with the US, and in 1988 the quota dropped to the lowest level since 1875. Today, canecutters are paid just $1.50 per ton of cane cut, and they live under conditions that have been likened to slavery.

COFFEE: The nation's second most important export crop was introduced in 1715. Most farms are located on steep or rolling hills between 1,000 and 3,000 ft. The three major growing areas are the mountainous slopes lining the Cibao Valley, the SE portion of the Cordillera Central between the towns of Baní and San José de Ocoa, and the NE slopes of the mountains S of Barahona. The nation's coffee, a variety of Arabica, is high quality but low yielding.

CACAO: Thought to have originated in the Amazon basin on the E equatorial slopes of the Andes, *Theobroma cacao*, the "food of the gods," has been cultivated for upwards of 2,000 years. After the

Yuca or manioc plant, staple crop of the Tainos

Spanish conquest, *cacao* (known as chocolate or cocoa in its refined form) became an important crop and the Dominican Republic remains one of the world's leading producers; it ranks as the third leading export crop. Much of the harvest comes from small farms in the Cibao and Yuna valleys and from the humid coastal lowlands near the towns of Sabana de la Mar and Miches.

OTHER VEGETABLES: Crops produced include rice, corn, red beans, peanuts, coconut palms for oil, *yuca* (manioc or cassava), sweet potatoes, limitied quantities of white potatoes, pigeon peas, and *yautia* (taro). Grain sorghum is growing in popularity as an alternative animal feed. Vegetable fibers such as cotton, henequen, and sisal are also produced. Bananas and plantains are produced by small growers. Irrigated crops such as cabbage, tomatoes, scallions, onions, radishes, and garlic are intensively cultivated in the Constanza valley. Tobacco, the only other significant export crop, is indigenous and cultivation by settlers began in 1531. Famous for its quality, cultivation centers in the Cibao.

AGROINDUSTRIES: Nontraditionals include citrus fruits, pineapples, chinola (passion fruit), oranges, melons, olives, cashews, and other vegetables. Dole's role is growing in the country. Dole Fresh Fruit International has invested another $41 million in the nation and intends to turn the country into a major pineapple exporter. Foreign Investment Law No. 61 limits foreign ownership of agroindustries to 49% of equity, a limit investors say hamstrings them Ironically, despite the push to develop crops for export, the nation is not yet self sufficient in very basic staples such as rice and beans.

The People

Caribbean culture is truly creole culture. The word "creole" comes from *criar* (Spanish for "to bring up" or "to rear"). In the New World, this term referred to children born in this hemisphere, implying that they were not quite authentic or pure. Later, creole came to connote "mixed blood," but not just blood has been mixed here. Cultures have been jumbled as well. Because of this extreme mixture, the Caribbean is a cultural goldmine. The culture of a specific island or nation depends upon its racial mix and historical circumstances. Brought over on slave ships – where differences of status were lost and cultural institutions shattered – the slaves had to begin anew. In a similar fashion, but not nearly to such a degree, the European, indentured or otherwise, could not bring all of Europe with him. Beliefs were merged in a new blend born of the interaction between different cultures – African and European. Today, a new synthesis has arisen in language, society, crafts, and religion: one which has been shaped by and which reflects historical circumstance.

INDIGENOUS INFLUENCES: Although the Indians have long since vanished, their spirit lives on – in traditions, in the feeling of dramatic sunsets, and in the wafting of the cool breeze. Remaining cultural legacies include foods (*casabe*), place names (Jaragua, Canoa), innumerable words (such as "hammock," an Indian invention), and in native medicines still in use. Even the Indian name for the island, Quisqueya (Mother of All Lands), is still in use. Many Spanish towns were built on old Indian sites; the *bateyes* of the Indians became the plazas of the Spanish. There are also a few remaining archaeological sites and a number of sites with pictographs and petroglyphs.

AFRICAN INFLUENCES: This has been the strongest of all outside influences on those Caribbean islands with large black populations. Arriving slaves had been torn away from both tribe and culture, and this is reflected in everything from the primitive agricultural system to the religious sects and cults that mirror the dynamic diversity of W. African culture. Although the African influence is less pronounced than in neighboring Haiti, it has still been very influential in shaping the culture.

SPANISH INFLUENCES: Spain was the original intruder in the area. Although the Spaniards exited the Dominican Republic in 1821 after more than 500 years of influence, the island's culture is still predominantly Spanish – as are neighboring Cuba and the Puerto Rico. Many Caribbean islands, whether the Spaniards ever settled there or not, still bear the names Columbus bestowed on them 500 years ago. And, although other European influences have had a powerful effect, Spanish continues to be the predominant language in the islands once controlled by Spain. Major Spanish architectural sites remain in the old parts of San Juan and in Santo Domingo. In the Dominican Republic, the Spanish legacy continues in the form of *personalismo*, the worship of leaders. Constitutions have often been ignored, elections have been contested, and often only lip service has been paid to democracy.

AMERICAN INFLUENCES: The history of the U.S. is inextricably linked with the Caribbean in general and the Dominican Republic in particular. Although American influence predates the American occupations, baseball, the national passion, was introduced by the Marines who also laid the path for the accession of Trujillo. Television and fast food continue to have their effect as have the migration and return of Dominicans to the mainland. The nation also remains economically dependent on the US.

Los Dominicanos/The Dominicans

As with so many of its neighboring islands, the Dominican Republic has forged a unique racial and cultural mix. The Taino Indians, the original inhabitants of the island, were forced into slavery by the Spanish *conquistadores* and exterminated. Other arrivals over the centuries have included Spanish, Italians, Germans, other Europeans, Africans brought in as slaves, escaped slaves from the US, Sephardic Jews from Curacao, Jewish refugees from Europe, Canary Islanders, Puerto Ricans, Cubans, other West Indians, Chinese, Japanese, and Lebanese. All of these diverse ethnic groups, intermarrying and multiplying, have helped forge modern Dominican culture. Over the course of time, a social structure has emerged. Although most Dominicans are of mixed racial ancestry, the upper class tended to be whiter and the lower class darker. Immigration of sugarcane workers has resulted in the *mulatización* of parts of the society ranging from food and religion to language. Each of the nation's different sectors (E, SW, and N) have developed their own special characteristics, even though these have developed into different subgroups within each area.

NATIONAL PSYCHE: Throughout history, Dominicans have felt a sense of inferiority, fatalism, and despair. Some writers have gone as far as to argue that the Dominicans have a fatal flaw or congenital defect which prevents them from achieving democracy and civilization. Some maintain that the Dominican complex regarding their mulatto background has also handicapped them in their dealings with the outside world. Trujillo's success as a leader came partially as a result of his promise of a release from this karmic cycle.

POPULATION: Some 60% of the population is mulatto with another 35% black and 5% white. Today, it is estimated that some 200,000 Haitians reside in the Dominican Republic. A large percentage of births are illegitimate. Its population density stands at around 145 people per sq km. Although the current growth rate hovers at 2.7%, the population skyrocketed from three million in 1960 to 6.3 million in the mid-1980s to an estimated 7.5 million today. And well over another million Dominicans live within the continental United States. Most have been compelled to migrate by economic necessity. Life expectancy in 1988 was 64 yrs. for men and 68 yrs. for women. The large portion of the Dominican population defined as black is the fastest growing racial category and is largely a result of increased Haitian immigration during the 20th C. Rural folk live 10 years less on average.

CLASS STRUCTURE: Owing to turbulence within the nation, a distinct ruling elite did not coalesce until the end of the 19th C. Up until the time of Trujillo a small, elite Spanish-blooded ruling class (today known as *de primera*) had controlled the nation's political, economic, and social life. Currently composed of some one hundred families, this group thrives in Santiago where its members are businessmen and property owners; its Santo Domingan counterpart is composed of politicians and professionals. Traditionally, they have been joined by the *gente de segunda* who have been slightly less wealthy. To their ranks have been added those who prospered in the Trujillo years as well as a more recent group who have prospered in light industry, banking, and tourism Encouraged by Trujillo, a small middle class – composed of military officers, government employees, businessmen, and industrialists – sprang up and challenged the position of the elite. Today the middle class comprises some 20% of the population. The vast majority of the population remains composed of lower class, uneducated, impoverished, and disenfranchised blacks or mulattos. A 1978 Dominican Planning Agency survey disclosed that 75% of the people have inadequate diets and 50% have diets that are seriously deficient. Only 55% have potable water available. In the rural areas, 80% are illiterate and unemployment rises to 50%.

DOMINICANS ABROAD: Approximately one out of every seven Dominicans now lives outside the nation. New York City has a half-million to a million of these *dominicanos ausentes* (absent Dominicans), and it is now the second largest Dominican city. Many borrow $2,000-10,000 for the trip and some finance it by mortgaging the family house at 10% a month. Many men make the move, slave and save, and visit their families once a year. Under tremendous financial and social pressure to succeed, some have turned to drug dealing as a quick way to make lots of greenbacks. Others have established themselves as outstanding members of the New York community. Many have also emigrated illegally to Puerto Rico where they blend in more readily. The passage is not without its hazards: in 1987 shipwrecked Dominicans just 20 miles off the nation's coast were eaten by sharks. Despite this, Dominicans continue to mount rickety *yolas* (small boats) and risk drowning and shark attacks to cross the dangerous Mona Passage. Paying up to $500 each, the smuggling has proved a popular and profitable business: there are an estimated 100,000-300,000 Dominicans on hand in Puerto Rico at any one time! Soon after arrival, they pick up a stolen or forged birth certificate and learn to talk like Puerto Ricans. Then, it's a simple matter to migrate to the States. It is estimated that these emigrés remit some $500 million annually, an income which is now the nation's largest source of foreign exchange. Although their influence is such that candidates for office in Santo Domingo now campaign in New York, emigrant Dominicans have not really been assimilated into the US, and their main motivation for emigration has been the relatively increased economic opportunities found abroad. However, Dominicans are having their influences on NYC: Dominican newspapers are sold on New York streets on their day of publication and popular Dominican TV series are aired simultaneously in NY and on the island. Returning Dominicans, however, are far from readily re-assimilated. They are branded "Dominican Yorks" or called *cadenús* (after the gold chains popular with drug dealers), and their children are referred to as "Joe." They are seen as bad eggs who are bringing crime to the island.

THE HAITIANS: Since 1915 when the internal agricultural system broke down during the US occupation of Haiti, a steady stream of Haitians have crossed the border to harvest the sugarcane (*zafra*).

While many have returned, about half a million remain. Forced to work an exhausting 12-hr. day at wages below the minimum, they are provided barrack housing (*bateys*) in which to live – concrete or wooden structures generally lacking in light, running water, or toilets. Food is lousy and bosses are abusive. For decades Haitians have been brought across the border in *Kongos* (work teams) through an arrangement with the Haitian government in exchange for a hefty recruitment fee. Trujillo initiated the process by signing an agreement with the Haitian government. In 1983, acting upon the request of the British-based Anti-Slavery Society, the International Labour Office sent a mission to expose the scandalous circumstances. While the report which followed was embarrassing, it did little or nothing to improve their lot. That same year Baby Doc was paid an estimated $2.25 million for supplying the workers. After Duvalier's fall in 1986, many Haitians refused to return to Dominican cane fields. In an effort to entice Dominicans into work in the cane fields, President Jorge Blanco went out and cut cane in front of the TV cameras. Today, some 20,000-30,000 Haitian *braceros* are lured (or even kidnapped) across the border by *buscones* (recruiters) who are paid $7-20 for each Haitian worker delivered. Under the short-lived presidency of Aristide, the Haitian government attacked Dominican abuses. President Balaguer responded by ordering the roundup of some 10,000 Haitians under 16 or over 60 and summarily expelling them from the country during 1991.

DOMINICAN ATTITUDES: Today, Haiti and the Dominican Republic are two countries with their backs turned toward each other. The long domination of the Dominican Republic during the 19th C, combined with the apprehension of inordinate racial dilution through "darkening" and "Africanizing," has spurred on racial antagonisms which are now being brought to bear upon the Haitians. Viewed with little sympathy, the Haitians are thought to be inferior serfs whose destiny is to harvest the Dominicans' sugarcane for them. One of the greatest proponents of racism against Haitians has been President Balaguer who once refused to open the borders, and ignored Haitian accomplishments in a 1984 book about Haiti and the Dominican "destiny." He has blamed deforestation on Haitians, and his administration has alleged that food shortages have resulted because of the Haitian presence. Today, the Haitians find themselves residing in a country that requires their labor yet rejects their presence. Ironically, many aspects of Haitian culture have become integrated into lower class Dominican life, including types of food, housing, and religious beliefs. Peña Gómez, leader of the PRD and a presidential candidate in

1990 and 1994, is also of Haitian ancestry, the son of immigrants who died in Trujillo's 1937 massacre. A final irony is that Trujillo, who cemented Dominican attitudes towards Haitians during his iron-fisted rule, himself had a Haitian maternal great-grandmother who settled in the Dominican Republic during the Haitian occupation.

RACIAL PREJUDICE: Although Dominicans may maintain that racial discrimination is nonexistent, there is a distinctly positive value attached to being white, a bias which accounts in part for the prejudice against Haitians. Women commonly apply color-lightening cosmetics, and facial features in photographs may be whitened. Expressions such as "Indian color," "light mulatto," and "good hair" betray a desire to be white. Still, a black can acquire status through education and financial success, so color does not constitute an impenetrable barrier.

MALE AND FEMALE RELATIONSHIPS: Most lower class Dominicans live together in a common law union. Often the girl is 14, 15, or even younger and already pregnant or a mother when she moves in with her boyfriend. All that's required is the consent of parents on both sides. A man may prefer to wait until a woman of higher status or lighter color comes along before he marries, and he may also live with more than one woman before he marries, often in middle age.

COMPADRAZGO: Literally "co-parentage," this important practice of social bonding resembles the system of godparents found in the States, but is much more solemn. Selected when a child is baptized, *compadres* and *comadres* can be counted on to help out financially in a pinch. A poor farmer may seek out a rich employer to be his child's *padrino*. The employer will assent because he knows that this will tighten the bonds between himself and his employee. Or such a relationship may be sought merely to cement a close friendship between males. It is considered treasonous to conspire against one's *compadre* or *padrino* – a belief crafty Trujillo exploited to his advantage by conducting mass baptisms at which he became the godfather of thousands of peasants' children.

MALES IN THE SOCIETY: The Dominican Republic is indisputably a male-dominated society (as are all Latin cultures). The male ethos rests on a trilogy of concepts: *personalismo*, the *patrón*, and *machismo*. Stressing individual uniqueness, *personalismo* values dignity and honor above responsiblility to a group and personal integrity over abstract rights and institutions. An important corollary is idealism (coinciding with the extolling of visionary ideals) while a correspondingly low value is placed on compromise, which is seen as a blot on one's character because it invokes skepticism as to the purity of one's ideals. Because individual honor is so sensitive, encounters are polite and cordial. Individuals are believed to shape the country – as Dominican history has borne out – and politicians attempt to portray themselves as dramatic and dynamic leaders as opposed to public servants. Although the *patrón* system originated under the plantation system, it permeates the entire society. In return for his guidance, the *patrón* demands unswerving and unquestioning loyalty. *Machismo* (maleness) reinforces these traditional values. Males are expected to be daring, forceful, virile, competitive, and to have a sense of humor and fatalism. This image is tied to the *caballero*, the gentleman-knight of 16th C. Spain. Deriding manual labor, the *caballero* styled himself as a cultured and artistic intellectual. While among the upper classes, the *macho* ideal is fulfilled through leadership, lower class males are at the bottom of the pecking order and must demonstrate their *machismo* through sexual and physical prowess.

FEMALES IN THE SOCIETY: The Dominican woman looks to the male for her definition, and the feminine ideal is the exact opposite of *machismo*. Traditional feminine ideals are gentleness, passivity, self-sacrifice, abnegation, and the identification of herself with her husband. A dedicated homemaker, she should devote her life to the welfare of her husband and children. Unlike the male, who is expected to be sexually promiscuous, women must be faithful regardless of their husband's behavior. Despite this, Dominican women are generally hardworking and, as many must rear their children without male support, they are also self-reliant. Sadly, owing to the economic situation and the lack of male responsibility for the children they father, many women have been forced into prostitution. There are an estimated 60,000 prostitutes on the island, and prostitutes have become a major export: some 7,000 work in Amsterdam alone. To the typical Dominican male, women are seen as a commodity, rather like cigarettes.

ATTITUDES TOWARDS AMERICANS: Generally, Dominicans have a favorable attitude towards US citizens. Unfortunately, many have a false image of North America and Europe, believing the streets to be lined with gold. Despite a singularly unfortunate historical legacy, there is little or no resentment. Western women, and American women in particular, are often courted by Dominican males who covet them because they possess the "three Bs": blonde hair, big boobs, and (most importantly) a blue passport.

THE MILITARY: Once at the forefront of the nation during the Trujillo years, the military establishment has exercised a lower profile since the Guzmán administration. While there has been a focus on a new "professional" military in recent years, the army has also been increasing its individual and institutional economic clout. The military is legendary not only for budget misuse and corruption but also for its alleged involvement in the nation's burgeoning drug trade. During Balaguer's first terms of office, many generals became millionaires, and the process of self-enrichment has continued since despite Guzmán's attempts to reform the military hierarchy. A US-subsidized "modernization" program has included training of an elite counter-insurgency unit known as the *Cazadores de la Montagne* (Highland Rangers) who were used to shoot the populace during the 1984 riots. While the military supports "democracy" such as it is in the nation, it may well have a different reaction should meaningful efforts be made to pull its hand out of the till.

OTHER GROUPS: Trujillo instituted an open-door policy towards Caucasian immigrants, and large numbers of Western Europeans arrived. Trujillo hoped that they would produce white babies as a bulwark against the burgeoning blacks. Hundreds of Japanese families were recruited by Trujillo in the 1950s and settled in many areas but today remain only in the villages of Constanza and Jarabacoa. Chinese arrived during the mid-1960s and invested in real estate and tourism. Today, large numbers of Syrians, Lebanese, and Turkish immigrants run clothing stores and restaurants in the cities. Refugees include a small number of Jews remaining in Sosúa, a colony of 5,000 refugees from the Spanish Civil War who arrived in 1940, and 600 Hungarians who fled the Soviet invasion following the 1956 elections.

Religion

Any visitor to the Dominican Republic will soon take note of the importance of religion, particularly among the womenfolk. Churches abound, even in small villages, and the country practically grinds to a halt during the Christmas and Easter seasons. While the majority are Catholics, evangelicals are playing an increasingly prominent role, and there are a small number of Jews, Muslims, and Ba'hais. Other sects include Mennonites, Jehovahs Witnesses, Mormons, *Vudu* practicioners, and Soka Gakkai International (SGI) – a Japanese Buddhist cult.

Catholicism

Some 93% of Dominicans are Catholics, and the Church's influence resounds throughout Dominican society. Every town, large or small, has its Catholic church, and the clergy have had an important historical impact.

HISTORY: Introduced with Columbus, the Catholic Church became a major national force only with the accession of Trujillo. *El jefe* entered into a smooth, mutually beneficial relationship with the Church. Out of shrewdly enlightened self-interest, he helped finance and supervise church construction, changed marriage from a civil to religious institution, permitted the Society of Jesus to return for the first time since the colonial era, and allowed clerics to become armed forces chaplains. He also signed a concordat with the Vatican. The first in the nation's history, it greatly strengthened the powers of the Church. In return, Trujillo gained a flow of positive propaganda, and the Church annulled his second marriage and bestowed a papal blessing on his third. To many Dominicans, the Church seemed to be another arm of his government. At the time of his assassination, the Church was as powerful in the Dominican Republic as anywhere in Latin America. At the top, the Catholic archbishop, as head of an electoral commission, prevented the controversy over the 1986 elections from erupting into civil war. At the local level, the Church operates hospitals, dispensaries, schools, old age homes, and orphanages. Some priests have even espoused Liberation Theology, in the past actively challenging the ruthless land acquisition policies of the Rosario Mining Company near the town of Pueblo Viejo and the expansionist policy of Gulf & Western in the E sugarcane fields. The government reacted negatively: the priests were subjected to police intimidation and repression. Unfortunately, priests of this high caliber are in the minority, and the bulk of the Church's energy has been regressively directed towards combatting progressive governmental policies such as family planning and divorce liberalization. While the Church had failed to rail against Trujillo – under whose sponsorship it prospered – until the tail end of his administration, its heirarchy wasted no time in branding Bosch a "communist" during his presidency. On the other hand, the Church spoke openly against the paramilitary units which were terrorizing the urban *barrios*. In recent years, it has also been outspoken on the mistreatment of the Haitian cane cutters. Since Balaguer's reelection in 1990, the Church has come under attack for allegedly displaying little concern over the country's economic crisis and for serving as an apologist for Balaguer. However, just before the 1990 elections and again in Dec. 1990, the Church criticized the widespread corruption, labeling it as the basic cause of the present crisis, and offering a forthright indictment of the current system in which a few elite live in unbelievable luxury while the vast majority wallow in misery, cut off from basic necessities.

PRACTICE: Catholicism here is a far cry from the dogmatic religion practiced in countries such as Italy. Dominicans have selected the rules and regulations they wish to follow while conveniently ignoring the rest. To them, being a good Catholic does not mean being dogmatic. Many strict Catholic couples, for example, have civil or consensual marriages and practice birth control. Many men don't bother to turn up in church.

ROSARIOS: These religious processions are commonly organized to pray for rain or request divine intercession in a common dilemma. An image of a saint or madonna is carried at the parade's head followed by a person who leads the singing and carries a large wooden rosary.

FORMULARIOS **AND** *ORACIONES:* Resulting from the synthesis of Catholic and African beliefs among the lower classes, these incantations may be used to stave off the evil eye or to draw good luck; they are generally sold in *botanicas*.

SANTOS **CULTS**: Another complement to Catholicism is the half-magical cult of the saints (*santos*). Most households have an image of one or two of these, usually St. Anthony and one of the Virgins. They are grouped together with the family crucifix and designated as the "Holy Family." Saints are selected in accordance with one's needs, and reciprocation is mandatory if devotions are to continue. The relation between saint and worshipper is one of *promesa* (promise or obligation); promises are made by the devotee and carried out if his wishes are granted by the saint. Certain goods are offered to the saint, who is expected to reciprocate by providing prosperity and good fortune. Rituals of devotion, termed *rosarios* (see above), are held to obtain relief from sickness or give thanks for recovery after an illness. *Noche Vela*, the "Night of the Saints," is used to call the Saints to earth.

Other Denominations

EVANGELICOS: In recent years Evangelical Protestantism has skyrocketed in popularity, attracting both immigrant Haitians and members of the lower and lower-middle classes. Associated with the middle-class, Protestantism is popular among family members because spouses are taught not to beat their wives or offspring nor fritter away their earnings on prostitutes and booze. It also provides the rural and urban poor a sense of emotional security in the face of a rapidly changing world. Formed in 1960 through the merger of other groups, the Dominican Evangelical Church is influential and the only indigenous denomination. Other major sects include the Asssembly of God, the Seventh-Day Adventists, and the Protestant Episcopal Church. Many well meaning US born-again Christians have come to visit, leaving behind a trail of dependency.

VOODOO: *Liborista* and the Brotherhood of the Congo are cults found in the outback. Brought to the nation by Haitian immigrants, *Vudu* (Voodoo), however, is more prevalent. As in Haiti, its rejection by the status quo has driven it underground. No religion in the world has been so misunderstood and vilified as Voodoo. A complex reblending of African religious beliefs with elements of Christianity thrown in for good measure, its name comes from a Dahomean word meaning "god." Worship takes place in *houmforts* where sacrifices are made and believers are possessed by *loas* (spirits). Many Dominicans also practice a form of spiritualism which is similar (see above). A good introduction is to visit one of the many *botanicas*, the supermarkets of spiritualism, which sell plants, herbs, oils, rubbing water, and spiritualist literature.

Language

Spanish is the norm throughout the island. Although a number of Dominicans can speak English, the more Spanish you can speak the better. Outsiders who can speak Spanish are more readily accepted by locals. Dominican Spanish is laden with local idioms, along with numerous Indian and African words. When speaking with Dominicans, keep in mind that the "*tu*" form of address connotes a high degree of familiarity; don't jump from the more formal "*usted*" until the relationship warrants it. "S" sounds are muted and may even disappear (as in *graciah* instead of *gracias*). The "ll" and "y" sounds are pronounced like the English "js." And the terminal "e" sound is often truncated (as in *noch* instead of *noche*). As a consequence, Dominican Spanish is also difficult for the uninitiated to understand; ask them to slow down.

HISTORY: The first settlers brought their native Spanish with them, the dialect of Andalusia. Later arriving Castillian *caballeros* had little influence on speech patterns. The Taino language quickly vanished but has left many words behind in the vocabulary. Haitian Creole has affected the speech of lower class Dominicans and those living near the border. Many English words have been incorporated into the language, especially those terms (such as "bar" and "leader") for which there is no Spanish equivalent. Today, there is a gulf between the speech patterns of the unschooled rural poor and the urban elite. Of the three regional dialects, *Cibaeña* – spoken by rural lower-class inhabitants of the N Cibao valley – is the most significant.

Arts and Crafts

Dominican culture is largely Spanish in origin with many African elements. While the Dominican Republic in its role as "cradle of America" had a cultural head start on other nations, both the quality and quantity of its artistic and literary work had begun to wane by the end of the 16th C. The Haitian occupation served to reinforce its sense of *hispanidad* (Spanishness). A number of Dominican authors wrote fine novels in the romantic and modern styles during the late 19th and early 20th C. Unfortunately, the ascension of Trujillo, the Kim Il Sung of the Caribbean, stymied the nation's culture. Since the late 1960s a movement known as *la nueva ola*, the new wave, has emerged.

ART AND ARTISTS: Dominicans have been influenced by the trends and schools found in the US. Indian and African influences are also found in the work. Some Spanish-born painters have become naturalized Dominicans; the most famous among them is the late José Vela Zanetti. Clara Ledesema is renowned for her landscapes and portraits. Ada Balcácer is noted for her sculptural pen drawings. Others of note include painters Jaime Colson, Darío

Suro, Mario Cruz, Aquiles Antonio Azar, Fernando Peña Defillo, Guillo Pérez, and wood sculptor Domingo Liz. A visit to the fine art museum in Santo Domingo is a must for visitors.

Music and Dance

As holds true on islands all over the Caribbean, Dominican music and dance combines African and European elements in a distinctive blend. Dancing is a popular pastime – indeed an avocation – and you may spot young boys laying down their *merengue* steps: Dominicans learn young!

MUSICAL INSTRUMENTS: Dominican musical history begins with the Taino. At least one instrument, the *güira* has been handed down by the Indians, and musicologists speculate that the *areytos* (Indian dance tunes) have also influenced the development of Dominican music. Traditionally a hollow, notched, bottle-shaped gourd played with a wire fork, today's instrument resembles a metal scraper. The double-headed *tambora* drum is covered on one side with the skin of an elderly male goat and on the other with the hide of a young female goat who has never given birth. The drum is tightened by dousing it with local rum The best place to hear these instruments is in the *perico ripiao* or *prí prí*, three-member bands of roving minstrels who play folk music. Another traditional instrument, the *marumbula* (a large thumb piano which the musician sits at and plucks) is also used at times. Also of note, and used to accompany traditional dance, are the *balsié* (accordion) and *pandero* (tamborine).

MERENGUE: Dating in its modern form from around the end of WWI, the *merengue* is the Dominican Republic's contribution to Latin Music. Popular in part because it is easier to dance to than *salsa*, the *merengue* has taken over many of the New York City dance clubs. It consists of three segments: a brief introduction (often deleted in practice) followed by two main sections – one of 16 bars and another African-derived segment consisting of two-bar phrases repeated over and over with slight variations. In its rural form a *merengue* band's instrumentation consists of the *melodeon* (an accordion-like instrument which supplanted the guitar in the 16th C), the *güira*, and the *tambora*. A *marumbula* is also sometimes used. The musical style can also be heard in Haiti where it's known as the *méringue*. Its predecessor was the *upa*, a dance introduced by Cuban regimental bands stationed in Puerto Rico which offended the authorities and was banned in 1848. Consequently, the *upa* was matched with new steps adapted from the *contradanza*. The word "*merengue*" was used in songs of this form from about 1850. Nearly all *merengues* are fast and many are satirical or humorous. Vocals are either solo or call-and-response. Played to a fast 2/4 rhythm, dancers move only below the waist. Two of the most famous *merengue* bands are those of Wilfredo Vargas and Johnny Ventura. Current hot bands include La Coco Band, José Esteban y la Patrulla 15, and Roka Banda. The most important Dominican performer is Jean Luís Guerra. His group plays not only *merengue* but also *bachata, soca, salsa*, gospel, North American folk, and pop. He is now immensely popular in Spain as well as the rest of Europe. Recent albums include *Bachato Rosa* and *Areito*. *Merengue típico* is a form originating in the Cibao; it has some similarities to Cajun zydeco. Acoustic, it features accordion and *güira* as part of its lineup. The newest and most popular form is *bachata*, a form which combines the rhythm of the Cuban *son* with the emotion of the Mexican *ranchera*. The most famous *bachata* artists are Luis Dias, Sergio Vargas, and Anthony Santos.

OTHER DANCES AND MUSIC: The *pambiche* is a simpler version of the *merengue* which consists of only the last portion. Coming from the nation's S, the *mangualina* is similar to the *merengue*. The *sarandunga* is an Africanized version of the fast tap Spanish dance called the *zapateado*. *Palo* drums play during one section, and a group of dancers perform a shuffle step instead of one couple performing a tap dance. Generally it's accompanied by accordion, *güira*, and *tambora*. Other forms also revolve around the *palos* or *congos* and the *cantos de hacho* (axe songs) of the S. The Cibao region features nearly pure, ancient Spanish *salves* and *tonados*. Their melodic qualities are similar to ancient Castilian vocal forms. A dance known as the *tumba* may still be found in some of the mountainous regions.

Festivals and Events

The nation's Latin nature really comes to the fore in its celebrations. Dominicans really know how to relax and have a good time. Most celebrations have a religious basis. Many are famous, including those at Higüey and Samaná. Every town on the island has its *fiestas patronales* or patron saint festival. They generally begin on a Friday, approximately a week before the date prescribed. Although services are held twice a day, the atmosphere is anything but religious. Music, gambling, drinking, and dancing take place on the town plaza, and food stalls sell local specialties. On the Sunday nearest the main date, *imahenes* or wooden images of the patron saint are carried around the town by four men or (sometimes) women. Flowers conceal supporting wires, and the base is tied to the platform to prevent it from falling.

JANUARY

New Year: The evening before *día de año nuevo*, the place to be is in Santo Domingo where thousands assemble along the Malecón, the capital's seaside boulevard. Bands blast *merengue*, fireworks explode overhead, and sirens sound. The partying continues until it's time to view the sun rise over the Caribbean.

Epifanía (Día de los Santos Reyes): Held on Jan. 6, this event denotes the end of the Christmas season. As with the North American Christmas, the parents lay out the gifts while the children sleep. In many places including Santo Domingo, there are processions featuring the Three Kings. The night before, children traditionally place boxes of grass along with candies and cigarettes under their beds to await the arrival of the Three Kings: Gaspar, Melchor, and Baltazar. After the camels eat all the grass, the kings leave presents in the now empty boxes.

Las Noches de Vela: A synthesis between the African-derived popular religion and formal Catholic liturgy, this night of prayer (*velas*) is performed in San José de Ocoa, Monte Plata, Villa Altagracia, Pedernales, Paraiso, and los Bajos de Haina around the 20th of Jan. Held in honor of the Virgin of Altagracia, the spiritual mother of Dominican *pueblos*, prayers are recited, hymns are sung, music is played, and everybody dances. Instruments used include *panderos* (tambourines), *güiras* (scrapers), *atabales* (kettledrums), *tamboras* (hand drums), and *maracas*. The next day is the festival of the Virgin of Altagracia in Higüey when thousands of pilgrims converge on the basilica. The following Saturday, services are also held at Los Zapatos church in Río Arriba. *Salves* ("Hail Mary!" chants) here are accompanied by *panderos* and *güiras*.

Día de Duarte: The celebration of the birthday of this national hero, born in Santo Domingo on Jan. 26, 1814, involves 21-gun salutes, flying the Dominican flag, services, floral offerings, and the like.

FEBRUARY

Ga Ga: Of Haitian origin, the *ga-gá*, a carnival-like mystical religious celebration takes place in the *bateyes* or sugarcane villages. Known in Haiti as *rara*, it has become especially popular in the areas around Haina, Boca Chica, and Barahona as well as in other locations. Here it is celebrated not only by Haitians but by thousands of Dominicans and represents a syncreticism of Haitian and Dominican cultures. It parallels *Miercoles de Ceniza* (Ash Wednesday) in February. Festivities also take place in selected locations (Barahona and Boca Chica to name a few) on or around Mar. 28 as part of Holy Week.

Carnavál: This is widely celebrated in the days surrounding Feb. 27, Independence Day, which often falls around Lent. Over half a million participate in Santo Domingo, and the highlight is a parade of some 30,000 down Santo Domingo's Malecón. Another prominent celebration is held in Santiago, and every Sun. afternoon in Feb., colorfully costumed *diablos cojuelos* take to the streets in La Vega.

APRIL

Semana Santa: A generally somber atmosphere prevails during Holy Week (*Semana Santa*), the week surrounding Easter, when processions and pageants are held island-wide. In some places a gigantic grotesque effigy of Judas Iscariot is burnt in effigy (*Quema de Judas*) to mark the culmination of Holy Week. *Los Cachúas,* a local version of the *Diablos Cojuelos*, takes place in the SW town of Cabral between Good Friday and Easter Monday. Costumed participants crack whips and bandy about.

JUNE

Espiritu Santo: Taking place around the first or second week of June, these celebrations involve African instruments like congo drums. The most interesting places to visit are Villa Mella (near Santo Domingo), Santa María (San Cristobal), and El Batey (San Juan del la Maguana).

JULY

Festival del Merengue: This festival takes place in the third week in July and generally continues into Aug. in order to coincide with the founding of Santo Domingo on Aug. 4, 1496. In addition to innumerable live musical performances, events include artisan fairs, a "gastronomic" festival, the Waiter's Marathon along the Malecón, Bartender of the Year competition, and a motocross competition.

AUGUST

Fiesta Patria del la Restauración: Held Aug. 16, Restoration Day commemorates the regaining of independence from Spain in 1863. Although there are celebrations nationwide, the largest are held in Santo Domingo and Santiago.

OCTOBER

Puerto Plata Festival: Similar to the *Merengue* Festival, celebrations here, held every Oct., include live bands, tents serving food, parades, and the like.

Descubrimento de America: Held each Oct. 12, this celebrates the "discovery" of America by Columbus. Festivities are held at Columbus's tomb in the Faro a Colón and at the Cathedral in Santo Domingo.

Bambúla: Held in honor of St. Raphael on Oct. 24, the *bambúla* is a traditional African-derived dance seen only in the Samaná region. It commences in the house of the descendants of Doña Vertil a Peña. The dance can also be wtnessed at the *fiestas patronales* of Santa Bárbara held on Dec. 4.

DECEMBER

Christmas: *Las Navidades* (the Christmas season) stretches approximately from Dec. 15 to Jan. 6 and is the liveliest time of the year. Marked by parties and prayers, it's a time to get together with friends. Everyone heads for *el campo* ("the country") to join in celebrating the occasion with friends and loved ones. Out in the countryside, groups of local musicians known as *trulla* roam from house to house singing *aguinaldos* or Christmas carols. *Nacimentos* (nativity scenes) are set up in homes and public places. On *Noche Buena* (Christmas Eve) most people attend midnight Mass (*Misa de Gallo*) before returning home to feast on the traditional large supper known as *cena*. Traditionally *campesinos* celebrated this holiday seated around a fire where a pig was roasted. *Manicongo* and *lerenes*, meat pies wrapped in plantain leaves and bread fruit, are eaten. Midnight mass is also attended.

National Holidays

Jan. 1:	New Year's Day
Jan. 21:	Day of Our Lady of Altagracia
Jan. 26:	Birthday of Juan Pablo Duarte
Feb. 27:	Independence Day
Mar.-April:	Good Friday (movable)
May 1:	Labor Day
June 17:	Corpus Christi
July 16:	Foundation of Sociedad la Trinitaria
Aug. 16:	Dominican Restoration Day
Sept. 24:	Feast of Our Lady of Mercy
Dec. 25:	Christmas Day

Fiestas Patronales
(Patron Saint Festivals – dates are approximate)

Jan. 1:	Santo Cristo, Bayaguana
Jan. 21:	Nuestra Señora de la Altagracia, Higüey
Feb. 2:	Nuestra Señora de la Candelaria, Barrio de San Carlos (Santo Domingo)
Feb. 11:	Nuestra Señora de Lourdes, Distrito Nacional de Peralta (Azua)
Mar. 18, 19:	San José: Bani, San José de Ocoá, San José de las Matas, Altamira, Río Grande, and San José de los Llanos
May 1:	San José Obrero, Jaragua (Baoruco)
May 13:	Nuestra Señora de Fatima: Galván (Baoruco), Arenoso (San Francisco de Macorís), Hondo Valle (Estrelleta)
May 15:	San Isidro Laboral: Luperón (Puerto Plata), Guayabal (Azua), El Plantón (Barahona), Los Calvelinis y Uvilla (Baoruco), El Llano (Estrelleta), Sanate y La Enea (Higüey), Las Caobas (Santiago Rodriguez)
May 30:	San Fernando Rey, Monte Cristi
June 13:	San Antonio: Sosúa, El Bonao (Higüey), La Lanza (Barahona), Tamayo and El Estero (Baoruco), Villa Riva (San Francisco de Macorís), Monción (Santiago Rodriguez), Villa Bohechío (San Juan de la Manguana), Tenares, Monte Plata, Laguna Salada (Valverde) & Miches.
June 14-24:	San Juan Batista: San Juan de la Manguana, Baní
June 29:	San Pedro Apostol: San Pedro de Macorís, Las Salinas (Barahona), Pedro Sanchéz (El Seibo),

	Jobo Palmarejo (Santiago Rodríguez, El Cercado (San Juan de la Maguana), El Plátano (Cotuí)
June 30:	San Pedro and San Pablo: Villa González (Santiago) and Bonagua (Moca)
July 4:	Santa Isabel, Isabela (Puerto Plata)
July 5:	San Felipe, Puerto Plata
July 15 :	Nuestra Señora del Carmen: Jabaracoa, Padre las Casas (Azua), El Palmar (Baoruco), Trinitario (Djabón), Castillo (San Francisco de Marcorís), Gaspar Hernandéz, José Contreras, and Cayetanao Germosén (Moca), Duvergé (Jimani), Los Amacigos (Santiago Rodríguez), Honduras and Majagual (Samaná), and Platanal (Cotuí)
July 22:	Santiago Apostol: Santiago, Paya (Baní)
July 25:	San Cristóbal, San Cristóbal
Aug. 2:	Nuestra Señora de Los Angeles, Atabelero (San Francisco de Macorís)
Aug. 3:	San Augustin, Bajos de Haina
Aug. 10:	San Lorenzo, Guayabín (Monte Cristi)
Aug. 11:	Santa Filomena, Rinconito (Estrelleta)
Aug. 15:	Nuestra Señora de Antigua, La Vega Nuestra Señora de Agua Santa, Sabana Grande de Boyá (San Cristobal)
Aug. 16:	San Roque, Jaibón Laguna Salada (Valverde)
Aug. 22:	Corazon de Maria, Chaquey Abajo (Cotuí)
Aug. 24:	San Bartolemé, Neiba (Baorucu)
Aug. 30:	Santa Rosa de Lima, La Romana
Aug. 31:	Santa Rosa and San Ramon, Partido(Dajabón)
Sept. 8:	Nuestra Señora de los Remedios: Azua, Cabral (Barahona), El Limón (Jimaní), Naranjo (San Juan de la Maguana)
Sept. 14:	Santisma Cruz, Mao (Valverde)
Sep. 24:	Nuestra Señora de las Mercedes: Constanza, Santo Cerro (La Vega)
Sept. 29:	San Miguel: Los Patos (Barahona) and Vaca Gorda (Dajabón)
Oct. 1-4:	San Francisco, Bánica (Santiago Rodriguez)
Oct. 4:	San Francisco: Las Rosas (Dajabón), Azlor (San Francisco de Macorís) Nuestra Señora del Rosario: Barahona, Moca, Dajabón
Oct. 14:	Santa Rosa de Jesús, Elías Piña
Oct. 15:	Santa Teresa de Avila, Comendador (Elías Piña)
Oct. 24:	San Rafael, Boca Chica
23-24:	Bambula (San Rafael), Samaná
Nov. 1:	Todos los Santos, Maguana (San Juan de Maguana)
Nov. 13:	Santa Lucia, Las Matas de Farfán (San Juan)

Nov. 18:	Nuestra Señora de la Esperanza (Valverde)
	Virgen del Amparo, Polo (Barahona)
Nov. 21:	Nuestra Senora de Regla, Baní
Nov. 30:	San Andrés, Andrés (Boca Chica)

Food

Combining African, Indian, and Spanish cuisine into a distinctly refreshing cuisine, the nation's food on the island provides a unique culinary experience. Although similar to Puerto Rican, Cuban, and other Caribbean cuisines, it has its own distinct flavor. Though it's not one of world's haute cuisines, it is hearty and tasteful – if a bit on the greasy side. And there are plenty of places to eat, including a variety of restaurants large and small. There are the ubiquitous fast-food joints and a considerable number of pizzerias which serve it up Dominican style. While international cuisine is scarce outside of the resort areas, Chinese food (or an imitation thereof) can generally be found just about everywhere.

TYPICAL FARE: As everywhere in the Caribbean, the staple dish is *arroz con habichuelas* (rice and beans), generally served with meat, chicken, or fish on the side along with some semblance of a salad. While Jamaicans refer to their "rice and peas" as the Jamaican "coat of arms," Dominicans fondly dub their version "the Dominican flag." Rich in vitamins A, B, and C, plantains are boiled or mashed with a bit of oil to make *mangú* which is often served with rice and beans. **soups and specialties**: *Sancocho* is a stew made with a variety of tubers, some greens, and meat (beef, chicken, and/or pork). *Asopao* is a soup made with rice and meat or seafood. *Lechon asado* or roast pig is another specialty. Served in local *lechoneras*, it's tastiest when the pig's skin is truly crisp and golden. *Chicharrones*, chunks of crispy skin, are sold alongside. Other pork dishes include *cuchifrito* (pork innards stew), *mondongo* (an African stew of chopped tripe), and *gandinga* (liver, heart, and kidneys cooked with spices). *Carne mechada* is a beef roast garnished with ham, onion, and spices. *Locrio de cerdo* (meat and rice) is another typical dish. Goat is also quite popular and *cabro* (young or kid goat) is considered a delicacy. *Fricase*, a dish made with stewed chicken, rabbit, or goat, is usually accompanied by *tostones*, plantains that have been fried twice. Another popular dish is *arroz con pollo* (rice and chicken). Similar but more savory, the *sopa criolla dominicana* includes stew meat, pasta, greens, onions, and seasoning. The

Dominican Food A to Z

Arroz con dulce – sweet rice pudding.
Arroz con pollo – rice and chicken.
Arroz con habichuelas – rice and beans (generally served with meat, chicken, or fish on the side).
Asopao – a soup made with rice and meat or seafood.
Batata – a type of sweet potato.
Cabro – young or kid goat.
Calabaza – a type of squash.
Cangejo – crab.
Carne mechada – a beef roast garnished with ham, onion, and spices.
Catibias – yuca flour fritters made with meat.
Chapin – trunkfish.
Chayote – a type of squash.
Chicharrones – chunks of crispy pork skin.
Chillo – red snapper.
China – sweet orange.
Chinola – passion fruit.
Cocido – soup made with meat, chickpeas, and vegetables.
Chicharrones de pollo – small pieces of fried chicken.
Cocos frios – green drinking coconuts.
Cuchifrito – pork innards stew.
Dulce de leche cortada – a sour milk dessert.
En escabeche – dishes pickled Spanish-style.
Ensalada de pulpo – a tasty salad centering on octopus.
Flan – caramel custard.
Fricase – a dish made with stewed chicken, rabbit, or goat.
Gandinga – liver, heart, and kidneys cooked with spices.
Gelatina – jello.
Guineo – banana.
Lambi – conch.
Langosta – local lobster.
Lechon asado – roast pig.
Lechosa – papaya.
Locrio de cerdo – meat and rice
Majarete – corn pudding.
Mero – sea bass.
Mofongo – mashed and roasted plantain balls (platános) made with spices and chicharrón.
Mondongo – an African stew of chopped tripe.
Name – African yam.
Naranja – sour orange.

> **Pastelón de vegetables** – a vegetable pastry.
> **Piña** – pineapple.
> **Pipián** – goat's offal cooked as a stew.
> **Pulpo** – octopus.
> **Sancocho** – a stew made with a variety of tubers, some greens, and meat (beef, chicken, and/or pork).
> **Sopa criolla dominicana** – a soup with stew meat, pasta, greens, onions, and seasoning.
> **Tostones** – plantains that have been fried twice.
> **Yuca** – manioc, cassava.

pastelón de vegetables (vegetable pastry) is a baked conglomeration of garden vegetables and potatoes that have been seasoned and thickened with eggs and flour prior to being cooked with fat or butter.

VEGETABLES: The Dominican Republic has a unique range of *verduras* (vegetables), including *chayote* and *calabaza* (varieties of west Indian squash), *yuca*, *yautia* (tanier), *batata* (a type of sweet potato), and *ñame* (African yam). All are frequently served in local stews. The indigenous *yuca* (manioc, cassava) can kill you if eaten raw. It's generally boiled, fried or prepared as *casabe*, a form of bread which the first Europeans found to be an acceptable substitute. *Catibias* are *yuca* flour fritters made with meat.

OTHER DISHES: *Mofongo* are mashed and roasted plantain balls (*plátanos*) made with spices and *chicharrón* (crisp pork cracklings). *Cocido* is a soup made with meat, chickpeas, and vegetables. *Chicharrones de pollo* are small pieces of fried chicken. *Pipián* is goat's offal cooked as a stew.

SEAFOOD: Although some seafood like shrimp must be imported, many others like *chillo* (red snapper), *mero* (sea bass), *pulpo* (octopus), *lambi* (conch), and *chapin* (trunkfish) are available locally. Fish dishes served *en escabeche* have been pickled Spanish-style. *Ensalada de pulpo* is a tasty salad centering on octopus. *Mojo isleno* is an elaborate sauce which includes olives, onions, tomatoes, capers, vinegar, garlic, and pimentos. The most famous dishes are *langosta* (local lobster), *cangejos* (crabs), and *ostiones* (miniature oysters which cling to the roots of mangrove trees). **note:** If ordering at a local restaurant in non-tourist areas, be sure to ask for your seafood to be cooked *sin sal*. For unknown reasons, Dominican chefs appear to pour an entire shaker of salt on their fish! Also, what may be referred to on menus as "salmon" is actually red snapper.

FOREIGN FOOD: Although often bland, Chinese restaurants are found throughout the land. The quality varies from gourmet to grease galore, but most feature the same menu: egg foo young, chop suey, rice and beans, steak, and sandwiches. You may want to ask them to leave out the *ajinomoto* (monosodium glutamate, MSG), a Japanese flavoring derived from soy sauce that, along with cornstarch, ruins the quality and flavor of traditional Chinese cuisine. Other nationalities have opened restaurants in Santo Domingo, Santiago, and in La Romana. In the resort hotels and towns such as Sosúa and Puerto Plata you can find many varieties of cuisine; Santo Domingo's network of restaurants caters to the nation's elite as much as, or more than, to tourists.

CHEESE, SANDWICHES AND DESSERTS: *Queso de hoja* is the very milky, mild-flavored, local soft cheese. It must be eaten fresh, and is often combined with the local marmalade, *pasta de guayava* (guava paste). Many types of sandwiches are also available. A *cubano* contains ham, chicken, and cheese inside a long, crusty white loaf. A *medianoche* ("midnight") contains pork, ham, and cheese. **desserts:** Desserts are simple but tasty if a bit too sweet. They include *arroz con dulce* (sweet rice pudding), *dulce de leche cortada*, a sour milk dessert, *majarete* (corn pudding), *gelatina* (jello), *flan* (caramel custard), *quesillo de leche y piña* (milk and pineapple flan), *cocoyuca* (a *yuca* flan with coconut chunks), *bizcocho* (sponge cake), *cazuela* (rich pumpkin and coconut pudding), *tembleque* (coconut pudding), and *plátanos horneados* (baked bananas).

Fruit

Called *yayama* by the Tainos, the pineapple was brought by Columbus to Europe and was introduced from there to the rest of the world, reaching India in 1550; Dominican *piñas* are much sweeter than their exported counterpart because they are left on the stem to ripen. Thought to have been introduced around 1740, the mango has its season in May and June.

Light to medium-green in color, the Dominican orange is sweet and seedy but nearly non-acidic. Brought by the Spaniards in the 16th C., the sweet orange is known as *china* because the first seeds came from there. Vendors will peel off the skin with a knife to make a *chupon* which you can pop into your mouth piece by piece. *Naranja* is the sour orange. Limes here are known as lemons. *Guineo* or (sweet) bananas, imported by the Spanish from Africa, come in all sizes, from the five-inch *niños* on up. Brought from southern Asia, the *platano* or plantain is inedible until cooked. The white interior of the *panapen* or breadfruit is roasted or boiled as a vegetable. Another fruit indigenous to the West Indies, *lechosa* or *papaya* is available much of the year. The oval *chinola* (passion fruit) has bright orange pulp and makes a delicious fruit drink. Brown and similar to avocadoes but with a sweet orange pulp, *zapotes* are another exotic fruit. Coconut palms arrived in 1549 from Cape Verde, Africa, via Dutch Guiana. Other island fruits include the *mamey* (mammee apple), *guanabana* (custard apple), *caimito* (star apple), *jobo* (hogplum), and the *jagua* (genipap). The *quenepa* or "Spanish lime" is a Portuguese delicacy about the size of a large walnut; its brittle green skin cracks open to reveal a white pit surrounded by pinkish pulp. Island avocados are renowned for their thick pulp and small seeds. *Acerola*, the wild W. Indian cherry, has from 20-50 times the vitamin C of orange juice.

Soursop (guanabana)

Drinks

Delicious fruit drinks are made from *chinola* (passion fruit) and many others including pineapple. These are generally found in small restaurants. Shaved ice is covered with tamarind or guava syrup and served in a paper cup. Cool *cocos frios* or green drinking coconuts are available just about anywhere. *Batidas* are milkshakes made with fruit. *Clamato* is clam juice mixed with water.

ALCOHOL: Locally brewed, high quality beers include Presidente, Quisqueya, and Bohemia. There's also a Dominican version of Heinecken. Miller ($1) and other imported beers are actively being promoted as well. Beers come in both large and small bottles, and prices are very reasonable. Prices are lowest at *colmados* (small stores) which are outside of tourist areas. Presidente is the most popular brew, but the others run specials: check the walls for posters. The most enjoyable way to have a beer is to have it put in a paper bag and sit or stand outside the store as the Dominicans do. The three most prominent types of rum are Brugal, Bermudez, and Barcelo. Others are Macorix and Carta Vieja. Blanco (light rum) is the driest. *Anejos* are selected golden rums which have been aged several years in wooden casks. Richest and most flavorful of the rums, they are smooth and sometimes compared to brandy. If ordering in a local bar or disco, you should know that *un servicio* is 1/3 liter with a bucket of ice and *refrescos* (soft drinks). Prices vary from city to countryside for this service. Whole bottles sell for around $2/liter and up. Of the many brands the author's favorite is Brugal's Viejo Anejo which comes in a dark bottle covered with yellow netting. Drinks such as *pina coladas* and banana daiquiris were developed especially for the tourist trade. *Pina coladas* are made by combining cream of coconut with pineapple juice, rum, and crushed ice. Brandy, gin and tonic, and cognac are also found.

CAFFEINE: Aside from alcohol, the most popular drink in the Dominican Republic must be coffee. It is served either as *café expresso* or *café con leche* (coffee essence with steamed milk) along with generous quantities of sugar. Another popular drink is *chocolate caliente* (hot chocolate). *Té Ingles* is also available.

Dining Practicalities

TAXES AND TIPS: Restaurants charge 8% value-added tax, plus an additional 10% for "service." When dining at small restaurants, locals sometimes leave an additional tip; you may do as you like; on occasion the poorly paid waitresses are genuinely surprised and pleased.

SOFT DRINKS: Colored sugared water is enormously popular in the nation; imbibers will find a choice selection practically everywhere. Brands include Sprite, Pepsi, 7-Up, Coke, Country Club, Mirinda, and Club Soda. *Extracto de Malta* is a malt extract drink. Milk is available in supermarkets, as is orange juice. Both are surprisingly expensive.

DINING OUT: If you're only into fine dining, it's better not to leave Santo Domingo or Santiago unless you're traveling to a resort. However, if you pass up local eateries, you'll also miss some of the best food and hospitality the nation has to offer.

BUDGET DINING: You'll find no lack of places to eat: there are a number of local restaurants in every town. It's best to ask locals for recommendations. In the cheapest eateries, expect to spend about $2-5 per meal, depending upon what you order. Tourist towns such as Sosúa are considerably more expensive. It's always best to ask the price of food before consuming.

BUYING FOOD: There are markets in every town, and you can bargain for your veggies. Avocadoes and other delicacies are frequently sold on streetcorners. There are also plenty of supermarkets and small stores.

TIPS FOR VEGETARIANS: The Dominican Republic is most definitely a carnivorous society so the more you are able to bend or compromise your principles, the easier time you'll have. If you're a vegan (non-dairy product user), unless you're cooking all of your own food, you will find it even more difficult, but the local fruits may be your salvation. The local rice and beans is a good staple, but it can get monotonous after a while. Salads (including ingredients as varied as avocado, tomato, cucumber, and string beans) are also widely available. Also try Chinese restaurants. If you do eat fish, you should be aware that locals eat it fried and that it (along with dishes such as *tostones*, green fried plantains) may have been fried in lard or in the same oil as chicken or pork. The best way to find out is to ask if something is "*sin aceite de jamon?*" An inadvertent positive repercussion from the economic downturn is that pork has become so expensive that lard isn't used. If you eat a lot of nuts, plan on bringing your own because (except for peanuts) those available locally are expensive. The same goes for dried fruits such as raisins. **note:** Places serving vegetarian food are frequently listed in the text.

TOBACCO: Nicotine junkies can choose their poison from several local brands. If you wish to cut down or quit, the Dominican Republic is an excellent place as single cigarettes are sold for a few cents.

Sports and Recreation

Water Sports

BEACHES AND SWIMMING: All beaches in the nation are public property, even if they are bordered by a resort or hotel. Some of the best beaches are found in the Samaná area. One of the better places here is Cayo de Levantado, a small island accessible by ferry from Samaná town. On Bahía Rincón, Las Galeras is a half-hour drive from town. Set to the NW of town, Las Terrenas is the peninsula's crown jewel. A large number of beach resorts have opened along the 20 miles E of Puerto Plata. On the E coast, the 15 mile stretch of white sand beaches from Macao to Punta Caña is punctuated by resorts at Bávaro and Punta Caña. The best beach near Casa de Campo is Playa Bayahibe. Although much of the S coastline is coastal limestone shelf which lacks sandy beaches, there are several great beaches near Santo Domingo, including the popular surfing beach of Guibia along Santo Domingo's Malecón. In the vicinity of the airport and on to the E are the popular Dominican tourist spot of Boca Chica, and the resort areas of Juan Dolio, and Guayacanes. SW of Santo Domingo, are Playa Monte Río (S of Azua) and La Saladilla and Los Quemaditos (S of Barahona). Other beaches near Barahona, such as Playa San Rafael, can be dangerous owing to undertows, strong waves, or steep drop-offs.

SAILING: Hotels rent out Hobie Cats and Sunfish. Marinas are located at Boca de Yuma and at La Romana of the S coast. At Boca Chica, some 45 min. E of Santo Domingo, the Club Náutico de Santo Domingo (tel. 566-4522) has a marina. The Punta Cana Beach Resort (tel. 686-0084/0886) also has a marina. Contact all of these for sailboat charters.

SCUBA AND SNORKELING: With coral reefs bordering all three coasts in places and over 400 wrecks, the Dominican Republic is made for scuba divers and snorkelers. There are few independent dive operators so you'll have to go through resorts. It's preferable to bring your own snorkeling equipment. Good spots for snorkeling are found along the E coast from Samaná Bay to Punta Cana (when the waves are not too strong). **dive spots:** With a large reef and wrecks, the N coast at Monte Cristi is one of the best places, but it's off limits from Dec. to March when strong northerlies blow.

Other prime locations are the breakwater at the mouth of the Río Haina, the Silver Bank 85 miles NE of Puerta Plata, Isla de Beata (off the coast of Pedernales province), Las Terrenas on the N coast of the Samaná Peninsula, and in the Bahia de Samaná. Isla Catalina at La Romana is the SE coast's premier dive spot. You can also try Bayahibe, E of Casa de Campo. Parque Nacional Submarino La Caleta (La Caleta National Marine Park), is near the Santo Domingo airport and features the purposely-sunk wreck of the *Hickory* and the reef which has sprung up around it. The reef slopes very gradually from 50-80 ft and then drops off to 120 ft A similar artificial reef has been created in Bahía de Ocoa, W of Santo Domingo. For more information on these spots, see their mention under the areas concerned in the travel section. **scuba companies:** Contact Dominican Divers (tel. 567-0346) in Punta Cana and Divers Cove Dominicano (tel. 526-1118, 556-5350) in San Pedro de Macoris, Juan Dolio, and La Romana.

SURFING: The best areas are Playa Grande near Río San Juan in the N and, less often, Sosúa, also on the N coast, and Macao on the W coast. The Atlantic waves at these locations are strongest during the winter.

WIND SURFING: The internationally-known beach at Cabarete, 14 km (eight miles E) of Sosúa, is the nation's best site. Most resorts here will rent boards. Facing the Atlantic, the E coast is also quite popular.

DEEP-SEA FISHING: A wide and phantasmagorical variety of fish reside offshore. Permits are required for all fishing. Offshore, world records have been broken. Although most numerous on the S coast in June and Oct., and on the N from Aug. to Oct., blue marlin can be caught all year-round. Abounding in the waters from Punta Espada to Punta Macao along the E coast, white marlin are most plentiful from March through June and one of the best spots for them is at Cabeza de Toro, offshore near Punta Cana also on the E coast. While wahoo appear year round, yellowfin tuna may be caught on occasion off the S coast during the winter, and white bonito, skipjack, and albacore appear during the spring months. Sailfish are caught on occasion. The prime area for deep-sea fishing is off of the SE coast at Bahía de Yuma along the Mona passage to the SE. A marina is found in this area at Boca del Yuma at the mouth of the Río Yuma, and the town holds an annual fishing tournament. Cabo Rojo and other areas off of the nation's SW tip are also good spots.

ANGLING: Bass and carp fishing is beginning to become popular in the dams and manmade lakes, and snook and tarpon can be found in river mouths and coastal estuaries. Bring your own gear.

Other Sports

HORSEBACK RIDING: In Santo Domingo contact the Rancho School (tel. 682-5482), the International Horseback Riding Club (tel. 533-6321), or the National Horseback Riding School (tel. 682-5482). Casa de Campo (tel. 523-3333, ext. 2249) has several thousand horses for trail riding and polo. The Punta Cana Beach Resort also features riding. The nation is well known for its Paso Fino horses, and competitions are held yearly at La Romana and at La Feria Ganadera in Santo Domingo.

POLO: Available only at Casa de Campo and in Puerto Plata, polo is similar to hockey or soccer except that it's played on horseback. Facilities at Casa de Campo include two 300-yard fields plus two fields for stick and ball practice. Its stables hold over 100 polo horses, and lessons are available.

GOLF: The nation has six golf courses. Two 18-hole courses designed by Peter Dye are at Casa de Campo at La Romana. Windy and therefore requiring control, Dientes de Pierro is a 6,774 yard course. Known as the "Links," the second course is inland and has narrow fairways. These two courses are said to be the Caribbean's finest. A third Dye-designed course has opened at La Romana Country Club to the E. All-inclusive packages are available. Designed by Robert Trent Jones, Playa Dorada's challenging 18-hole course is along the ocean. Another Robert Trent Jones course is at Punta Goleta in Puerto Plata. Another is at Costambar, on Puerto Plata's outskirts. Access to Santo Domingo's Country Club's course can be gained through your hotel. Santiago also has a golf course.

TENNIS: Tennis courts are a standard feature of all major hotels and resorts in the republic. Most courts are clay and many have night lights. Generally, pros are available for coaching. Although it probably won't be necessary, it's not a bad idea to bring your own tennis balls. The major international tournament is the Marlboro Cup.

BASEBALL: This sport is the passionate and nearly obsessive national pastime, and the nation has supplied so many ballplayers to the US that currently there are more Dominican players on US major and minor league teams than from any single US state or any other Latin American nation. Introduced during the occupation, the Dominicans first took on Puerto Rico in 1922. San Pedro de Macorís is the nation's most famous baseball town and has become practically synonymous with the sport on the island.

Practicalities

WHO SHOULD COME: The Dominican Republic offers something for practically every type of visitor. Large resorts provide every amenity for the well-heeled tourist, and there are a number of inexpensive options for those on a budget as well. Hikers and naturalists will revel in the country's national parks; swimmers, snorkelers, and divers will love its beaches. Most definitely a Latin American nation, the Dominican Republic is also a great place to study, improve, or use your Spanish.

WHEN TO COME: When you should come depends upon your motives for coming. The best time is definitely off-season when rates for hotels plummet and there are few visitors to be found in the more popular spots. The rain is heaviest May through Sept. and in Nov. If camping and hiking are important items on your itinerary, it would definitely be preferable to arrive during the dry season. And, if you travel to the more inaccessible or untouristed towns, parks, and reserves, crowds shouldn't be a problem no matter what the season. The times the average visitor will *not* want to arrive is at Christmas and Easter when Dominicans themselves go on holiday or visit loved ones, and both hotel rooms and flights from the States are frequently booked.

PLANNING EXPENSES: If you are planning to stay in tourist-oriented hotels and eat at resort-style restaurants, you should plan on spending as much as you would for a similar trip in Florida. If you dine at local restaurants, you'll find your costs substantially reduced. **low budget travel:** Expect to spend from $10 pp, pd at a minimum for food and accommodation. Generally, you'll find yourself spending at least $20 total and, depending upon your needs, probably more. Differences in price from top to bottom reflect upon facilities and the level of comfort, so the more you can do without the cheaper you can travel. The best way to cut down on expenses is to stay in one (relatively inexpensive) location for a time.

Arrival

BY AIR: International flights run by the major carriers arrive at Las Américas International Airport in Punta Cauceda near Santo Domingo on the S coast and at Puerto Plata International Airport between Puerto Plata and Sosúa. There are four other "international" airports (La Romana's Cajuile, Punta Cana, Santo Domingo's Herrera, and Barahona), but these are limited to small aircraft (American Eagle does fly to La Romana's Cajuile and to Punta Cana; Barahona's airport is scheduled for expansion). The best way to get a deal on airfares is by shopping around. A good travel agent should probe around to find the lowest fare; if he or she doesn't, find another agent, or try doing it yourself. If there are no representative offices in your area, check the phone book – most airlines have toll-free numbers. In these days of airline deregulation, fares change quickly so it's best to check the prices well before departure – and then again before you buy the ticket. The more flexible you can be about when you wish to depart and return, the easier it will be to find a bargain. Whether dealing with a travel agent or directly with the airlines, make sure that you let them know clearly what it is you want. Don't forget to check both the direct fare and the separate fare to the gateway city and then on to Santo Domingo or Puerto Plata; there can be a price differential. Although it might be ideal for you to fly in to Santo Domingo and exit from Puerto Plata (for example), airlines generally will make you pay a hefty surcharge for this privilege. Taxes – amounting to some $32 – will be added to your ticket. Some of this will go to the Dominican government and the rest will, presumably, help pay off the S&L scandal. When calculating the misleading fares placed in newspaper ads, be sure to double the fare and add the tax. Allow a minimum of two hours connecting time when scheduling. Airlines flying here include Dominicana de Aviacion (from Miami), Carnival (800-274-6140, from Miami, NY, Orlando, and San Juan, PR), and American Airlines (daily from New York and Miami to Puerto Plata and Santo Domingo). Minneapolis-based TransGlobal Tours (800-338-2160) offers seasonal charters for around $339-$429 RT not including taxes. Packages are available. **from Puerto Rico:** American Airlines and American Eagle fly from San Juan to Santo Domingo. American Eagle also flies from San Juan to La Romana, Punta Cana, and Puerto Plata. Air Puerto

Rico flies from San Juan and Mayaguez into Santo Domingo and also to La Romana. **from Canada:** Charters are cheap and abundant; contact your travel agency. Charter companies flying to Puerto Plata include Montreal-based Vacances Air Transat and Royal. The other alternative is to fly to the States first. **from Central and South America:** With a connection or two, it's a cinch to get to the Dominican Republic from anywhere in Latin America save Cuba. Avianca, Dominicana, COPA, Viasa, and ALM fly. **from Europe:** Generally, you must fly to Miami or another gateway city and make connections. Iberia flies from Madrid four times a week. Dominicana flies from Vienna and Milan to Santo Domingo. Air France flies twice weekly from Paris. Lufthansa flies from Germany via San Juan, Miami, and NY. KLM and Air Portugal also fly.

BY SEA: There is currently no regular service between Hispaniola and other islands. Cruise ships call at Puerto Plata and at Samaná, but these don't allow you the freedom you need to explore the island.

PACKAGE TOURS: As they say, all that glitters is not gold. This cliché may be old but it still applies when it comes to package tours. If you want to have your every need and whim catered to, then package tours may be the way to go. However, they do have at least two distinct disadvantages: Most decisions have already been made for you, which takes much of the thrill out of traveling, and you are more likely to be put up in a large characterless hotel (where the tour operators can get quantity discounts), rather than in a small inn (where you can get quality treatment). So think twice before you sign up. Also read the fine print and see what's *really* included and what's not. Don't be taken in by useless freebies that gloss over the lack of paid meals, for example. If you want isolation rather than exploration, you will choose to stay at the all-inclusives – where you won't have to meet a Dominican who isn't waiting on you. But if you really want to experience Dominican life, you'll spend only part of your time in the resort areas and the rest traveling around and experiencing the heartfelt hospitality of the Dominican people.

DEPARTING BY AIR: The $10 departure tax must be paid in US dollars. Dominican citizens and residents pay a comparative pittance to leave.

Internal Transport

BY AIR: A new airline, **Bávaro Sunflight** (tel. 320-2202, fax 320-2204) began operating between Las Américas and Herrera airports in Santo Domingo and Punta Cana, Samaná, Santiago, and Puerto Plata. **Columbus Air** (tel. 320-6950, fax 320-6951) runs day tours between Puerto Plata and Santo Domingo. Local charters also fly between Santo Domingo's Herrera and locations as diverse as La Romana, Casa de Campo, Puerto Plata, Barahona, and Santiago. However, as roads are in good condition, the scenery is lovely, and travel times are reasonable, there's little incentive to use these services. The major companies operating charter service from Herrera Airport are Faxa Air Taxi (tel. 567-1195), Servicios Aereos Profesionales (tel. 565-2448), Servicios Aéreos Turísticos (tel. 566-1696, 567-7406), Transporte Aéreo (tel. 566-2141), and Uni Charter (tel. 567-0481/0818). Prieto Tours (tel. 685-0102, 688-5715) operates an air taxi service to and from Portillo. Agencia Portillo (tel. 565-0832) provides air taxi services to Puerto Plata and Punta Cana for around $35 including transfers and a meal. A division of National Jets, the Airborne Ambulance Service (tel. 567-1101/4171, Av. Tiradentes 52) rents executive jets in addition to their 24-hr. ambulance service.

BY BUS: Regularly scheduled buses ply the main routes; these leave on time, and tickets are sold in advance. Known as *guaguas*, minibuses run throughout the nation, though service is best along the main arteries. Passengers often sing along with the latest *merengue* and *salsa* tunes. On the rural routes, you might share the bus with chickens. Be at the stop half an hour before departure. These leave only when full and run from approximately dawn to dusk. The buses' back seat is known as *la cocina* because it's a center for gossip. Buses share the roads with *públicos*, and to some destinations only *públicos* are available. Both are frequently jam packed. Private cars (*carros*) painted red and blue or blue and white are among the vehicles operating as *públicos*. *Público* rates are fixed by law. They'll give you a speedier ride but may cost slightly more. There are generally three of you in the front; your leg may be jammed against the stick shift. You'll ride along to the thumping rhythms of *merengue*. Be sure to settle the fare before accepting. From Santo Domingo, expect to spend around $7 to Puerto Plata, $4 to Santiago, $4 to Barahona, $2 to Boca Chica, $6 to La Romana, $7 to Rio San Juan, and $5 to San Juan de la Maguana. Travel times anywhere within the country are reasonable, but regular buses are slow. Keep a close watch on your things while in transit. Baggage can be a problem Although some buses may have storage below, many do not – including the local buses. Overhead racks inside won't hold large backpacks or suitcases; it's preferable to carry as little as possible. If you're planning on traveling on weekends or during three-day holidays, it's advisable to obtain tickets in advance when possible.

BUS ROUTES: Travel is faster on the better roads, and there is good bus service to all the major towns. But, on the rougher rural roads, fares and travel time escalate. You'll need to have patience! One problem with bus travel is that buses to more remote areas may leave only once or a few times per day. Your hotel and a shop, bar, or restaurant near the bus stop are good sources for information on departures. But, if you're on a tight schedule or have an early departure, you would do well to double-check.

BOATS AND FERRIES: There are boats from Sabana la Mar across to Samaná. You may wish to rent a boat to explore the Samaná Peninsula. While the the *canoa* is a small dugout, the *yola* is a medium-sized rowboat which takes up to 10, while a *bote* takes 20 or over.

HITCHING: Owing to the lack of cars, hitchhiking is slow but very possible and a good way to pass the time while waiting for buses in the boonies. In some places, where there are no buses, it may be the only means aside from a charter.

ON FOOT: With the exception of Santo Domingo's urban sprawl, walking is unquestionably the best way to experience Dominican life. Old Santo Domingo can best be explored on foot, and no place in the central area of any of the towns is too far to walk. One thing you'll find everywhere is that the street names repeat themselves: Independencia, Beller, Separación, Duarte, Ariza, Sánchez, 12 de Julio, J. F. Kennedy, and so on.

BY TAXI: Cabs are meterless. Be sure to agree on the price before getting into one. Especially if you have a group of people, taxis can also be a reasonable alternative to renting a car, but you should negotiate as well as ask around. A less expensive alternative to taxis, empty *públicos*, hired by one person or a group, are known as *carreras*. Fares rise around Christmas. *Motoconchos* or *motocochas* are motorcyclists who take passengers – up to three on pillion. In Samaná, *motoconchas* tow four-seat covered rickshaws. This is potentially a dangerous form of transportation: you ride at your own risk! Be careful not to get a "Dominican tattoo," a leg burn from the hot exhaust pipe.

RENTING A CAR: Owing to high import duties and operating costs, car rentals are very expensive here. A substantial deposit or a major credit card is necessary, and it may be required for you to fill out your credit card form with the amount of payment not specified. It's better to rent from the better known companies in order to avoid hiring a clunker. You can use a valid US or international driver's license here for up to 90 days, but you must be 25 to rent a car. Insurance, in the form of "collision waver" at around $6 per day, is generally not comprehensive, and you may be expected to pay the first $500-750 of a claim against you. Cars may also be rented at the airports. Prices are very high; rates vary but you can expect to pay around $50/day or $250/wk. for a good but inexpensive model. Don't rent a 4-wheel drive vehicle (4WD) unless you really need it to get where you're going. As you should do everywhere, read the contract thoroughly – especially the fine print. Ask about unlimited mileage, free gas, late return penalties, and drop-off fees. Check the car over for dents and scratches and make sure that the agent notes any damage so you won't be charged later. **motorbikes:** These or mopeds may be rented with ease for about $15/day in the tourist areas. Be sure to lock it up at night, and challenge larger vehicles at your peril. Note that there is no insurance, and scooter stealing is popular in resort areas such as Sosúa.

DRIVING: The nation has an extensive network of roads. Major highways in good condition include the Carr. Duarte, from Santo Domingo to Puerto Plata (soon to be four lanes); the Santiago-Monte Cristi road; and the Santiago-Dajabón road. Many of the others have potholes, broken pavement or gravel and dirt surfaces. Avoid driving at night if possible. Speed limits are 40 kph in the city, 60 kph in the suburbs, and 80 kph on the main roads. Dominican drivers can be crazy, and motorcyclists are the worst. Tolls are charged on all of the main roads from Santo Domingo. Always keep in mind that with few exceptions service stations (*bombas*) are not open late (most close at 6, others at 10), and many close on Sundays or are open only half a day. Be sure to fill up at the main towns before heading out to the sticks where there may be no service stations. Road signs are few and far between, and it will be difficult to get around without being able to speak some Spanish. Road maps may be out of date, and you may find secondary stretches to be impassable. An essential reference tool is the topographic map from the Instituto Geográfico Universitaria (tel. 682-

2680), Instituto Autonoma de Santo Domingo, Calle de las Damas, Old Santo Domingo. You may expect to be stopped by police at the entrances and exits to towns. Sometimes you'll be expected to pay a few *pesos* bribe; fees rise around Christmas. All towns have unmarked speed bumps so beware! Most stations run from dawn to dusk. Bring a rag to wipe the inside windows in the rain. Gas is around $1.75 per gallon.

TOURS: One option for visitors without much time or with an urge to savor a few different experiences is to take a tour or excursion. Most of these include hotel pickup, meals, and dropoff in their pricing and cost around $50/day. This is fairly expensive, but the high cost can be partially attributed to the exorbitant duties on imported vehicles. The advantage of tours is that you avoid crowded buses, you can cover a lot of territory, and your driver may be very informative. The disadvantages include the added expense, the isolation from locals, and the loss of flexibility. Tours do provide an easy way to visit many of the national parks and other attractions. In addition to those listed in the text, hotels may offer their own tours for guests.

Accommodations

The Dominican Republic has hundreds of hotels, totalling more than 26,000 hotel rooms – everything from luxury resorts to simple inns. It all depends what you want, and what you want you can find. Rooms with a private bath run for a minimum of $6. The five-star hotels charge an average of $140 plus 23% for service and tax. Apart-hotels charge $50-130 for two. If staying for a while, inquire about a lower weekly or monthly rate. If you're traveling on business, you should try to get the special "*la tarifa comercial*" rate. As the towns are small, it's not a problem to walk from hotel to hotel checking out the rooms. Some hotels and resorts will have their own generators. **types:** *Apart-hotels* (spelled varyingly "Aparta Hotel," "Apar-Hotel," "Apart-Hotel," or "Aparte Hotel," are rooms or suites which are fully equipped with a kitchen or kitchenette. *Cabañas* are generally cabins. A *pensión* is a low cost hotel which may be family-run. Motels are for short-term sex and are for rent by the hour. **on a budget:** If you're content to live simply, prices are inexpensive compared to the rest of the Caribbean or the States. Truly low-budget travelers will wish to avoid the resorts and stay in the cities, mountain towns, or less-developed coastal towns. Among the difficulties you might encounter in the truly low-budget hotels are blaring TVs, clucking chickens, mosquitoes, spiders, and cockroaches. Some of the rooms are dimly lit. In spite of this, the smaller hotels offer a genuine Dominican experience, one which often brings you closer to the local people and their lives. Your neighbors will be ordinary, hardworking folks, and not wealthy tourists on holiday. Hoteliers are generally quite hospitable and, if you speak Spanish, you can have some remarkable conversations. If you try it, you'll find that you can survive quite well without a/c; a fan or sometimes no fan will suffice. The major difficulties are the irregular power supply and, less frequently, problems with the water. Before staying in a cheap hotel, ask about the electricity (*la luz*), making sure that it has a backup generator (*planta*) and ask about continuity of the water supply. If they do not have a generator, you can probably expect blackouts. Finally, you should be aware that some of the cheapest hotels are unmarked.

TAXES: A 7% sales tax is added to your bill along with a 6% value-added tax, and all tourist-oriented hotels and resorts add a 10% service charge as well. The very cheapest hotels are tax and service charge free (or include the taxes in theri rates). **making reservations:** Reservations should be in advance during the Christmas season and are preferable during the winter. During the remainder of the year, reservations are a good idea, but you generally can have your pick of rooms. Couples should state if they prefer twin or double beds. Rooms with a shared bath down the hall are the least expensive. Remember that most tourist-oriented hotels give a 20-30% discount during the low season. The major resorts and hotels have two or three or more sets of rates. The least expensive hotels often do not take reservations. Be sure to figure out the total price when condsidering a hotel. **pricing:** For the reader's convenience prices (generally inclusive of 13% tax and 10% service where applicable) are listed in US dollars. They are subject to fluctuation and should be used only as a guideline. Wherever you go, there are likely to be one or more newer places not listed in this guide. Local hotels generally charge per room. Tourist-oriented hotels generally price singles at the same rate or only slightly lower than doubles. Establishments for which no prices are listed in the text are classified as follows: **low budget** ($2-10), **inexpensive** ($11-30), **moderate** ($31-50), **expensive** ($51-80), and **luxury** (over $80).

CAMPING: There are no organized campgrounds, but camping is possible. If you decide to camp make sure that your things are kept in a safe place.

Visas, Services, and Health

VISAS: All visitors require an onward ticket. American and Canadian citizens may enter with a passport or proof of citizenship and stay for 90 days maximum. In lieu of a visa, a $10 "tourist card" for entry and departures is sold at the airport or from your airline. You may be able to avoid this charge by applying for a tourist visa at an embassy or consulate. US legal residents must show an alien card in addition to their tourist card. Persons under 18 traveling alone or accompanied by only one parent/legal guardian or other adult(s) are required to present written, notarized consent from the absent parent(s) or guardian(s) which grants permission to travel. **for other nationalities:** Citizens of Great Britain, Germany, Italy, Switzerland, Spain, Denmark, Sweden, Norway, Finland, Luxembourg, Liechtenstein, Israel, Costa Rica, Argentina, Aruba, Ecuador, Netherlands, and the Netherlands Antilles may stay for 90 days without a visa.

EXTENDING YOUR VISA: Go to the Immigration Office (tel. 685-2505) in the Huacal Bldg. in Santo Domingo. An extension costs a few dollars.

INFORMATION: Tourist information centers are at the airports and major towns. The **Ministry of Tourism** (tel. 221-4660, fax 682-3806) main office in Santo Domingo is open weekdays 9 to 2:30. It's located at Av. México and 30 Marzo inside a modern complex of new buildings; it's in the one on the far left. For toll-free information from the US call (800) 752-1151, from Germany call (800) 815561, from Britain call (800) 899805, from Spain call (900) 995087, and from Holland call (06) 022-3107.

ORGANIZATIONS: The Caribbean branch of **Oxfam International** (tel. 682-7585, 687-1010, fax 689-1001; Apdo. 20271, Santo Domingo) does a lot of good work in the country. **Earthwatch** is an organization that allows you to visit the country, participate actively in valuable research, and contribute financially at the same time. One project, held in 1994, involved exploring a wrecked ship off the coast near Monte Cristi. For more information, call (800) 776-0188. A very unusual organization working to change the face of world tourism is the **Ecotourism Society**. It publishes a set of guidelines for nature tour operators, a newsletter, and a number of other publications. Membership is $15 students, $35 ecotourists, $50 professionals. For more information write Box 755, North Bennington, VT 05257. In Britain, **Tourism Concern** is an organization devoted to uniting British people who are concerned with the effects of tourism; it advocates the kind of tourism that puts long-term social and environmental health of areas affected in front of short-term pecuniary gain. For more information write **Tourism Concern**, Froebel College, Roehampton Lane, London SW15 5PU, UK or call 081-878-9053. A project of Creighton University, a Jesuit-run medical school, **Latin American Concern** (tel. 402-280-32179) sends teams of medical students for five-week sojourns in the nation's outback, where they form close ties with locals as they help them with their health care. Each of the six teams generally includes two medical students, two dental students, one nursing student, and a pharmacy student. Each group is supervised by three or four professionals from these fields.

LAUNDRY: Laundry services are available only in major towns and cities, but your hotel can usually arrange to do laundry or hook you up with someone who will. Otherwise be prepared to do it yourself.

TELEPHONE SERVICE: Operating since 1930, *Compañia Dominicana de Teléfonos* (Codetel) is a GTE subsidiary, and international calls can be dialed directly. Probably because it is not run by the government, there are few problems with the service. Recently, competition has appeared in the form of Tri Com and All-America Cables and Radio which offer cheaper long distance and internal fax service. There are a reasonable number of pay phones which charge 25 *centavos* for a local call; they require the old-style 25 *centavo* coins or a combination of five *centavo* coins and 10 *centavo* coins. A bilingual Spanish/English business phone book is available, and you can reach a bilingual operator by dialing "O." In case of emergency, dial 711. While collect overseas calls can generally be made from your hotel, you may have to go to the local telephone office if you wish to pay. The number for local information is 411. Finally, where there is no pay phone available, there is generally a pay-by-time phone. Ask around. **using Codetel:** To make long distance calls both within the country and abroad, you should visit a Codetel branch office. Dialing is now direct and computerized.

Enter a booth and dial "1." After you give the number, you will be connected to your party. When you finish your call, you'll go up to the desk and pay after the printer, connected to a computer, prints out your number along with the cost. **calling from abroad:** Direct dial service is available from both the US and Canada. To call the Dominican Republic, the country code is 809.

POSTAL SERVICE: Window services at the (General Post Office), run from 7-1:30 on weekdays and 7-noon on Sat. Other offices are located nationwide and are normally open weekdays from 7-1:30. Mail generally takes at least a week to the US, Canada, or Europe but may take months. Sea mail usually runs about four to six weeks to North America. To ensure prompt delivery, mail from your hotel desk or a main post office. Be sure to have your letters stamped at the PO because employees have been known to steam off the stamps and resell them for supplementary income. International mail and parcel services are available, but they are very expensive. You can have mail sent to you at your hotel or to *Lista de Correos* in any other town. Post boxes are unreliable. Postal rates internally are incredibly cheap. It's worth it to use *entrega especial* (special delivery) for overseas mail. It has its own window.

FAXES: Faxes are growing in popularity and many hotels now have them. The Codetel offices also offer fax service as do Tri Com and All America.

BROADCASTING AND MEDIA: There are 10 daily newspapers. Seven are published in the morning and three in the afternoon. Among the morning papers are *Hoy, El Listin Diario , El Siglo,* and *El Caribe. El Nacional, La Noticia,* and *Ultima Hora* are published in the afternoon. *La Información* is published in Santiago in the morning. *Vanguardia del Pueblo* is a weekly put out by Juan Bosch's Dominican Liberation Party. The only English-language press is *The Santo Domingo News,* a weekly. *The Miami Herald, The New York Times,* and *The Wall Street Journal* are available as are *Time* and *Newsweek.* There are eight TV stations. In additon to NBC and CNN, there are 18 other cable TV stations operating 24 hrs. a day. The most popular programs are *telenovelas* (soap operas) and variety shows, both locally produced and imported. Many hotels have their own satellite dishes. There are 179 AM and FM stations. At 91.7 FM, Melody FM is an "adult contemporary" station serving the N coast.

Medical Emergencies – 24 Hour Service

SANTO DOMINGO
Ambulance, Fire, Civil Defense,
Police – 711

Ambulancia Aérea y Terrestre
Tel. 567-1101/4171

Red Cross
Ensanche Miraflores. Tel. 682-4545

Centro Cardiovascular
Josefa Perdomo 152, Tel. 682-6071

Centro de Intoxicaciones
Tel. 532-6511

Centro Medico UCE
Máximo Gómez 66. Tel. 682-0171

Clinica Abreu
Independencia. Tel. 688-4411

Clinica Corazones Unidos
Fantino Falco 21. Tel. 567-4421

Clinica Gómez Patiño
Independencia 701. Tel. 685-9131

Pharmacies
Los Hidalgos
27 de Febrero 241. Tel. 565-4848

San Judas Tadeo
Independencia 57. Tel. 689-6664

NORTE
SANTIAGO
Hospital José Ma. Cabral y Báez
Av. Central. Tel. 583-4311

PUERTO PLATA
Centro Médico Dr. Bournigal
Antera Mota. Tel. 586-2342

Hospital Ricardo Limardo
J.F. Kunhart. Tel. 586-2210

ESTE
SAN PEDRO DE MACORIS
Hospital Oliver Pino
Tel. 529-3353

Hospital Oncológico de la UCE
Tel. 529-6111

LA ROMANA
Centro Médico Oriental
Sta. Rosa. Tel. 556-2555

HEALTH: The water is not generally safe to drink from the tap. Restaurants and hotels will supply purified water (*agua filtrada, agua purificada*), and two brands of bottled water are Agua Sana and Agua Cristal. When uncertain or in the parks, water purification tablets should be utilized. Also take basic precautions such as washing both your hands and pocketknife before peeling fruit. For sunburn apply locally manufactured Savila, which includes aloe. No immunizations are required, but you might want to catch up on your polio and tetanus injections. There's also no malaria so pills are not needed. There are plenty of pharmacies around should you require medicine, but most medications are imported (largely from Europe and the US) and are expensive by Dominican standards.

HEALTH CARE: The best thing to do is not to get sick here. If you should, ask your hotel for a referral or go to one of the clinics listed in the text. There is only one doctor for every 1,700 Dominicans. Public hospitals are legendary for their horrific conditions and are a last resort. You must bring your own sheets, your own food, and your own medicine at times! In the countryside near the Haitian frontier, local healers known as *curiositas* practice. If you're adventurous, give it a try!

PROTECTION AGAINST INSECTS: Although scarce at higher altitudes, mosquitos are prevalant in the lowlands. A mosquito net is a handy appurtenance as are the boxes of mosquito coils which keep the numbers down when you relax or sleep. Avoid inhaling the smoke. Try antihistamine cream, Euthrax, or Caladryl to help soothe bites. Repellents (with the possible exception of Avon's Skin So Soft or a similar product) are ineffective against sand gnats; use some antibiotic ointment and, as is the case with all bites, avoid scratching or risk infection. In summary, prevention is the best cure. Take the precautions listed here, and wear adequate clothing.

GETTING DIVORCED: A cottage industry of the Dominican Republic is the quickie, mutual consent divorce – legislation designed to attract US citizens. Expect to spend $1,000-$1,500. One party needs to stay in the Dominican Republic for a minimum of two weekdays; the other must grant the power of attorney to a Dominican lawyer. For more information you should contact the American Chamber of Commerce (tel. 533-7292, 532-7414) or the US Embassy (tel. 682-2171) in Santo Domingo.

Money and Shopping

MONEY: Monetary unit is the Dominican *peso*. The current exchange rate is approximately $1=D$12.50; the peso will probably have been devalued by the time of your visit. Change only as much money as you think you'll need because most banks are not permitted to change funds back into foreign currency. One way to do it is to present your exchange receipt, air ticket, and passport at the Banco de Reservas in Santo Domingo or at the airport. Paper money is issued in notes of 1, 5, 10, 20, 50, 100, 500, 1000, and 5,000 *pesos*; the coins are 1, 5, 10, 25, and 50 *centavos*. Be sure to carry plenty of smaller bills when visiting rural areas. **changing money:**

The easiest currency to change is US dollars, and the Dominican *peso* is tied to the dollar. Most banks are open Mon. to Fri. from 8:30 to 1:30. Although they will exchange travelers checks, hotels will not accept personal checks. You can exchange your dollars upon departure at the airport; you'll lose around 2-3%. You can change back only about 30%. **black market:** A once-flourishing black market died down in 1991. It may, however, be resurrected at some future date. Beware of street changers who will definitely rip you off. They'll follow you down El Conde offering to change money at as much as 35% above the official rate. Don't do it! They are very fast and count very quickly. If you count the money, they'll pull it back and count again and a hundred or so will disappear. A very popular tactic is to exclaim that "the police are coming," hand you back your money, and take off. You will unfold your $100 note to find it magically transformed into a dollar bill!

CREDIT CARDS: Although there are a large number of establishments accepting credit cards, don't make them your chief source of cash. Frequently, a 5% surcharge is attached to your bill when you use a credit card, and they are of very limited use out of Santo Domingo and major tourist hotels. At the American Express office in Santo Domingo you may be able to write a personal check to purchase traveler's checks in dollars if you have one of their credit cards. You should also be able to get cash from any of the banks if you have a major credit card. **note:** Be sure you investigate *all* of the charges before going this route.

SHOPPING: Opening hours vary but stores are generally open 8-noon or 1 from Mon. through Fri., with most stores closing from noon or 1 to 3 in the afternoon and reopening at 2 or 3 until 6-6:30 PM. Most close down Sat. afternoons and are closed on Sundays. Since government workers must have an outside job in order to survive, offices have a *jornada único* from 7:30 to 1:30 or 2:30. Souvenirs you *won't* want to bring out are things fashioned from tortoise shell or black coral. Tortoise shell will be seized by US customs, and the harvesting of black coral destroys the reef. You can bring back a bottle of local rum, cigars to destroy the lungs of a hated relative, or a faceless doll. Probably the best buys are the rum – which you should purchase in town, rather than at the airport – and the local version of Amaretto. Other unusual and inexpensive souvenirs include cocoa, coffee beans (ground and whole, $1/lb.), cinnamon, and nutmeg. As is the case with all luxury items, there's an import tax on photographic equipment and accessories, so bring your own. **craft items:** There are a good selection of craft items in the nation, and specifics and locations of shops may be found in the travel section text. Wood, wicker and rattan furniture are well made here. Some handicrafts are imported and then sold at inflated prices. Haitian paintings and other crafts are common. **duty-free shopping:** There are a number of duty-free shops. When purchasing goods, you'll have to pay a couple of days before your departure and pick the things up at the airport on your way out of the country.

AMBER: This rock-like fossilized resin from the West Indian locust tree is mined from caves found between Santiago and Puerto Plata in the N. Found in relative abundance in the Dominican Republic, this lustrous resin is one of the most mysterious and magical substances known to man. Warm to the touch, it burns like wood. When rubbed against silk, it becomes charged with electricity – a property which caused the ancient Greeks to call it electron. It has long had a place in legend. While Roman gladiators used it for protection in the arena, early Christians used it as a talisman against evil spirits. Aristotle was the first to classify it as fossilized tree resin. Over the centuries medicinal properties were attributed to it, and it was used in treating asthma and fevers. About one piece in 100 found in the Dominican Republic contains an inclusion, fossilized plants and insects trapped by the once fluid sap. Possibly the most famous inclusion yet unearthed is a *Coprintes Dominicana*, the earliest known gilled mushroom. Be aware that amber embedded with plant or insect fossils technically requires an export permit from the Museum of Natural History, but no one will check your bags upon departure. Traditionally used by artisans worldwide, Dominican amber – some of which dates back as far as 120 million years – is famed for its resilience and its range of colors: clear white, ruby red, lemon yellow, caramel, near black, and cobalt blue. The rarest shade is milky white. Found in Sabana la Mar in 1979, the largest piece yet discovered weighs around 18 lbs (8 kg) and measures 18 by 8 in. Amber is found in shops islandwide. In Santo Domingo be sure to visit Joyas Criollas at Plaza Criolla and in Puerto Plata the Amber Museum. **larimar:** Another semiprecious gemstone, similarly used in jewelry-making, larimar is a light blue rock similar to turquoise which is mined in the Bahoruco mountains. Actually a variety of pectolite found only in the Dominican Republic, the cobalt oxide present during its formation accounts for its color. The stone gained its moniker in 1974 when a Peace Corps volunteer brought a sample to jeweler Miguel Mendez. He named the stone by combining "Lari," for his daughter Larissa, with *mar* (sea).

BARGAINING: Although most of the stores have fixed prices, you can bargain in market stalls and in smaller stores. It's better to start with what you would consider to be a ridiculously low price and slowly work your way up.

AMERICAN CUSTOMS: Returning American citizens, under existing customs regulations, can lug back with them up to $400 worth of duty-free goods provided the stay abroad exceeds 48 hours and that no part of the allowance has been used during the past 30 days. Items sent by post may be included in this tally, thus allowing shoppers to ship or have shipped goods like glass and china. Over that amount, purchases are dutied at a flat 10% on the next $1,000. Above $1,400, duty applied will vary. Joint declarations are permissible for members of a family traveling together. Thus, a couple traveling with two children will be allowed up to $3,200 in duty free goods. Undeclared gifts (one per person of up to $50 in value) may be sent to as many friends and relatives as you like. One fifth of liquor may be brought back duty-free as well as one carton of cigarettes. Plants in soil may not be brought to the U.S. If you're considering importing a large number of items contact the customs agency before you travel.

CANADIAN CUSTOMS: Canadian citizens may make an oral declaration four times per year to claim C$100 worth of exemptions, which may include 200 cigarettes, 50 cigars, two pounds of tobacco, 40 fl. oz. of alcohol, and 24 12-oz. cans/bottles of beer. In order to claim this exemption, Canadians must have been out of the country for at least 48 hours. A Canadian who's been away for at least seven days may make a written declaration once a year and claim C$300 worth of exemptions. After a trip of 48 hours or longer, Canadians receive a special duty rate of 20% on the value of goods up to C$300 in excess of the C$100 or C$300 exemption they claim This excess cannot be applied to liquor or cigarettes. Goods claimed under the C$300 exemption may follow, but merchandise claimed under all other exemptions must be accompanied.

BRITISH CUSTOMS: Each person over the age of 17 may bring in one liter of alcohol or two of champagne, port, sherry or vermouth plus two liters of table wine; 200 cigarettes or 50 cigars or 250 grams of tobacco; 250 cc of toilet water; 50 gms (two fluid ounces) of perfume; and up to £28 of other goods.

GERMAN CUSTOMS: Residents may bring back 200 cigarettes, 50 cigars, 100 cigarillos, or 250 grams of tobacco; two liters of alcoholic beverages not exceeding 44 proof or one liter of alcohol over 44 proof; two liters of wine; and up to DM300 of other items.

Conduct

Christopher Columbus described the native Tainos as "very open hearted people who give what they are asked for with the best will in the world and, when asked, seem to regard themselves as having been greatly honored by the request." Today, one may find the same to be true of many Dominicans. Attempt to maintain this good will by treating them respectfully and fairly. Try to keep in mind that Latin and other conservative cultural mores prevail here. Men and women alike tend to dress conservatively. If you want to be accepted and respected dress respectably: skirts or slacks are appropriate attire for women in towns and villages. Bathing attire is unsuitable on main streets, as is revealing female attire which will solicit unwanted attention.

CULTURAL DIFFERENCES: If you find yourself face-to-face with an urban Dominican who's making hand gestures and speaking loudly, it's not that he believes you to be deaf: it's simply that the *el campo* tradition of speaking loudly to overcome distances has been passed on, unmodified, to city dwellers. If out in the countryside, you ask someone directions and are told that it's *alli mismo* (right over there), bear in mind that it may be miles away. **hustlers:** As everywhere in the Caribbean and Latin America, prostitutes are accompanied by thieves and pimps. Hustlers, in the form of self-appointed "guides," sometimes won't leave you in peace, but dealing with them means trouble. If your tip is unsatisfactory, they may threaten to tell the police that you had approached them to deal in drugs. They also are on the in with street money changers who frequently defraud tourists. **drugs:** With the exception of alcohol, coffee, and tobacco, all drugs – from marijuana to cocaine – are treated as narcotics. Penalties are severe, and you can expect to spend a few unpleasant weeks rotting in a cell before you see a judge. You would also do well to steer clear of terrorist activities. According to the government tourism guide, "if you are part of a group smuggling arms, explosives, or drugs, it is possible that you will meet face to face with an INTERPOL agent." **tipping:** If a service charge is added to your restaurant, nightclub, or hotel bill, it's not necessary to leave a tip, although you may. Nor is it

Dominican Republic Dos and Don'ts

• Don't condescend to locals. Do treat the local people with the same respect you would like to receive yourself. Try to speak Spanish – even if it is only a few words. Do try local food.

• Don't make local children into beggars by acting like Santa Claus and dispensing gifts and money. Never pay for photos.

• Don't just stay lounging around your hotel. Do get around and explore. But don't overextend yourself and try to do too much.

• Don't dump your garbage at sea or litter in town. Do protect the environment and set a good example for others.

• Don't remove or injure coral, spear fish, remove tropical fish, annoy turtles or touch their eggs. Do not feed fish.

necessary in small, family-run restaurants. A doorman or porter should be tipped as well as taxi drivers.

BUYING LAND: Although it is possible for foreigners to buy land here, don't expect to do so easily or quickly. Even Dominicans have a difficult time purchasing land here; a foreigner is even worse off. Land titles are a problem here: many have been falsified or are forgeries. You must check with a lawyer to make sure that they are correct. Beware of deeds which resemble land deeds but actually aren't. Be sure you understand what's written in Spanish. Some of the land is sold two or three times over.

WOMEN TRAVELING ALONE: Dominican men have a definite propensity for courting western women. However, you'll find that you'll receive the most attention at beach resorts like Sosúa. Many local lads there specialize in bedding bored foreign tourists (especially German women) in exchange for money. Many of them are quite successful. Don't be a sucker. Relationships between Dominican men and western women seldom work out long-term. If you should desire a fling, make sure the guy uses a condom; some of the male prostitutes are reportedly bisexual. If, on the other hand, you wish to deflect attention, there are a number of appropriate responses.

THEFT: Problems include pickpockets and hotel break-ins. Nevertheless, you should be fine if you take adequate precautions. The very best prevention is being aware that you might be a victim. By all means avoid the slum areas, don't flash money or possessions around and, in general, keep a low profile – avoid looking affluent. Keep track of your possessions, and *never* leave anything unattended on the beach. Avoid carrying anything in your back pockets. Women should carry purses that can be secured under their upper arm. Never, never leave anything in an unoccupied vehicle, not even in a trunk. Make sure that you keep a sharp eye out on your bags while at the airport – never entrust them to anyone, and be certain to lock your bags before checking luggage. Remember that locals who form sexual liasons with foreigners often do so with pecuniary gain in mind. And, if you give one of them access to your hotel room, it can be a bit sticky to go to the police and make a charge afterwards! It's useful to photocopy your passport and keep it separately along with the numbers of your travelers checks and any credit cards. A useful precaution is to secure unnecessary valuables in the hotel safe; a more effective precaution is to leave your jewels and Rolex watch at home.

TRAVELING WITH CHILDREN: The Dominican Republic is as safe as anywhere for children, and locals love foreign kids. Just take care that they are not overexposed to sun and that they get sufficient liquids. Remember to bring whatever special equipment you'll need. Disposable diapers and baby food are available but expensive. Be sure to enquire at your hotel as to extra charges for children and whether they'll even be wanted. Finally, keep an eye on the kids while they're in the water. Good places to visit with children include the zoo, aquarium, and botanical gardens in Santo Domingo, and the capital's Parque de Tres Ojos, the nation's most accessible national park.

ENVIRONMENTAL CONDUCT: Respect the natural environment. Take nothing and remember that corals are easily broken. Much damage has already been done to the reef through snorkelers either standing on coral or hanging onto outcroppings. It's wise to keep well away just for your own protection: many corals will retaliate with stings and the sharp ridges can cause slow healing cuts. Also exercise caution while snorkeling, scuba diving, or anchoring a boat. While diving or snorkeling resist the temptation to touch fish. Many fish secrete a mucous coating which protects them from bacterial infection. Touching them removes the coating and may result in infection and death for the fish. Also avoid feeding fish. Dispose of plastics properly. Remember that six pack rings, plastic bags, and fishing lines can cause injury or prove fatal to sea turtles, fish, birds, and other marine life. Unable to regurgitate anything they swallow, turtles and other sea creatures may mistake plastic bags for jellyfish or choke on fishing lines. Birds may starve to death after becoming entangled in lines, nets, and plastic rings. Remember that the parks and reserves were created to preserve the environment and refrain from carrying off plants, rocks, animals, or other materials. Buying black coral jewelry also serves to support reef destruction and turtle shell items come from an endangered species. Finally, remember to treat nature with all due respect.

BOATING CONDUCT: In addition to the behavior patterns detailed above, always exercise caution while anchoring a boat. Improperly anchoring in seagrass beds can destroy wide swatches of seagrass which take a long time to recover. If there's no buoy available, the best place to anchor is a sandy spot where relatively little environmental impact can occur. Tying your boat to mangroves can kill the trees, so it is acceptable to do so *only* during a storm In order to help eliminate the unnecessary discharge of oil, maintain the engine and keep the bilge clean. If you notice oil in your bilge, use oil-absorbent pads to soak it up. Be careful not to overfill the boat when fueling. Emulsions from petrochemical products stick to fishes' gills and suffocate them, and deposits in sediment impede the development of marine life. Detergents affect plankton and other organisms which throws off the food chain. When you approach seagrass beds, slow down because your propellor could strike a sea turtle. Avoid maneuvering your boat too close to coral reefs. Striking the reef can damage both your boat and the reef. Avoid stirring up sand in shallow coral areas. The sand can be deposited in the coral and cause polyps to suffocate and die. If your boat has a sewage holding tank, empty it only at properly equipped marinas. Avoid using harsh chemicals such as ammonia and bleach while cleaning your boat; they pollute the water and kill marine life. Use environmentally safe cleaning products whenever possible. Boat owners should avoid paint containing lead, copper (which can make molluscs poisonous), mercury (highly toxic to fish and algae), or TBT. Finally, remember that a diver-down flag should be displayed while diving or snorkeling.

Other Practicalities

WHAT TO TAKE: Bring as little as possible, i.e., bring only what you need. It's easy to wash clothes in the sink and thus save lugging around a week's laundry. You can leave your hairdryer at home. The electricity can be counted on to fail at times, and a few minutes in the sun will effectively dry your hair. Remember, the simpler the better. Set your priorities according to your needs. With a light pack or bag, you can breeze through from one town, resort, or region to another easily. Confining yourself to carry-on luggage also saves waiting at the airport. And, if a second bag of luggage gets lost, you at least have the essentials you need until it turns up. If you do pack a lot of clothes, you could leave things at your hotel and pick them up later. When packing it's preferable to take dark, loose clothing. If you're going to wear shorts, bring long and loose ones. If you're planning on dining in expensive restaurants or attending church, you may wish to bring along some formal clothes. Be sure to bring plenty of reading material because books can be hard to come by and expensive. **protectives:** Avon's Skin-So-Soft bath oil, when diluted 50% with water, serves as an excellent sand flea repellent. Sunscreen should have an 8-15 or greater protection level. A flashlight is essential, and you might want to bring two, a larger one and one to fit in your handbag or daypack. Feminine hygiene items are rarely found outside the major population centers; bring a good supply. Likewise, all prescription medicines, creams and ointments, and other items should be brought with you. **others:** Books are twice US prices so you'll also probably want to stock up before arrival. It's a good idea to have toilet paper with you, as the least expensive hotels and park restrooms may not supply it. Film is very expensive so be sure to bring a good supply. Plastic trash bags and an assortment of sized baggies will also come in handy. **budget travel:** If you're a budget traveler, you'll want to be sure to bring along earplugs, some rope for a clothesline, towel and washcloth, toilet paper, cup, small mirror, a universal plug for the sink, and a cotton sheet. A smaller pack is preferable because a large one may not fit on the overhead rack above the bus seats; there are luggage holds only in some buses, and the smaller vans may be awkward. **hikers and backpackers:** If nature is your focus, you'll want to bring a rain parka, walking shoes or hiking boots, a day pack, canteen, hat, binoculars, and insect repellent as well as a bird book or two. Loose cotton

What to Take

CLOTHING
socks and shoes
underwear
sandals, thongs, or windsurfing thongs
T-shirts, shirts (or blouses)
skirts/pants, shorts
swimsuit
hat
light jacket/sweater

TOILETRIES
soap
shampoo
towel, washcloth
toothpaste/toothbrush
comb/brush
prescription medicines
chapstick/other toiletries
insect repellent
suntan lotion/sunscreen
shaving kit
toilet paper
nail clippers
hand lotion
small mirror

OTHER ITEMS
passport/identification
driver's license
travelers checks
moneybelt
address book
notebook
Spanish-English dictionary
pens/pencils
books, maps
watch
camera/film
flashlight/batteries
snorkeling equipment
earplugs
compass
extra glasses
umbrella/poncho
rubber boots
laundry bag
laundry soap/detergent
matches/lighter
frisbee/sports equipment
cooking supplies (if necessary)

trousers are recommended; jeans take a long time to dry. **anglers:** Necessities include sleeved shirts and pants, raingear, a wide-brimmed hat, and effective sun protection. It's better to bring your own equipment. Bring a 20 lb. or stronger line for saltwater fishing.

MEASUREMENTS: Electric current is 110-120 volts AC. You can expect periodic failures as a matter of course. Hotels may have backup generators; check to see if yours has one *before* you check in. While some villages are without electricity, other villages (and resorts which have their own generators) have electricity only part of the day. The major reasons for the shortages are mismanagement and corruption; the electrical output produced in 1990 was only 70% of the output in 1987. Compounding the problem is the fact that only 40% of all users pay their bills. The Dominican Republic operates on Atlantic Standard Time (Eastern Daylight Savings Time) all year, but attitudes towards time are distinctly different from North American or European standards. It may be a good idea to request something earlier than you need it, and you should reconfirm requests. Gasoline and motor oil are measured in US gallons, but cooking oil is sold by the pound. Fabrics are measured by the yard. While land in urban areas is measured in square meters, the outback employs the *terrea*. Colloquial measures also apply: *una rumba* is a lot, *un chin* is a little bit, and *un chin-chin* is a tiny bit. **conversions:** A meter is equal to three feet and three inches. A kilometer equals .62 miles (about 6/10 of a mile), a square km is equal to about 3/8 of a square mile. To convert centigrade to Farenheit, multiply the °C by 1.8 and add 32.

PHOTOGRAPHY: Film is expensive here so you might want to bring your own. Kodachrome KR 36, ASA 64, is the best all around slide film. For prints 100 or 200 ASA is preferred, while 1000 ASA is just the thing underwater. For underwater shots use a polarizing filter to cut down on glare; a flash should be used in deep water. Avoid photographs between 10 and 2 when there are harsh shadows. Photograph landscapes while keeping the sun to your rear. Set your camera a stop or a stop and a half down when photographing beaches to prevent overexposure from glare. A sunshade is a useful addition. Keep your camera and film out of the heat. Silica gel packets are useful for staving off moisture and mildew. Replace your batteries before a trip or bring a spare set. Because local developing is very expensive and of generally poor quality, it's better to take your film home for developing. The best place to practice underwater photography is at La Caleta National Marine Park to the W of Santo Domingo. Finally, remember not to subject your exposed film of ASA 400 or greater to the X-ray machines at the airport. Hand carry them through. **note:** Ask permission of soldiers before photographing military installations.

VISITING THE NATIONAL PARKS AND RESERVES: Many consider these treasures to be some of the nation's greatest attractions for visitors. Combined, they are larger than Rhode Island. However, they're generally difficult to get to if you don't have your own transportation and, in many cases, you'll need your own food as well. Trails in many of the parks are neither marked nor maintained. One alternative to visiting on your own may be to visit the parks with a tour. Although not always charged, admission is D$50 (US$4) for foreigners and D$20 for Dominicans.

Santo Domingo

Introduction

Santo Domingo, capital and chief seaport of the Dominican Republic, is a sprawling, thriving metropolis of 2.5 million. The focus of wealth, banking, finance, money, and the seat of government, it is the nation's hub. This is a city of contrasts, where Spanish ruins compete with large office buildings, and Porsches share streets with the *chiriperos* (pushcart vendors). With the largest concentration of people in the country, it also has the highest growth rate. The population has more than tripled in the past 30 years. This city is more exciting than any other Caribbean capital. Old Santo Domingo retains much of the flavor it had when it was the first Spanish capital of the Americas. Overlapping with Old Santo Domingo and seeming to sprawl endlessly, the new city contains the museums, numerous parks, and the *cinturon de miseria* ("belt of misery"), the vast, squalid slums which are home to thousands of Santo Domingo's rural poor. The modern sector, with its broad boulevards, ultramodern museums, and embassies, is a world unto itself. Yesterday's soldiers of fortune and missionaries have given way to swarms of Japanese businessmen and Venezuelan oil salesmen.

ARRIVING BY AIR: Las Américas, the international airport, is 23 km from the city. A tourist office is to your R after arrival and near it is an office selling tourist cards. If you need one, be sure to pick it up here. A bank is just past immigration. It takes 30 min by taxi from Las Américas, and the fare is around D$200 (US$16). To get to town by bus or *público*, walk to the R about 25 min. to the main highway and then cross. The stop is at Restaurante La Caleta to the L. Buses pass every half-hour during the day, but are less frequent during the evening. Another alternative is to walk down to Av. de las Américas and try to stop any passing bus or *público*. *Públicos* also leave from the top level of the airport. **internal flights:** Charter flights arrive at Herrera, in the W end of town, from cities such as Santiago, Barahona, and La Romana.

GETTING AROUND: When feasible, walking is the thing to do. Public transportation is excellent but confusing. There is no Santo Domingan alive who knows all the routes. Ontrate, the public bus company, has yellow *guaguas* (buses) running throughout the city, but these are rarely seen these days. Private companies also run on

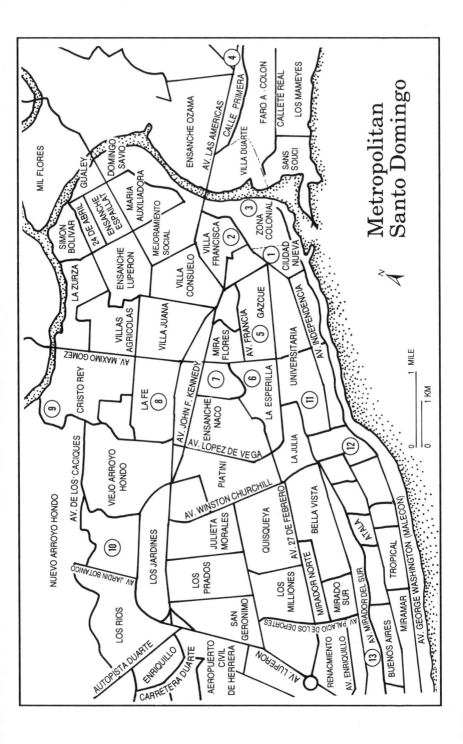

Metropolitan
Santo Domingo

some routes. You must have exact change. Painted red and white, *públicos* (D\$2,16 cents) also run throughout the city. These may take the form of vans or even passenger cars. A central location for public transportation is Parque Independencia which is surrounded by *públicos*, but you must find where to stand: ask a local. From Parque Independencia, *públicos* head E on Av. Bolivar and return via Av. Independencia. When standing on Av. Bolivar or another main artery, signal to a passing *público* with your hand whether you wish to turn L or R or go straight ahead. If traveling on the other side of the Río Ozama, you have to catch something along Av. 27 de Febrero or Av. Paris. Again, ask a local. You should note that when taking public transportation you'll be asked to pay when you get off as the vehicle nears its terminal. **streets and areas:** Many major hotels such as the Jaragua are on the Malécon, a seaside boulevard formally known as the Av. George Washington. It stretches clear along the coast from the old town through to the W. Paralleling it, running closer in some places and farther in others, is Av. Independencia which begins at Parque Independencia. The next major street running E-W is Av. Bolivar which turns into Prolongación Av. Bolivar before becoming Av. Romulo Betancourt. Av. 27 de Febrero and Av. John F. Kennedy (which eventually becomes Autopista Duarte) are the two other main arteries. The major roads running N-S are Av. Duarte, Av. Máximo Gómez, Av. Abraham Lincoln, Av. Winston Churchill, and – farther out to the W – Av. Nuñez de Caceres and Av. Luperón. The colonial section is centered in the SE, and three bridges (the Mella, Duarte, and Sánchez) span the Río Ozama. On the other side are the Parque Mirador del Este, Faro a Colón (the Columbus "lighthouse"), and the aquarium. The major road heading E is Av. Las Americas.

TAXIS: A less expensive alternative to taxis, empty *públicos*, hired by one person or a group, are known as *carreras*. Private cars are among the vehicles operating as *públicos*. Be sure to settle the fare before accepting; \$4 is average, but they may well want more. Fares rise around Christmas. Less expensive and safer than street taxis, radio taxis should be called 20-30 min. in advance. They are: Taxi Fácil (tel. 685-2202), Taxi Radio (tel. 562-1313), Taxi Raffi (tel. 689-5468), Servbús (tel. 686-6868), La Paloma (tel. 567-1412, 567-1437), and Micromóvil (tel. 689-2000). Most hotels have a set fare taxi or limo service which goes through the city and to the airport. A hotel doorman will summon a taxi for you, and you can arrange to have a taxi take you to a restaurant, wait for you, and then return you to your hotel. Taxis may also be rented by the hour, morning, or afternoon. *Motoconchos* are motorcyclists who take passengers – up to three on pillion. **tours:** With desks at nearly every hotel, it's easy to find a city tour. Expect to spend around $10 for a three hour tour. The **Museum of History and Geography** (tel. 688-6952, 686-6668) offers city and other tours.

CAR RENTALS: Cars may be rented at the airport, on the road to Santo Domingo, and on the Malecón. These include Auto Rental (tel. 565-7873), Avis (tel. 533-9295, Av. Abraham Lincoln), Budget (tel. 562-6812, Av. George Washington on the Malecón), Ford (tel. 565-1818), Honda (tel. 567-1015), Nelly (tel. 535-8800, Av. José Contreras 139), Pueblo Rent-a-Car (in front of Hotel Jaragua along Av. Independencia, (tel. 685-4127/4128, 689-9720/2000) Rent-a-Matic (tel. 685-6073), Rentauto (tel. 565-1140). Expect to spend $60-170 per day including insurance; mileage is free. Most offer a shuttle service to your hotel.

HISTORY: Founded On Aug. 4, 1496 by Columbus's brother Bartholomé, Santo Domingo was the first outpost of the Spanish in the New World, where the first street, university, hospital, church, and mint were established. From here Ponce de León sailed to colonize Puerto Rico, Hernando Cortez set out on his invasion of México, and Diego de Velasquez headed out to colonize Cuba. Originally known as Nuevo Isabella, the name of the town was changed either in honor of Columbus's father (whose name was Domingo) or for the day the town was founded (Sunday). In 1502, it was destroyed by a hurricane and its second founder, Frey Nicolás de Ovando, moved that settlement to the W bank of what was later named the Río Ovando in his honor. In 1508 Santo Domingo became the first New World settlement to be declared a "city" and granted its own coat of arms. From 1509-1524 under the governorship of Diego Columbus (Columbus's oldest son), Santo Domingo reigned as the capital of the Indies and the New World's principal outpost. After his departure, the settlement slumped as Spanish explorers were lured towards the silver and goldmines of México and Peru and as other nations arrived to put down stakes in the Caribbean. Santo Tomas de Aquino, the first university, was founded here in 1538. After a devastating earthquake in 1562, Santo Domingo was demoted to way station status. In 1586, Sir Francis Drake along with his crew of brigands, sacked the city, burning much of it and departing with its jewels and other treasures. Trujillo changed the city's name to Ciudad Trujillo in 1936; it reverted to Santo Domingo in 1961.

Old Santo Domingo Sights

This is a gem. Most of the old buildings have been restored by the government (at a cost of some $10 million) in cooperation with local residents. Walking is the best way to see the sights, and no place is too far to walk. Almost eerie at night, the town makes an immediate and indelible impression. **streets:** Once known as C. Fortaleza because it runs past Ozama fortress, C. Los Damas ("Street of the Ladies") was named because the women of the viceroy's court lodged here. El Conde, the main shopping street, cuts right through the old town, and Av. Mella borders one side. Another main shopping street, Av. Duarte, traverses the old town at a perpendicular. The Malecón runs along the S edge of the area.

PARQUE INDEPENDENCIA (EL CONDE): This walled-in park is the first thing you come to if entering the old town area from the W. Formerly delineating the city's limits, Puerta El Conde (Gateway of the Count) was converted by the Count of Peñalva, Captain General of Hispaniola, into a bastion in commemoration of the Spanish victory he gained over an English incursion in 1655. Also known as the Baluarte de 27 de Febrero, the gate's Latin inscription roughly translates as "It is sweet and fitting to die for one's country." Carved in bronze, the "nautical star" set into the walkway just past the gate contains the 32 directions in which the horizon is divided as well as a mark indicating "kilometer zero" – still used as the point from which all distances to and from the city are measured. Standing in the center of Parque Independencia, the modern concrete and marble mausoleum was built in 1976 to house the remains of revolutionary heroes Duarte, Sánchez, and Mella. Its eternal flame is safeguarded by a military sentry. **nearby sights:** The ruins of the fortress nearby were originally part of the city walls, and the main defense on the city's NW side. The **Puerta de la Misericordia** (Gateway of Mercy), corner of Palo Hincado and C. Arzibispo Portes, gave protection to the masses in the face of natural disasters. Here, Mella fired the first shot of the revolt against Haiti on Feb. 27, 1844. The ruins of Fuerte de la Concepción (1543) still stand at the cor. of Av. Mella and C. Palo Hincado. Currently housing a bank, the building at the corner of El Conde and Arz. Meriño was originally the town hall and still houses murals by Spanish artist Vela Zanetti who arrived in exile during the Spanish Civil War. The **Historical Archives of Santo Domingo and the Ibero-American Library** are slated to be stored here.

Farther S, the ruins of **Fuerte de San Gil** are on C. Padre Billini near the end of C. Pina.

CATEDRAL PRIMADA DE AMERICA (CATEDRAL DE SANTA MARIA LA MENOR): First and oldest in the Americas, this cathedral was constructed between 1523 and 1545. Its first stone was laid by Christopher Columbus' son, Diego. Although construction was begun by Bishop Alexandro Geraldini, the building was completed by Rodrigo de Bastido's son, also a bishop, who used part of his inheritance to finance the structure. It stands in Parque Colón which has a large statue of Columbus. Installed in preparation for the 1992 celebrations, the new gargoyles and sculptures at the gates portray the Tainos at the time of conquest. Above the entrance, a remarkable frieze is decorated with horns and mythical figures. Pass through the 2.5-ton main door. In the first chapel to the R of the altar, see where Sir Francis Drake nodded out in his hammock during his 1586 stay. He chopped off the hands of the bishop's statue and chipped off the nose of another during a fit of anger. Drake left the bishop's mahogany chair alone, and this is thought to have been the work of Taino artisans. St. Peter's chapel was

Old Santo Domingo
1. Catedral Primada del America (Santa María la Menor)
2. Fortaleza Ozama/Torre del Homenaje
3. Hostal Nicolás de Ovando
4. Panteón Nacional
5. Capilla de Nuestra Señora de los Remedios
7. Reloj de Sol
8. La Ataranza/Museo de Jamón
9. Alcázar de Colón/Museo Maritimo
10. Casa de Colón
11. Museo Duartino
12. Ruinas de Monasterio San Francisco
13. Iglesia Convento de Santa Clara
14. Casa de Tostado (Museum of the Dominican Family)
15. Convento de los Dominicanos
16. Capilla de la Tercera Order
17. Iglesia de la Regina Angelorum
18. Iglesia de Carmen
19. Puerta de la Misericordia
20. Puerta del Conde (Parque Independencia)
21. Iglesia de la Mercedes
22. Iglesia de Santa Barbara
23. Hotel Palacio de Colonia

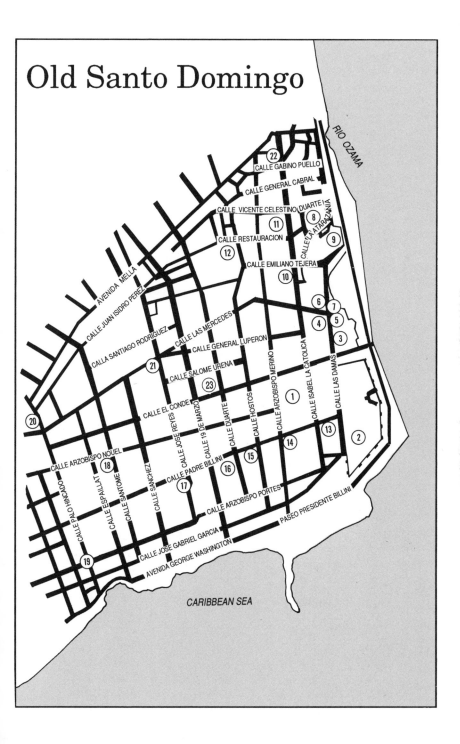

turned into a jail cell. The remaining 13 chapels also contain Romanesque arches and Gothic vaults. Other items of note include life-sized wooden animals and a wonderfully abstract Jesus in a manger. The cathedral's treasury contains a large number of priceless religious artifacts and jewelry along with jewels donated by Simon Bolivar's great grandfather. It's open from 9-4. Exit via La Callejón de Los Curates, a small alleyway, to 308 C. Isabela la Católica where **Museo Duartino**, the former home of the independence leader, contains mementos of the revolution. In this house Maria Trinidad Sánchez, the Dominican Betsy Ross, sewed the first flag which was unfurled over El Conde's gate on Feb. 27, 1844.

ALCAZAR DE COLON: Built without the use of a single nail, this home was constructed in 1510-14 by order of Don Diego Columbus (Columbus's son) during his tenure as viceroy. It was once a crumbling ruin. Opened to the public on Columbus Day 1957, it has been magnificently reconstructed at a cost of $1 million, using stone of the same type as the original. Inside, in the Museo Virreinal (Viceregal Museum), an armored knight rides a wooden horse; antique pottery, furniture, and musical instruments (including a 15th C clavichord) abound. The authentic furnishings from Spain give you a real feeling for the Spanish colonial era. Note the three 17th C tapestries depicting Columbus's story, the 16th C tiled kitchen, and the ivory-encrusted desks. Also view the 16th C Flemish carving of the death of the Virgin. It was shattered into some 40 pieces by gunfire during the 1965 civil war; experts toiled for a decade to piece it back together. Open Mon. to Sat, 9-12; 2:30-5:30. The Alcázar is closed on Tues. and the *museo* on Mon.

FORTALEZA OZAMA: On C. las Damas, oldest street in the New World, a children's library, and Planarte, a small but superb crafts shop, are located within the Casa de Las Bastidas inside and to the L. Crafts fairs are held seasonally in Gonzales Fernandez de Oviedo Plaza here. Gonzales Fernandez de Oviedo's statue dominates the inner square. The author of *Chronicle of the Indies* – the first history of the New World – Oviedo was once the warden here, and legend has it that the keys to the gaol had to be pried from his hands upon his demise. Dominating all this is the grim and somber **Torre de Homenaje**. Oldest fortress in the Americas and constructed by Nicolás de Ovando in 1503, ships were once hailed from its top. Diego Columbus and his wife lived in the warden's lodge here after their arrival. Prisoners were incarcerated here in the warden's lodge during the Trujillo era. It holds a museum/gallery which features temporary exhibits. The tower is open Tues. to

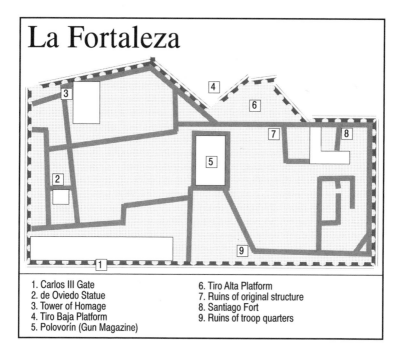

La Fortaleza

1. Carlos III Gate
2. de Oviedo Statue
3. Tower of Homage
4. Tiro Baja Platform
5. Polovorín (Gun Magazine)
6. Tiro Alta Platform
7. Ruins of original structure
8. Santiago Fort
9. Ruins of troop quarters

Sun., 8-7. Nominal admission charged. *Conquistador* and explorer Rodrigo de Bastidas, who built **Casa de Bastidas,** was also governor of Santa María (the present-day nation of Colombia). Its Romanesque arches surround the interior patio and garden. Known as the house of Hernan Cortes, **Casa de Francia** down the street on the L is the home of the Alliance Francaise, the French cultural center. To the R nearby **Hostal Nicolás de Ovando** is a 16th C mansion transformed into a hotel; visitors are welcome. It is split into two houses: the colonial residence of Gov. Ovando and the home of the Davila family. Restoration united both homes around a central pool area which overlooks the Río Ozama and the port. It once had its own private church and fort; the watchtower overlooks the pool. Before and after pictures of the restoration process are on display upstairs. Built in 1714, the **Panteón Nacional** (National Pantheon), across the street from the Hostal, was originally the Convento de San Ignacio de Loyola, a Jesuit Convent; after the Jesuits were expelled, it later served as a tobacco warehouse, and then as a theater. Now heroes and public figures are buried here, honored with a small eternal flame, a wall inscription, and an elaborate candelabra. During the Trujillo era, it was festooned with gifts received by Trujillo in commoration of its restoration. The Italian government donated marble tiles surrounding the eternal flame, Spain's Generalissimo Franco donated the imposing copper chandelier hanging in the cupola. Festooned with Latin crosses – rumored to have been swastikas removed from a Nazi prison after the war – the iron grills on the second floor were donated by Germany. Although this memorial was originally prepared for Trujillo, he is not buried here. It's open Mon. to Sat., 9-6.

CAPILLA DE NUESTRA SEÑORA DE LOS REMEDIOS: The Chapel of the Remedies, where the earliest residents attended Mass, has stark and simple interiors. Now restored, it was built in the early 16th C. It's open Mon. to Sat., 9-6.

MUSEO DE LAS CASAS REALES: Also on C. Las Damas, this "Museum of the Royal Houses" is one of the finest small museums in the Caribbean. An anchor from a salvaged Spanish galleon leans against one of its walls. During the colonial era, the building variously housed the Palace of Governors and Captains General, the Royal Audience and Court of Appeals, the Royal Counting House, and the Treasury. It was inaugurated by Balaguer in 1976 in the appropriate company of Spain's King Juan Carlos I and Queen Sofia. Enter below the heraldic shield of Emperor Charles V. See superb collections of handblown glass, armor, and weapons, intricately decorated crossbows, even samurai armor. There's also a beautiful apothecary shop, military dolls and models, and a monolith-sized milestone that delineated the border between the Spanish and French sides of Hispaniola. The Voluntariado de Casa Reales features contemporary art exhibits. (Open Tues. to Sun., 9-noon, 2:30-5:30). **Reloj de Sol**, a sundial built in 1753, is across the street and next to the Chapel of the Remedies. It was so positioned in order that the judges seated in the court across the way could always tell the time. **La Ataranza**, first commercial center of the New World, is farther up the street next to the Alcázar. These eight 16th C former warehouses have been turned into shops, restaurants, and bars. Stop in at **Drakes**, **Café Montesinos**, **Nancy's Snack Bar**, **Rita's Café**, or the **Museo de Jamón** here. One nice place to have a bite to eat is the attractive **Salon de Te** just across from the Museo Maritimo.

MUSEO MARITIMO: This maritime museum highlights sunken treasure – artifacts and treasures salvaged from the *Guadeloupe* and *Conde de Tolosa* galleons, both of which were wrecked off of Samaná in a 1724 hurricane. Because they were carrying mercury, they have been nicknamed the "quicksilver" galleons. Only 40 of the 600 passengers lived to tell the tale of the disaster. Another major exhibit illustrates life on the *Concepción*, a Spanish galleon which capsized off the Dominican coast in 1641 enroute back to Spain with a cargo of silver bullion and coins. Finds displayed here are absolutely enthralling. You'll find ceramic pipes, a brandy bottle, bars of silver, a lump of fused coins and pottery shards which weighs in at 14 lbs., silver bases used to hold then-exotic coconut cups, Ming Dynasty porcelain, copper bowls and pots, and contraband cargo including an eight-day bracket clock from London. It's open Wed. to Sat. 9-5 and Sun. 9-1.

CASA DEL CORDÓN: This "House of the Cord" is located opposite the Palacio de las Communicaciones building on C. Isabel de la Católica. Constructed in 1503 for Don Francisco de Garay – one of the early colonizers who later became governor of Jamaica, this was the first stone structure built in the New World. Its name stems from the belt of St. Francis engraved over the door. Diego Columbus and his wife lived here while they awaited construction of the Alcázar. In 1586 Sir Francis Drake besieged and looted the capital, and then demanded a ransom of 25,000 ducats to return it to the Spanish. The rich brought their jewels here to be weighed, but they were not quick enough for Drake: he systematically burned and tore down parts of the town as well as looting churches and – for good measure – hanging several friars before setting sail for greener pastures. It's now the Banco Popular, and tours are free during business hours: Mon. to Fri., 8:30-4:30.

RUINAS DE SAN FRANCISCO: Located at Hostos at the cor. of Emilio Tejera. The carved white cord, symbol of St. Francis, also decorates this monumental 16th C complex, first monastery in the Americas. It is believed to have had an underground passageway which connected it with the Alcázar and port, a characteristic shared with many other colonial structures. Sacked by Drake, it was devastated again by the 1673 and 1751 earthquakes. It was also damaged during the 1930's St. Zenon hurricane. An insane asylum was founded by Father Billini here in 1881. Portions of the cells remain along with chains used to secure the inmates. Evenings are said to echo with the howls of deceased madmen on occasion. Interred here are the remains of Bartolomew Columbus and some other *conquistadores*. The Taino leader Enriquillo was educated here and artists, fleeing from the chaos of the Spanish Civil War, sought asylum within these walls. Today, ballets and concerts are performed here on occasion.

CALLE PADRE BILLINI: On this street, heading toward Palo Hincado, are a number of sights. **Iglesia Convento de Santa Clara** was built in 1522 and served as asylum and church for the Clarissa sisters. One of the most genteel colonial residences, early 16th C. **Casa de Tostado** has a unique geminated (double) window. Once this was the home of scribe Francisco Tostado. Inside is the Museo de la Familia Dominicana (Museum of the Dominican Family). In its collection are 19th C mahogany antiques and Victorian wicker furniture. Be sure to visit the well in the garden. Inexpensive admission charged. Popularly known as "El Convento," the **Convento de los Dominicanos,** founded 1510, was granted the title of University by Pope Paul III in 1538, making it the first in the Americas. It is now called the Universidad Autónoma de Santo Domingo although the university has actually relocated to suburban surroundings. This formidable building is constructed of squared stone, faced with brick, and decorated with 16th C Spanish tiles. Although the Gothic style predominates, it also employs early Renaissance and Plateresque decorative elements. Note the rose motif around the window and the decorative vines. Its altar was a gift of Ferdinand and Isabela's grandson, Spain's Emperor Charles I. Its altarpiece features the Hapsburg eagle because he simultaneously served as Emperor Charles V of Germany! Be sure to visit the Rosary Chapel whose unique ceiling illustrates the medieval concept linking the elements of the universe, Christian icons, and classical gods in one unified system. The four evangelists represent Mars, Mercury, Jupiter, and Saturn while the Sun personifies God. Also portrayed, the 12 signs of the zodiac are believed to represent the 12 apostles. It's open Tues. to Sun., 9-6. The 18th C Chapel of the Third Order is where Eugenio María de Hostos founded the Escuela Normal, a teacher training school, at the end of the 19th C. It's located next to the **Iglesia de la Regina Angelorum** (1537), corner of C. Padre Billini and C. José Reyes, where the remains of philanthropist Father Billini are interred; the latter has a wall of silver near one of its altars. The first female poets in the New World, Leonor de Ovando and Elvira de Mendoza, lived here. To enter you must ask permission of the resident nuns. It's open Mon. to Sat., 9-6. The small **El Museo de la Porcelana**, devoted to antique ceramics, is at C. José Reyes 6. It's opened Tues. to Sun. from 10-6. Inexpensive admission charged.

IGLESIA DEL CARMEN: On C. Arzobispo Nouel at the side of Capilla de San Andrés, this 18th C church contains an interesting wooden sculpture of the Nazareno (Nazarene), a type of Christ. Christened the Plazoleta de La Trinitaria, its atrium served as a meeting ground for the Dominicans who led the revolt against the Haitian occupying forces in 1844. Capilla de San Andrés contains a statue of this saint, to which miraculous qualities are attributed.

If the chapel is closed, enter through the Padre Billini Hospital next door.

OTHERS: Iglesia de las Mercedes (the Church and Convent of Our Lady of Mercy), cor. of C. Mercedes and C. José Reyes, was built in 1555 and sacked during Drake's 1586 attack. Far to the N, off Ave. Mella to the L near C. J. Parra, are the unique uneven towers and accompanying fort of **Iglesia de Santa Bárbara**. Built in 1574 to honor the patron saint of the military, it was sacked by Drake in 1586 and, in the usual pattern, destroyed by the 1591 hurricane. It was reconstructed at the beginning of the 17th C. Visit the ruins of the fort here which command a good view. Although the fort has been restored, maintenance has been lax, to say the least. It's open Mon. to Fri., 8-noon. The ruins of **Iglesia de San Antón** are off Av. Mella at the cor. of C. Vincente Celestino Duarte.

CAPILLA DE LA VIRGEN DE ROSARIO: Set on the other side of the Río Ozama towards the Molinos Dominicanos at the end of Av. Olegario Vargas, this was the first church built in the Americas. It was restored in 1943.

HOSPITAL-IGLESIA DE SAN NICOLAS DE BARI: Located on Hostos between Mercedes and C. Luperón, this structure was built at the behest of Nicolás de Ovando between 1509 and 1552. Legend has it that it was built on the former home of a black woman who had once nursed the sick. This church's hospital was the first stone-built hospital in the Americas; it was sacked by Drake. Its walls were demolished in 1911 because they endangered passersby. The chapel has become incorporated into the Church of Our Lady of Altagracia. **Raffles** and **Village** pubs, both of whose structures date back to the 1500s, are across the street from the ruin.

Metropolitan Sights

GAZCUE: Stretching W of the Zona Colonial as far as Av. Máximo Gómez, his serene residential area sports the houses of the rich dating from the 1930s and 40s which incorporate Spanish, Republican, Tudor, and Victorian styles. To get here follow Av. César Nicolas Penson which runs in a straight line in an area just S of the Palacio Nacional to the Plaza de la Cultura.

PALACIO NACIONAL: Following the traffic flow from the park, you come to Av. Bolivár. Turn R on C. Dr. Delgado to find the

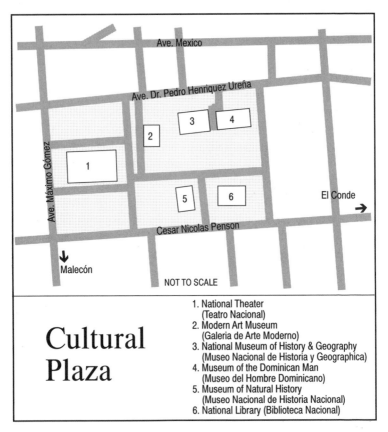

1. National Theater
   (Teatro Nacional)
2. Modern Art Museum
   (Galeria de Arte Moderno)
3. National Museum of History & Geography
   (Museo Nacional de Historia y Geographica)
4. Museum of the Dominican Man
   (Museo del Hombre Dominicano)
5. Museum of Natural History
   (Museo Nacional de Historia Nacional)
6. National Library (Biblioteca Nacional)

Cultural Plaza

National Palace. Used as executive and administrative offices and to house visiting foreign dignitaries, it has never been the presidential residence. Designed by Italian architect Guido D'Alessandro, this castle-like rose-colored marble structure was inaugurated in 1947. Inside, the palace was furnished with old mahogany, gold inlays, Samaná marble in various shades, beautiful mirrors, and elaborate crystal. Its best known room is the "Room of the Caryatids" in which 44 draped sculptured women rise column-like in a hall decked with mirrors and Baccarat chandeliers. To make an appointment for a free guided tour (available on Mon., Wed., and Fri.) call 686-4771, ext. 340 and 360. However, the building may not be open to just *anyone* so you should think up a good excuse.

PLAZA DE LA CULTURA: Take a *público* along Av. Máximo Gómez or turn R on C. Bolivar and then L onto César Nicolas Penson until you reach this complex of ultramodern buildings in a park-like setting. This area was once the personal property of Trujillo. You can easily spend the better part of a day here roaming

Dominican girl

Coast at Monte Cristi (above)
Constanza (opposite)
San Cristobal (below)

El Conde Entrance, Old Santo Domingo (above)
Old Santo Domigo (opposite)
Schoolgirls in Old Santo Domingo (below)

Las Terrenas (above)
On the Way to Constanza (opposite)
Constanza (below)

Rural Transport (above)
Casa de Caoba, San Cristobal (opposite)
Cathedral, Santo Domingo (below)

In San Cristobal (above)
House, Puerto Plata (opposite)
Getting Around in Puerto Plata (below)

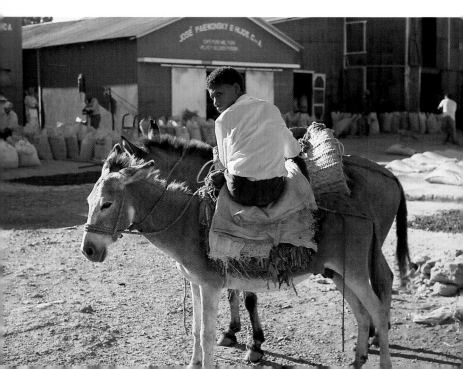

about from place to place. What's more, you find yourself sharing this place only with the staff. Even on Sundays, it doesn't seem to attract a crowd.

MUSEO DEL HOMBRE DOMINICANO: This "Museum of the Dominican Man" is the best of the lot. It contains poignant photos of life in a sugarcane village, the unique throne cars the pope rode during his 1979 visit, an extensive collection of Taino artifacts, carnival displays, etc. It serves as a good introduction to the pulse and tempo of the crazy pastiche of African, Spanish, and Taino cultures that make up Dominicana. The first floor contains a bookstore (good maps of the nation) and a room with Taino monoliths. From there you take an elevator up to the third floor, which has numerous Taino artifacts such as grinding stones, axes, carved necklaces, pottery, and a burial site under glass. There's also the stone head of Mictantecuhti, the god of the region of the dead. A diorama shows the slaughter of a beleaguered manatee, and another shows women cooking while the men lazily lounge in hammocks; even way back then the Dominican women were doing most of the work. One section depicts the ways and means of hallucinogenic intoxication. A diorama shows men snorting and a chief in a trance. *Duhos*, thrones for sitting and inhaling, are shown along with related paraphernalia. The fourth floor illustrates Spanish and African influences on the island. There's a *Vudu Dominicano* altar, a collection of *oraciones*, depictions of *santos* (saints), and a display of musical instruments. Photos show ceremonies at such cultish churches as the Iglesia Maravillosa o de Boca de Mai at Villa Altagracia. There's also a model *casa de un campesino* and a display illustrating similarities to African architecture. A fine display shows *carnavál* costumes from all across the land. In direct contrast is a portrait of a stiff German couple posing in front of their Hotel Aleman in Sánchez on the Samaná peninsula. It's open Tues. to Sun., 10-5, tel. 687-3622. Inexpensive admission charged.

GALERIA DE ARTE MODERNO: Located on Pedro Henriquez Ureña, this gallery contains fantastic woodcarvings, oils, mixed media works, and photographs. The display and arrangement here is excellent. The collection's highlights include Antonio Guadalupe's Tilapia, Manolo Pascual's portrait of a squid, Adolfo Piantini's "Sadismo-Masoquismo," Santiago Sosa's futuristic oils, and Alberto Ulloa's "Lamento Americano." Its fourth floor features rotating exhibits that may range from stained glass to moving wooden sculptures. There's also a library open from Mon to Sat. The museum itself is open Tues. to Sun., 10-5, tel. 682-8280. Inexpensive admission charged; Tuesdays are free.

Near Constanza

MUSEO NACIONAL DE HISTORIA Y GEOGRAPHICA: Right nearby on César Nicolas Penson, this museum is worthwhile chiefly for its comprehensive collection of Trujillo memorabilia on display in *sala* three. It's one of the few places, you'll see this despot's name mentioned directly. One of the first things you'll come to is the *gírocóptero* that Tirso Garcia flew from Bayamon, Puerto Rico to Santo Domingo in 1983. Sala de Historia 1 (1822-1861) features a ship model, weapons, depictions of the Haitian occupation including details of various battles, and a coffee cup designed with moustaches in mind. The next room covers 1861-1916 and offers more weapons, memorabilia relating to dictator Ulises Heureux, old uniforms and money, and Juan Isidro Jiménez's presidential sash. Sala de Historia 3 (1916-1961) contains photos of the American occupation including a legendary portrait of a torture victim, a reproduction of an electric chair, and a stupendous collection of Trujillo artifacts: his wallet, passport, *cedula* (identification card), medals, shoes, an ivory straight edge razor with his name inscribed on it, sashes, combs, briefcase, death mask, and a finely polished thick slice of a mahogany tree trunk with Trujillo's portrait etched on it; one of the three cars used in Trujillo's assassination is right behind the ticket desk as you enter. The museum is open Tues. to Sun. 10-5. Inexpensive admission is charged.

MUSEO NACIONAL DE HISTORIA NACIONAL: This museum's Spanish-labeled exhibits encompass space, geology, and zoology. There are dioramas, a gemstone section, and an amber collection. It also has whale skeletons, stuffed animals, and displays of the cosmos. It's open Tues. to Sun., 10:30-5:30. Inexpensive admission charged.

BIBLIOTECA NACIONAL: Right on César Nicolas Penson, the national library operates Mon. to Fri. from 9 to 11 PM. It houses tons of books along with a small art gallery.

TEATRO NACIONAL: A center for opera and symphony, this is on Av. Máximo Gómez (tel. 682-7255). Its main hall holds 1,600, and a smaller one holds 170.

MUSEO NUMISMATICO: On Pedro Henriquez Ureña at Leopoldo Navarro and housed in the Central Bank, the Numismatic and Philatelic Museum contains one of the Caribbean's most valuable complete coin and stamp collections. Open Tues. through Sat. from 9 to 5.

JARDIN BOTANICO NACIONAL (NATIONAL BOTANIC GARDENS): Set in the city's NW corner, this large park is a favorite picnic spot. Just off the central plaza, the Aquatic Plant Pavilion features displays of plants in tanks and in pools. You'll find water lilies, marsilea, cattails, azolla, horsetails, pickerel-weed, and over 200 species of palm, along with West Indian mahogany, the national flower featured on the currency. A series of artificial ponds, the Gran Canada is great for birdwatching. Ducks share the water with rented rowboats, and heliconia and ginger bloom along the banks. The gardens' national herbarium has displays of medicinal and poisonous plants along with a small library. The Bromeliad Pavilion features guess what? Open Tues. to Sat. from 9-5. Inexpensive admission charged.

PARQUE ZOOLOGICO NACIONAL: One of the largest and most majestic zoological parks in the Americas, this zoo has beautiful landscaped gardens where animals can roam freely over a 400-acre area. Monkeys swing from poles on an artificial island across from dromedaries munching on grass. There's an authentic African feel to the place. Beautifully designed and covered with netting, the walk-through aviary features native and exotic species, including the Hispaniolan parrot and palmchat. Be sure to visit the serpent and reptile house where you can see hutias and solenodons. Open Tues. to Sat., 9-5. Inexpensive admission charged.

PARQUE MIRADOR DEL SUR/PASEO DE LOS INDIOS: Located on a narrow stretch of land between Ave. Anaconda and Ave. Mirador Del Sur, this five-mile tree-lined boulevard and park was built to commemorate the Indians. Situated atop a long limestone terrace, it's perfect for viewing the city, jogging, cycling, picknicking, and watching sunsets. Kite-flying contests sometimes take place here. One of the parks's largest caves, the Cueva del Paseo de Los Indios was formed when the limestone underlying the terrace dissolved. Bats are occasionally found in one of its large domed rooms. Visit here during the daytime. For refreshments try the food stands or the **Mesón de la Cueva**, a restaurant and nightspot. Newer and more celebrated is the **Guacara Taina** disco (see "entertainment").

PARQUE LOS TRES OJOS DE AGUA (THE THREE EYES OF WATER): A series of four interconnected underwater ponds of volcanic origin with numerous stalactite and stalagmite formations, this is one of the city's major natural attractions. It's located in the **Parque Mirador del Este** which borders the airport road. The large and spectacular *cenotes* (sinkholes), set in a limestone terrace facing the sea, account for its name. Each cavern's water is colored differently. You can walk around the circumference of the largest and then descend the steps to a boat that takes you across to the other side. There's also a recently discovered fourth lake. Outside, vendors flog sculptures carved from stalactites. From the park, the Avenida de las Américas, running to Boca Chica, is lined with flags from all the western hemisphere's nations. **getting there:** From El Conde take a *público* along Av. Bolivar to Winston Churchill and from there take one in the direction of the sea.

ACUARIO NACIONAL: A product of the Balaguer administration, this small aquarium features tanks you can walk *under:* an arched passageway leads beneath the tropical-fish-filled tanks. Open concrete ponds contain turtles, starfish, and anemones. There's also a small outdoor cafeteria. Open 9:30-6 from Tues. to Sun., it's located in the Parque Littoral del Sur which is between C. Cuarta and 28 de Enero along the coast just to the S of Parque Mirador del Este.

FARO A COLÓN: Also across the Río Ozama, most of this monstrous lighthouse – a huge hunk of fortress-like reinforced concrete – is impossible to ignore. It is perhaps Balaguer's attempt to mimic Java's Borobudor or Cambodia's Angkor Wat. It contains the remains of Christopher Columbus. The six museums and libraries within are dedicated to Columbus, and its searchlight shines over a 60 mi. radius with 149 Xenon Skytrack lasers projecting a cross onto the city skyline. Naturally, in a nation with chronic shortages of electricity, it has its own generator; plans call for it to converted to solar power. **history:** The project was first dreamed up in the 19th C by Dominican writer and historian Antonio Delmonte y Tejada who called for "a statue...a colossus, like that of Rhodes" in his *History of Santo Domingo,* published in 1852. In 1923 the Fifth International American Conference, held in Santiago de Chile, resolved that a lighthouse should be constructed in Santo Domingo. One J. Gleave, an architectural student from Manchester submitted the winning design in an international contest. In 1937 a four-airplane goodwill flight – designed to promote the lighthouse construction – set out on a grand tour of the Americas. Unfortunately the three Cuban planes crashed into a mountain while flying from Colombia to Ecuador; only the Dominican craft was spared. Although ground was broken under Trujillo in 1939, WWII intervened and construction was abandoned; some say that he had heard the story of a jinx on Columbus's name and events such as the plane crash and the earthquake that commenced during the 1946 Columbus pageant convinced him of its veracity. To this day,

Dominicans refer to the *fucu* (Arawak for "curse" of Columbus) and refer to him only as "The Discoverer" and "The Admiral." Balaguer ordered renewed construction in 1987. Construction is estimated to have cost more than $70 million, and parts of the interior remain uncompleted. **the inauguration:** The government had intended the lighthouse to serve as a beacon for tourism and investment, asserting the Dominican Republic's place in the Western Hemisphere – a major miscalculation. In an attempt to forge a religious connection, the government termed the event a celebration of "The Discovery and Evengelization of America." Instead of attracting luminaries such as American right wing comedian Bob Hope (who had originally been scheduled to emcee a variety show) and the King and Queen of Spain, only Argentina's Carlos Menem attended the dedication. Although he later conducted a mass from behind the structure on the day before Columbus Day, the Pope disassociated his visit from the celebrations. The dedication was moved up from Oct. 12 (Columbus Day) to Oct. 6. After Balaguer's 73-year-old sister Emma Vallejo suffered a fatal heart attack just after touring the lighthouse, Balaguer cancelled his appearance at the dedication! The celebration was marked by nationwide protests with demonstrators chanting "Colón Ladron" ("Columbus is a thief"). A group of priests protested, a protester was shot in Azua by an undercover cop, and a human rights lawyer was shot dead by six police officers from the secret service branch of the National Police. In preparation for the dedication, some 50,000 residents of the area were evicted and 10-ft.-high walls erected along the road to the site in an attempt to camouflage the poverty. Dubbed the "Wall of Shame," it has aroused great controversy. As one resident said, "It shows that we are still Indians, symbolically speaking. We are still the people Columbus came to kill." Another asserted that "the government is treating us as garbage that must be swept under the rug." **sights:** The first thing that comes into view as you enter is the elaborate marble and bronze tomb of Christopher Columbus which was formerly housed in the cathedral. No one knows if it actually contains the bones of the 15th C navigator or not: another elaborate chapel in Seville, Spain makes the same claim. Believed to have been first brought here by his daughter-in-law in 1544, the alleged remains were found during restoration work in 1877 by Padre Francisco Billini, and the tomb (donated by the Spanish government) was made in 1898. Friezes around the base depict important episodes in Columbus's life. Passing by the tomb, you come to a long outdoor passageway flanked on either side by beautiful mahogany doors with brass handles. These lead to the museums. They depict the history of the lighthouse, with a library dedicated to Columbus and his voyages, maps of the Americas, a

Columbus museum, one on underwater archaeology, and a sixth displaying 15th C ceramics. The monument is covered with thousands of crosses: Juan Bosch has said there is one cross for every Indian killed.

MALECÓN SIGHTS: The titanic scupture along the *Malecón* (waterfront) is of Fray Anton de Montecrios who protested the Spanish exploitation of the Indians. It was a gift from México in Oct. 1982. Two obelisks are farther down. The first commemorates payment of the national debt to the US during the negotiations between Trujillo and US Secretary of State Cordell Hull. The second and larger one commemorates the renaming of the city as Ciudad Trujillo during the height of the despot's reign. Constructed in a record 17 days, it is popularly known as "Obelisco Macho." Located on one side of the street, Parque Eugenio María de Hostos has been restored to its 1940-era design. Though it was originally designed as the Plaza Columbiana where Columbus's remains were to be interred, plans were changed and it became Parque Infantil Ramfis after Trujillo's oldest son.

OTHER SIGHTS: The Museo de Trujillo is a private museum in Store 7 at Plaza Criolla. Housing pre-Columbian artifacts, the **Museo Pre-hispanico** is set at Av. San Martin 279 (near the intersection of Máximo Gómez and 27 de Febrero) and run by the 7-Up Company; this small museum is open 8-noon, Mon. to Sat. Past the Santo Domingo Hotel, **Centro de Los Héroes**, presently a collection of rundown government office buildings, was the setting for the 1955-56 Feria de Confraternidad (Fair of Peace and Fraternity of the Free World), on which Trujillo squandered an incredible $40 million, a third of that year's national budget. It now houses the Senate and Congress. At the opening of the fair, the dictator's 16-year-old daughter Maria was crowned Queen Angelita I. She wore an $80,000 satin coat with a 75-ft. Russian ermine train. If you wish to see a dramatic counterpart to the Faro a Colón, you should visit the Ciudad Universidad to the W of Gazcue. The **Universidad Autonomal Santo Domingo** (UASD) here has a large but delapidated campus. Never popular with Balaguer (he was ousted from a professorship here), the university is virtually free but vastly underfunded. Posters display protest demands, and conditions are quite bad. It's really insightful to see where the government puts its priorities.

Citywide Practicalities
Santo Domingo Hotels

With so many places to choose from, it's not an easy task to decide upon a hotel. Factors include your pocketbook and your interests. The place to be is in Old Santo Domingo, but accommodation there is limited to a few hotels. Another nice area to stay in is Gazcue.

LUXURY: Most of the accommodation listed in this section is priced at over $100 pn. The 316-room a/c **Dominican Concorde** (tel. 562-8222) is on Av. Anaconda and has two restaurants, an Olympic-sized pool, an attractive casino, and eight tennis courts. A recently renovated classic, the 355-rm. **Ramada Renaissance Jaragua Resort and Casino** (tel. 221-2222, fax 686-0528) is on Av. George Washington 367 and is set on 14 acres. The hotel's rooms have marble bathrooms, hair dryers, color TVs, and computerized door locks. Other facilities include a nightclub, ballroom, the nation's largest casino, a European-style spa, five restaurants, an Olympic-style pool, four tennis courts, and a convention center which can service up to 1,000. Prices range from $110 for a "standard" room to $1,500 for the penthouse, and this does not include 23% tax and service. You can call (800) 228-9898 toll free in the US and (800) 331-3542 toll free in the Dominican Republic. Renovated and enlarged in recent years, the 220-room a/c **Gran Hotel Lina** (tel. 563-5000; 800-942-2461) is at the corner of Av. Máximo Gómez and 27 de Febrero. Its rooms have radio and cable TV. Other amenities include bars, a nightclub, pool, solarium, gym, and sauna. The 260-rm. **Sheraton** (tel. 221-6666, 688-0823, fax 687-8150, 686-0125; Box 1493) is at Av. George Washington 365. Rooms here have cable TV with remote control and most command views of the sea. Its facilities include gym, sauna, pool, tennis court, convention rooms, disco, casino, and three restaurants. Call (800) 325-3535 in the US. The 316-room a/c **Hotel El Embajador** (tel. 533-2131, 800-457-0067, fax 532-4494/5306) is on Av. Sarasota. Its rooms are equipped with radio and cable TV. Facilities include a restaurant, coffeeshop, nightclub, casino, pool, shopping arcade, beauty parlor, massage and sauna services, car rental, babysitting services, and taxi service. It can accommodate up to 350 conventioneers. At Av. George Washington 218 (corner of Pasteur), the **V Centenario's** (tel. 687-2933, 800-223-5652) 230 rooms include 30 suites; all rooms face the sea. Facilities include restaurants, tennis, squash, pool, gym, sauna, disco, casino, and piano bar. Set right next to each other in the W side of town, the Hotels Santo Domingo and Hispaniola share common owners, and their meal plans are interchangeable. The colonial-style 220-rm. **Hotel Santo Domingo** (tel. 221-7111), Av. Independencia and Av. Abraham Lincoln, offers elegant interior decoration by designer Oscar de la Renta. The rooms have lots of lush red lacquer work and Dominican mahogany furniture. With 69 rooms, its "premier floor" is designed for executives and features a breakfast lounge along with additional facilities in the rooms including a hairdryer and TV remote control. Renting for around $725 pn, the huge presidential suite on this level includes a business meeting room. Facilities include restaurant, pool, night club, tennis and volleyball courts, sauna and massage, beauty parlor, and boutique. Call (800) 223-6620 in the US. The Santo Domingo's less elegant and less expensive sister, the 160-rm **Hotel Hispaniola** (tel. 535-7111), Independencia at Av. Lincoln, has comfortable a/c rooms with cable TV and radio, a restaurant, bar, disco, pool, three tennis courts, beauty parlor, car rental, gift shop, and massage. Built in 1956, it still has manual elevators with operators – a nice blast from the past. Call (800) 223-6620 in the US.

EXPENSIVE: Centrally located in the old part of town at C. Las Damas 53, **Hostal Nicolás de Ovando** (tel. 687-3101/3107) is a restored 16th C mansion which once belonged to the famous *conquistador* and Hispaniolan governor of the same name. It has a pool and is a/c. The seafront 72-rm. a/c **Hotel Napolitano** (tel. 687-1131, fax 689-2714) is on Av. George Washington. It has a terrace restaurant, 24-hr. cafeteria, disco, pool, and a beauty salon. The 180-rm. a/c **Hotel Cervantes** (tel. 686-8161, fax 686-5754; Apdo. 2768), C. Cervantes 202, has a swimming pool, steakhouse, and nightclub. Rooms have cable TV, a/c, and radios. Priced at around $20 s and $28 d., **Hotel Alameda** (tel. 685-5121/5122) is at C. Cervantes 157. The 87-rm. **Hotel Comodoro** (tel. 541-2277), Av. Bólivar 193, has a pool; rooms are a/c with cable TV and refrigerators; other facilities include a French restaurant, cafeteria, nightclub, car rental, taxi service, and convention facilities for up to 300. The 39-rm. **Hotel Caribe I** (tel. 688-8141), Av. Máximo Gómez (corner of Ramirez), has a pool and an Italian restaurant. Rooms have radio, cable TV, and are a/c. The 100-rm. **Hotel Continental** (tel. 688-1840, 689-1151-59), Av. Máximo Gómez 16, offers a/c rooms with radio and cable TV. Its facilities include a French restaurant, disco, bar, small pool, and babysitting service. In the US call (800) 223-1900. The 72-rm. **Hotel San Geronimo and Casino** (tel. 535-1000/8851), Av. Independencia 1076, has a/c rooms with cable TV and radio. There's also car rental, pool, cafeteria, and restaurant.

MODERATE: Priced at around $50 s or d including tax and service, the 75-rm. a/c **Hotel Comercial** (tel. 682-8161; Apdo. 787, Santo Domingo) is at C. El Conde 201 at Hostos. It has a cafeteria and bar and all of its rooms come with private bath. On C. Danae in the Gazcue area, 24-rm. a/c **Hotel la Residence** (tel. 682-4178, 686-2828) is a European-style hotel with TV, a/c, wall-to-wall carpeting, and your choice of bed size – from double to king. Newly opened in 1993, **Hotel Restaurante La Casona Dorada** (tel. 221-3535, fax 682-1832) is a small and quite elegant hotel. It's at Av. Independencia 255 (cor. C. Osvaldo Báez). Another new hotel is the **Hotel Casa Vapor** (tel. 221-8888. fax 686-6216). Designed to resemble the shape of a ship, it is at Av. Francia 40 and C. Dr. Delgado. Rooms (about $50 s or d) are very attractive, and it has a restaurant and disco. Finally, **Hotel Delta** (tel 535-0800/9722, fax 535-6957) is at Av. Sarasota 53. It has 75 a/c rooms with TV, refrigerator, bar and restaurant, plus a solarium with Jacuzzi. In the DR call toll free 1-200-1288 or write Apdo. 1818, Santo Domingo.

INEXPENSIVE: At C. Presidente Vicini Burgos 58 in Gazcue a half-block from the obelisk on the Malecón, 13-rm. **Hotel El Señorial** (tel. 687-4367, fax 687-0600) is renowned for its relaxed and social atmosphere. Its comfortable rooms (priced at around $30 s or d) are a/c, with cable TV. It has a nice dining room and good food. The staff are affable and easygoing. Priced from $20 s and $27 d, **Hotel Palmeras del Caribe** (tel. 689-3872, 682-0959) is on the Malecón at C. Cambronal 1. It has small but attractive rooms with b&w TVs. The Dominican management is very friendly, and the location is ideal. In Gazcue at C. Danae 26, **La Mansion** (tel. 686-5562, 682-2033, 689-8758) has rooms for around $20 and up. Just nearby at C. Danae, **Hotel La Residence** (tel. 682-4178) is a dollar or so more expensive but better value. Back in the old town, attractive, extremely atmospheric, but aging **Hotel David's** (tel. 688-8538, 685-9121/9123, fax 688-8056), Arz. Nouel 308, offers TV and refrigerator in its rooms which are priced at around $40 s or d. **Hotel Anacaona** (tel. 688-6888), Palo Hincado 303, has rooms with a/c, private bath, and hot water. **Hotel Bolivar** (tel. 685-2200), Av. Bolivar 62, has rooms with bath, fan, and TV. **Hotel Antillas** (tel. 685-4672, 686-8383) Av. Independencia 53, offers rooms with bath and fan. Inexpensive **Hotel Aida** (tel. 685-7692, 687-2880), El Conde 464 at Espaillat, has a/c rooms and less expensive ones with fans. Offering a terrace restaurant with Jacuzzi, at Av. Duarte and Teniente Amado Garcia, the **Royal Hotel** (tel. 686-5852/1717, fax 686-6536) offers 64 a/c rooms with phones for around $32 s, $35 d, $40 d. Set at Estrelleta 267 near Arzobispo Nouel and Parque Independencia, the recently-renovated **Independencia** (tel. 686-1663) has a roof terrace, art exhibits, and a language school across the street. On the old town's Malecón above the restaurant of the same name, the **Llave del Mar** (tel. 682-5761) offers rooms for about $18 s or d. Located near the Terra Bus terminal, **Hotel Rosal** (tel. 596-5033, 597-2066) is at C. Marginal 9, Alma Rosa 2.

LOW BUDGET: Best of the very cheap hotels that aren't used for short-time prostitution is **Hotel "La Fama,"** (tel. 689-1275), Av. Mella 609. Many Haitian smugglers stay here; it's clean and secure with fan and sink in rooms. **other options:** Try **Pensión Dominicana** (tel. 689-0722) at El Conde 454 and **Pensión Gilette** (tel. 685-7815) at El Conde 505. Also try to look for rooms in *casas de pensión* and in hotels by consulting the classified listings in the daily *Listin Diario*. Finally, be aware that many of the cheapest places are unmarked, so ask around.

APART-HOTELS: Among these there is one clear standout in design, service, and location. German-owned and operated a/c **Hotel Palacio** is set in the heart of the old town at C. Duarte 106 (corner of Salome Ureña). Opened in the fall of 1991, its 10 rooms are furnished Castilian style. There are also two single rooms and a large suite which has a private Jacuzzi. The seven regular rooms feature remote-control color cable TV, wardrobe, phones (one for the room and one for the bath), furnished kitchenette, and minibar. Other facilities include secretarial service, fax, tourist guide service, bar, small gym, and a patio. The hotel is actually a restored home which was once the private house of the offspring of Buenaventura Báez who served five times as president between 1848 and 1878. It has a pleasant patio facing a courtyard. Rates run from $50. A 10% discount is offered to readers of this book. To reserve, call 682-4730, fax 800-687-5535, or write Apdo. 20541, Santo Domingo. Nearby, less expensive and much more spartan, **La Arcada** (tel. 686-7456), C. Arz. Meriño 360, has apartments with cooking facilities from around $12 pn; a discount is offered for longer stays. Featuring 28 suites fully a/c with color TV and kitchenettes, **Apart-Hotel Drake** (tel. 567-4427) is at Augustin Lara 29 near Plaza Naco. At Plaza Naco, the **Plaza Hotel and Casino** (tel. 541-6226) is administered by the Naco chain. The tallest hotel, it features 54 suites and 165 efficencies, all of which come with kitchenettes. At Av. Tiradentes 22, a convenient mid-town location, its rooms also include cable TV, radio, and a complete kitchenette; and other facilities include a pool, cafeteria, restaurant, casino, and babysitting service. In the US call (800) 223-6510 and in Canada call (800) 424-5500. The **Apart-Hotel Aladino** (tel. 567-0144/0140), H. Pieter 34 (Ens. Naco), has both fan and a/c rooms available. At Av.

Bolívar 230, **Plaza Florida** (tel. 541-3957/4742, fax 540-5582) offers 32 spacious a/c and fully equipped one-bedroom apartments.The **Aparta-Hotel Plaza del Sol** (tel. 688-5596/5497/5686, fax 542-5454), José Contreras 25-A, offers fully furnished studios. On Av. 27 de Febrero, **Apart-Hotel Arak** (tel. 567-4267) offers fully equipped a/c apartments with power plant, maid, elevators, and 24-hr. security. In Gazcue, **Apart-Hotel Plaza Colonial** (tel. 687-9111, 685-9171, fax 686-2877), C. Luisa Pellerano at the cor. of Av. Jules Verne, offers a/c fully equipped one- and two-bedroom apartments, pool, and restaurant. Located near the Olympic Center, at C. Gustavo Mejia Ricart 8-A, **Aparta-Hotel Turey** (tel. 562-5271/5446) provides tasteful a/c studios and one-bedrooms with kitchenettes. There's also a pool and snack bar. Set at the intersection of Av. 27th de Febrero and Av. Winston Churchill, **Plaza Central** (tel. 565-6905/6706) offers 25 "Club Plaza" executive suites which cater to business travelers. Telex, secretarial services, and seminar facilities are available. **Aby** has three apartment hotels; one is at C. Padre Pina 104 (tel. 685-9729); another is at C. 23 Este Esq.; 25 Este la Castellana, Los Prados (tel. 541-0876/7116); and a third at C. 6 No. 9 Ens. Evaristo Morales, near the corner of Winston Churchill and 27 de Febrero (tel. 565-7184). **Aparta-Hotel Laurel** (tel. 530-4724/3859), C. Caonabo 41, features color TV in all apartments, a/c, and a restaurant. Set on the edge of the Malecón, **Apart-Hotel Sea-View** (tel. 221-4420/4319/4119) has units from around $45. Others include **Apart-Hotel Plaza Florida** (tel. 541-3650, Av. Lara 29) and **Apart-Hotel Mi Retiro** (tel. 598-0028, Del Pez 13).

OUT OF TOWN: Staying in Boca Chica is an alternative to the capital. Public transportation to and fro is quite good during the day. The 54-room Italian-run **Hotel Acuarium** (tel. 595-6755/fax 593-4484) is outside of town on the way to the airport. It has a restaurant, bar, pool, and conference rooms.

Santo Domingo Dining and Food

DINING OUT: The more expensive restaurants here may require that men wear a jacket. **hotel dining:** Each of the major hotels has its own special restaurant. At the Santo Domingo and designed by Oscar de la Renta, the **Alcázar**, with its 20-ft. tented ceiling, resembles a Moroccan palace. It's known for its fish dishes, buffet lunches here are less expensive, and a champagne brunch is featured on Sun. Also try the Las Palmas here. **La Piazetta** at the Hispaniola features Italian specialties. Gran Hotel Lina's **Lina**, Av. Máximo Gómez and 27 de Febrero, offers seafood, beef, excellent paella, and Spanish food; the cook used to work for Trujillo. The **Hotel Comodoro**, Av. Bolivar 193, has **Le Gourmet** which serves international and Dominican dishes. **note:** Many of the hotels offer lunchtime *buffets ejecutivos* for about $10.

OLD TOWN DINING: At the end of El Conde between Damas and Parque Colón, Argentinean-owned **Ché Bandoneón** (tel. 689-2105) features elegant Argentinean, French, and Dominican food served outdoors to the accompaniment of tangos. **La Cocina** is nearby. Serving local and international cuisine, the **Fonda La Ataranza** (tel. 689-2900) is at La Ataranza 5. The **Meson de la Ataranza** offers outdoor gourmet dining; naturally enough, it's also near the Ataranza. The Hostal Nicólas de Ovando's **Extremadura**, C. Las Damas 52, serves Spanish food. Also with Spanish-style cuisine, **América** (tel. 682-7194), is at C. Santome 201 at Arzobispo Nouel. Serving English-style food in a formal setting, **Café Coco** is at C. Sánchez 153 off of El Conde. Down at the Malecón on the old town side are a number of restaurants, including **Restaurant del Mar** and the **Restaurant la Llave del Mar** which offers piano music and decor including a stuffed crocodile, sea turtles, birds on the ceiling, corals, and stuffed fish. It claims to be a "paradise," but it's a marine life lover's nightmare. Classy outdoor **Manresa** is across the road. The a/c **Les Jardines de Bagatelle** is next door and **La Bahía** is farther down the road. If none of these last few appeal to you, you can always snack it up at the **Pizza Capri**.

ON THE MALECON: At Av. George Washington 1, **La Bahía** is renowned for its seafood including conch, lobster, and shrimp. Specializing in steak and seafood, **El Castillo del Mar** is at Av. George Washington 2. Specializing in French cuisine, **Les Jardins del Bagatelle** are at Av. George Washington 39. Folkloric shows are presented on the patio from time to time. With two locations at 459 and 123, spacious **Restaurant El Caserio** specializes in seafood. The Sheraton's **Antoine's**, George Washington 365, features international and seafood dishes. A classic restaurant and continually bustling, **Vesuvio I**, Av. George Washington 521, features Italian and international cuisine. A great location for peoplewatching, its outdoor section is the place to see and be seen. Smaller and similar though less atmospheric, **Vesuvio II**, a second establishment, is at Av. Tiradentes 17. Outdoors on the Malecón at Av. George Washington 553, **La Parilla** specializes in BBQ.

NEAR THE MALECON: Featuring Peruvian-style seafood and local cuisine, the renowned **Jai-Alai** (tel. 685-2409) is at Av. Independencia 411, to the rear of the Jaragua and Sheraton hotels. Also behind the Jaragua and Sheraton hotels at Av. Independencia 407, **La Mezquita** offers Spanish food in an informal but comfortable environment. Serving Dominican, Italian, French, and Spanish food, **Restaurante Tonde de Tasis** is also in the vicinity of the Jaragua. Outdoors and overlooking the Malecón, **Le Café**, JM Heredia, offers light meals including crepes and desserts. Popular with baseball aficionadoes, the **Lucky Seven**, C. Pasteur 16, has steaks and seafood. Next to Lucky Seven on C. Pasteur at Casimiro de Moya, **Marbella** offers seafood specialties. Also with Spanish cuisine, multi-level **El Toledo**, C. Pasteur at the corner of Casimiro de Moya, serves seafood dishes and other specialties. At C. Santiago cor. C. Pasteur, **Don Pepe** has Spanish atmosphere and cuisine. The **Bronco Steak House** at the Hotel Cervantes, C. Cervantes 202 at Bolivar, serves American-style steaks and chops; it has an extensive wine list. Another beautiful converted home in the Gazcue area, **D. Luis**, C. Santiago 205, has an international menu and a separate bar. At Av. Independencia 54, **Cantábrico** is popular with the exec lunch bunch and has good paella, seafood, and meat dishes. **La Reina de España**, C. Cervantes 103, serves Castillian and international food as well as innovative cuisine such as sea bass served in apple cider.

OTHER LOCATIONS: Offering steaks and other grilled foods, **La Pyramide** is at Av. Romúlo Betancourt 352. The **Delcías Diner** is also on Av. Romúlo Betancourt. The **Parrillada Don Miguel** on Marta Montés, is noted for its charcoal grilled meat. For German food try **Aubergine** on Av. Tiradentes. At Av. Máximo Gómez 9 near the Continental and Caribe hotels, **D'Agostini** serves very expensive international food. It's well known for its *ceviche* and its cooked *mero* (bass). At C. Gustavo Mejia Ricart 7, **Juan Carlos** has been transformed from a local eatery into a Spanish-style formal restaurant. At Av. Abraham Lincoln 605, **Piccolo Gourmet** offers seafood, pasta, and beef dishes in a congenial and casual setting. Inside Plaza Criolla on Av. 27 de Febrero, **La Fromagerie** dishes up crepes, fondues, and bouillabaisse. At Centro Europa to the rear of the Palacio del Cine on Av. 27 de Febrero, **El Picnic** offers seafood dishes as well as a deli/pastry shop. A bit off the beaten track but very convenient if you're visiting the museums at the cultural plaza, **Maniqui** features Sunday all-you-can-eat buffets for $6. The Japanese restaurant, **Restaurant Samurai**, is at Av. Abraham Lincoln 102. Probably the most unusually situated restaurant is **Mesón de la Cava** (tel. 533-2818), Parque Mirador, which is set in a cave and entered by a spiral staircase. Noted for its dancing and steaks, it's very popular so reservations are a must. On Av. Anacaona across from the Dominican Concorde, the **Lago Enriquillo** is in the same park and features Oriental and international cuisine.

At Plaza México on Av. México, the **Aubergine** restaurant specializes in German cuisine. Apart-Hotel Plaza Florida's family-style **Boga-Boga**, Av. Bolivar 203, serves up Spanish dishes including seafood; tapas are served at five. For pastas and snacks try **Café Atlantico**, Av. México 152. Specializing in intriguing dishes such as BBQ rabbit, **Asadero los Argentinos** is at Av. Independencia 809 (near Av. Máximo Gómez). On the second level of Galerias Comerciales at Av. 27 de Febrero, **Café Galeria** combines displays of artwork with crepes. Attractively designed, **Café St. Michell**, Av. Lope de Vega 24, has French and continental cuisine. Also on Av. Lope de Vega, **Remini** serves Italian pasta and pizza. Situated on Av. Independencia just behind the Hotel Hispaniola, **Le Bistro** offers authentic French Cuisine.

CHINESE FOOD: One of the best restaurants, reasonably priced, accessible, and attractively designed, **Salon de Te** is at C. Duarte just by the Maritime Museum in the old town. It's run by exceedingly friendly Anita and her sisters who all speak fluent English. **Mario's** is at Av. 27 de Febrero 299, and **Restaurant Gran Chop Suey** is on the same avenue at No. 356. Relatively inexpensive **La Gran Muralla**, Av. 27 de Febrero, is popular for its Sunday buffets and all you can eat tariff. Inexpensive **Comedor Buen Pastor** is at Av. Duarte 32. Inside the Hotel Embajador, the **Jardín de Jade** doubles as a miniature museum of Chinese ethnography with crowns, costumes, and weapons from China. Spacious and heavily a/c, **Chino de Mariscos** is at Av. Sarasota 38A near the Hotel Embajador. At C. Gustavo Mejia Ricart 64, **Lee's Kitchen** is an informal eatery which offers N Chinese and Taiwanese food.

PIZZA: Pizza Capri is on the old town part of the Malecón, and there are a number of pizza joints along El Conde. On Av. George Washington, **Il Capo del Malecón**, offers pasta as well as pizza. Another location is in the Embajador Gardens. Featuring *tacos* and *tamales* in addition to pizza, **Taqueria Antojiots** is at Av. Lope de Vega 49. Located at the Merengue Plaza on the corner of Av. 27 de Febrero and Av. Tiradentes, open air **Pala Pizza** has a second location on Winston Churchill.

LOCAL FOOD: Good and inexpensive, **Cafeteria Dumbo** is on C. Nouel behind Parque Independencia. At. C. Hostos 153 between C. Arz. Nouel and El Conde, **El Sarten** has a great atmosphere and red and white decor. **Pala Pizza** is next door. On Arz. Nouel at Hostos, the **De Nosotros Empanadas** offers fast-food *empanadas* – just the thing for a snack. The **Naiboa** is at Av. Bolivar 730 near Av. Máximo Gómez. On Felix E. Mejia, the **Comedor "Franklin"** offers creole cuisine. Less pricey are **El Burén** on Padre Billini, and **Pacos Café** near Parque Independencia. One reasonably priced restaurant is the **El Conuco** on Casimiro de Moya, situated approximately behind the entrance to the Jaragua. **Palacio de Mofongo** (Av. Independencia, tel. 688-8121) or the **Casa del Mofongo**, more distant on Av. 27 de Febrero, specialize in *mofongo*. For traditional Dominican sweets and cider visit **Dulces Criollos Doña María** at Plaza Criolla, Av. 27 de Febrero. At Lea de Castro 205 in the old town, **Casita Dulce** has *pasteles in hoja*, *dulces*, and desserts. **Delicatesa**, across the street, sells pastries and bread. *Chimchurri* (spiced sausage) is sold from stands all over the city.

VEGETARIAN DINING: Your best bet is the cafeteria-style **Ananda** (tel. 682-4465) which is at Casimiro de Moya 7 at Pasteur and is open daily for lunch and dinner. It is a branch of a worldwide Indian guru sect. The food is plentiful and quite good. They also have a set lunch of three items for less than $2, but it's more fun to mix and match on your own. You can order and combine your own dishes. Another good choice with longer hours is **Nutrivida** (tel. 686-2985) which offers a set lunch (for around $2.25), milkshakes, and entrees such as ravioli and cheeseburgers. It has a utilitarian atmosphere, but the staff is friendly and the food is fresh and well prepared. It's open daily from 8 AM to midnight. Also try **El Terrenal** (tel. 689-3161), Malecón and Estrelleta, which features some vegetarian dishes. For gourmet dining, **Las Ojas** (tel. 682-3940) is in C. Jonas Salk near Bolivar and is within walking distance from the Plaza Cultural. Food here is exceedingly delicious but the accent on cream and cheese in many dishes is a bit heavy for cholesterol and fat watchers. One good alternative is the gluten shish kebab. Entrees are around $2-3. Lunches ($4) are served all-you-can-eat cafeteria-style. It's open 12-3 and 6-9, but is closed Sat. evening.

BUDGET FOOD: Many *cafeterias* clustered around the vicinity of El Conde are open late. Seedy in appearance (and therefore redolent in atmosphere), **Cafeteria Colonial** is on C. El Conde and is good for breakfast and lunch. **Cafeteria Viejo Roma**, Av. Bolivar across from Puerto El Conde, serves great lunch and dinners. Street vendors hawk peanut brittle, *dulce de leche* (a traditional sweet), and other goodies for a few cents and up. You can get a slice of pizza at a variety of places in El Conde, but you may not find it to your taste. On C. José Reyes, **Mr. Burger** offers the "first American style hamburgers, sandwiches, and breakfast in the Dominican Republic."

FOOD STORES: At C. Luperón 9 (corner Arzobispo Meriño), **Restaurant Bethel** (closed Sat.) sells good whole wheat bread and sugary peanut butter in its shop; it's also good for lunch in a pinch but is hardly *haute cuisine*; you do get a free Jehovah's Witness pamphlet with lunch however. At the junction of a small park with Luperón, **Vita Naturaleza**, C. Mercedes 255, sells health food. There's also a health food shop along the side street garage entrance at Plaza Naco. The best place to buy vegetables is at the back of the **Mercado Modelo** on Av. Mella.

SUPERMARKETS: In the old part of town, a medium-sized good grocery store is the **Casa Velasquez** at Gran Luperón and Arzobispo Meriño. **Supermercado Extra** is at Nicolás de Ovando 385 (corner of Av. Máximo Gómez). **Supermercado Avenida** is at Av. Duarte 379. **Supermercado Nacional** has locations at Av. Mella 119, Av. Abraham Lincoln at Av. 27 de Febrero, and on Av Nuñez de Caceres. In Gazcue, **Serpermercado Savica** is at Benito Moncíon 51. The **Super Asturias** is in Centro Commercial Naco, Av. Tiradentes, and at Av. 27 de Febrero at Juan Baron Fajardo. Innumerable others are listed in the yellow pages.

Santo Domingo Entertainment

There's plenty of good nightlife here although the frequent blackouts can make getting around a pain. Be sure to bring a flashlight with you before venturing out at night. *Perico ripeao*, groups of three or four street musicians, serenade all up and down the *Malecón*, the waterfront boulevard. Dominicans traditionally welcome in the New Year here; the *carnavál* and Mardi Gras festivals also take place here, and the wide stretch is lined with cafes, bars, restaurants, clubs, and movie theaters. You can snack on everything from pizza to cashews as you stroll or take a horse and buggy ride. Dominicans cruise along the stretch in Toyota convertibles.

CONCERTS AND THEATER: The **Teatro Nacional**, Av. Máximo Gómez, offers musical and other events including performances by the National Symphony. Recitals and chamber music performances are held in the smaller Sala Ravelo. The ticket office (tel. 682-7255) is open from 9:30-noon daily, and tickets are inexpensive. Local and international performances are also held in the **Palacio de Bellas Artes** (Palace of Fine Arts, tel. 682-6384) on Av. Independencia at the corner of Máximo Gómez. Located at the corner of El Conde and Las Damas, the **Casa de Francia** (tel. 685-0840) offers concerts, films, and other activities. The Instituto Cultural **Dominicano Americano** (tel. 533-4191), Av. Abraham Lincoln 21, offers theater performances and concerts. **Casa de Teatro** (tel. 689-3430, 686-7840), a drama workshop and experimental theater formed in 1975, is at C. Arzobispo Meriño 110. It also has regular art exhibits and performances. The **Teatro Nuevo** in Barrio Don Bosco has performances all year. Set in the Parque Mirador Sur, the **Guacara Taina** (tel. 530-2666) offers folkloric dances on Tues. to Fri. from 7-10 PM.

DISCOS: There are many discoteques in town. Large and most luxurious, the **Babilon disco** is at Av. George Washington 1005. Nearby, **Le Regine** also presents occasional fashion shows and live music. Inside the Jaragua, try **Jubilee**. Also on Av. George Washington, elegant **Bella Blue** (next to Vesuvio's) features loads of *merengue* and sometimes has fashion shows and live bands. Luxurious and featuring *merengue* groups on occasion, the Hotel Sheraton's Omni spins *merengue, salsa*, ballads, and rock. At the Hotel Hispaniola, **Neon 2002** caters to a young crowd. At. C. La Guardia 25, **Kuora Disco** features "sensurrom" sound. A yuppie crowd collects at **Alexander's**, C. Pasteur 23, which chiefly features rock. **Exquesito** (tel. 540-5477) is a dance spot on Av. Tiradentes. On Robert Pastoriza near the cor. of Av. Abraham Lincoln, the two-story **Gasolina** resembles a 1950s gas station; half of a car is attached to a wall on its first level. At Av. Máximo Gómez 60 across from the National Theater, **Columbus/Club 60** features merengue, rock, and ballads. Set atop the Plaza Naco Hotel and commanding a breathtaking view of the capital, **Top's** is another classy and popular disco. The Hotel Continental features the **Tiffany Club**, a bar and disco. With three bars on three levels and two dance floors, **Guácara Taina** is the largest disco around. It's set in Parque Mirador Sur near Nuñez de Caceres. Music pounds from 9 or 11 to dawn. **others:** You can also try Hotel El Embajador's **Hipocampo**; **Opus Discoteca** (merengue, salsa, etc.), Av. Independencia 624. Featuring daily live entertainment, **Bottom's Lounge** is on the first floor of the Plaza Naco Hotel on Av. Tiradentes at C. Presidente González. **Lapsus** is at Av. Independencia 503; **Punta Final** on Av. Pasteur. At Sánchez Valverde y Balthazar de los Reyes in Villa Consuelo, El Rincón Habanero has Cuban son music from the 40s and 50s. At Baltazar de los Reyes and Pimentel, one block away, the Secreto Musical Bar is similar. It's the headquarters of the Club Nacional de Soneros. Merengue, rock, and ballads are also played here. Also try **La Vieja Habana** in Villa Mella on the city's N outskirts.

BARS AND CLUBS: There are plenty of places to take others and display your sense of sophistication. **Drake's Pub** is across from the Alcázar in the old town. **Café Montesino** is also here, as are **Nancy's Snack Bar, Rita's Café,** the **Candray Bar,** and also the **Bar-Meson Museo de Jamón,** which features flamenco dancing to recorded music on Thurs. and Sun. at 10 PM. The last takes its name from the batallions of smoked hams hanging from the ceiling – a surrealistic work worthy of a Marcel Duchamp. Worthy of any city in the world, unforgettable **Chez Duke** has a living room atmosphere and a chess table. Offering live jazz weekly, it's at Arz. Portes 99 at Meriño which is near the cathedral. Dark and romantic, **Disco Momento** is down the street. It's just the place for some hot petting. The **Meson Nuevo Mundo** is on C. Los Damas in front of the National Pantheon. An attractive place with tremendous atmosphere, the **Maubo-Café** is at El Conde 151 – near the end of the street. The **Village Pub** and **Raffles** are on C. Hostos opposite the ruins of the hospital. At Padre Billini and Las Damas, **La Taberna** features classical music. Situated at Palo Hincado 101 at Arz. Portes which is across from the Puerta de la Misericorda, the **Clasico Delicatessen** serves as a liquor store during the day and takes on the character of a classy bar at night. The **Karamba**, Isabel la Católica, has a DJ spinning pop and *merengue* tunes. At the corner of Av. México and Av. Abraham Lincoln, **Café Atlantico** serves Mexican snacks during its happy hour. It also has occasional live bands and theme parties. It plays everything from jazz to samba to *salsa* to *merengue* to African pop. On Av. Sarasota 53-8, inside the Delta Hotel, **Delta's Café** is where the white collared come to relax after work. On C. Roberto Pastoriza 14, **D'Golden Club** is an upscale bar with a happy hour and live entertainment. Set next to the Café San Michel on Av. Lope de Vega, the **Grand Café** caters to a younger crowd. Jazz, rock, and *merengue* bands perform here. On Av. Independencia one block E of the Sheraton, the **Mento Bar** is a popular watering hole. **Ibiza** is at the corner of Av. Tiradentes and C. Roberto Pastoriza. D'Golden is next door. Popular with Spaniards as well as university students, **No Lo Se** is on Av. Bolivar near the corner of Av. Máximo Gómez. Another popular venue is the **Stone Bar** in La Ataranza. Footballheads will want to visit the **Sports Center Bar/Restaurant** (tel. 688-3215/2369), 30 de Marzo 31 where you can watch all your favorite US teams in season. Bets are taken. Another alternative is the **Restaurante Banca Para Apuestas Deportivas** (Polo Ground Sports Center) a bar-restaurant at C. El Conde 159 (corner Hostos) in the old town which features international sporting events. **hotel bars and clubs:** The Hotel El Embajador's classy **Embassy Club** requires a jacket and sometimes has live entertainment. Another exclusive joint is the Sheraton's **El Yarey**, also with live entertainment. The **Sol Bar** is on the 12th F of the Hotel Naco. You can also try Hotel Jaragua's **Salon La Fiesta**, Hotel El Napolitano's **Disco Piano Bar**, Hotel Dominican Concorde's **La Azotea**, Hotel Comodoro's **Salón Rojo**, and the **Maunaloa Night Club and Casino** (Centro del los Héroes).

MOVIES: Movies in English are shown at the Independencia in the rear of the Puerto del Conde and at theaters along the *Malecón*. Check the newspapers for listings and ask at your hotel or check the phone book for the exact locations.

GAMBLING: Casinos are found mostly at major hotels and are generally open from 4 to 4. Bets may be placed in US or Dominican currency, and Las Vegas odds and rules apply, with some variations. The staff is bilingual. Casinos are found at the Hispaniola, V Centenario, Concorde, Santo Domingo, San Gerónimo, the Sheraton's Omni, El Embajador, Naco, Lina, and in the Jaragua. Also gamble at the Maunaloa Night Club in Centro de los Héroes.

BOAT TRIPS: The *Wonder* (tel. 221-4551) offers nightly excursions on the Río Ozama for D$50 pp. Board the boat on the river in back of the Alcazar.

BOWLING: This can be found at the **Bolera Dominicana** (tel. 566-3818) in Plaza Naco. It's open from 9:30 to midnight.

SPORTING EVENTS: Baseball games are held at the stadium. **Horseraces** are held year-round on Tues., Thurs., and Sun. at the Perla Antilla near the baseball stadium. **Greyhound** races are held on Wed. through Sat. at 7 and Sun. at 4 at Canodromo El Coco (tel. 567-4461, 565-8333), 15 min. N of Santo Domingo at Duarte Hwy. Km 13 (La Yuca, Av. Monumental). There are 400 dogs participating in 12 races an evening. Admission is minimal. **Cockfighting** can be found on Av. Luperón; call 566-3844. **Wrestling** events are held on occasion at Estadio Eugenio Maria de Hostos. **jogging:** Joggers should visit the Olympic Center and stadium on Av. 27 de Febrero across from the Hotel Lina and the Mirador/Paseo de los Indios to the rear of the Hotel Embajador. **health clubs:** These can be found at the Jaragua, York Caribe, Lina, and Sheraton. The most complete club is Club Body Health (tel. 565-5156) on Av. 27 de Febrero. Jazz, modern, and aerobic classes are offered by Taller

Dansa Moderna (tel. 567-8261) at Centro Comercial Paraiso on Av. Winston Churchill.

Santo Domingo Shopping

Santo Domingo is by far the best place to shop in the nation and, perhaps, in the entire Caribbean. Remember, if you go into a shop with a guide, you will pay more. Bargain hard and watch out for slick bag snatchers and pickpockets. Around the old town, you'll find many stores along Aves. Duarte, Melia, and on C. El Conde (Street of the Count). Now a pedestrian mall, the last is the city's oldest shopping area, with a profusion of stores selling everything from furniture to records to clothing to toys. It's a good place to shop for shoes, jewelry, and hand-embroidered children's clothing. Av. Duarte also has a large number of stalls.

DUTY-FREE SHOPPING: In order make a purchase, you must shop a few days ahead and present your airplane ticket; your purchases will be available after you clear customs. You may shop for duty-frees in The Centro de los Héroes, La Ataranza, shops in the Santo Domingo, Sheraton, and Embajador hotels, and in the airport departure lounge. All purchases must be paid for in US currency.

MARKETS: Mercado Modelo, Av. Mella at Santomé, is chock full of stalls offering leatherwork, ceramics, *dulce* (sweets), boats made from cow's horn, and amber necklaces. *Merengue* tapes are less than $2 after bargaining. Upstairs are huge sausages, whole barracudas, severed pigs heads and feet; the thump and crack of cold steel hitting bone reverberates throughout. A few *botanicas* sell Fortune Teller, Gambler's Amour, and other good luck seasonal sprays to believers in spiritualism. Out back, the market overflows with tomatoes, peppers, eggplants, cucumbers, potatoes, carrots, pumpkins, and tropical fruits. **La Sirena**, Av. Mella 258, is a large discount store selling toiletries and innumerable household items. Set on Av. Winston Churchill about three blocks N of the 27 de Febrero intersection, **La Hortaliza** is a smaller and quieter market. A bit more expensive, it sells produce, brass beds, baskets, ceramics, glazed decorative tiles, and other goods. Granix natural foods are also sold here.

DEPARTMENT STORES: Puerto del Sol and **Gran Via** on El Conde. **La Opera** on El Conde and **González Ramos** at El Conde 252.

SHOPPING CENTERS: Located on 27 de Febrero at Máximo Gómez across from the Olympic Center, **Plaza Criolla** is a split-level arcade designed as a mock village complete with clock tower. Its plaza houses a small fruit and vegetable market, and there are a wide variety of shops. On the plus side, it's air conditioned, you can use credit cards, and there's a good selection. The downside is that it's very pricey, and you can't bargain as much. On 27 de Febrero just a few blocks down, **Galerias Comerciales** features two levels of specialty shops. On C. Duarte, **Plaza Lama** offers a wide range of goods. A combination market and supermarket, **Centro Comercial Nacional** is at the intersection of Av. Abraham Lincoln and Av. 27 de Febrero. One of its highlights is the flower market in its parking lot; it also has a supermarket. Just across the way, **Plaza Lincoln** specializes in high quality boutiques and home furnishing shops. Nicknamed the "Golden Apple," the three-story **Plaza Central** is one of the Caribbean's largest malls, located at the corner of Av. 27 de Febrero and Av. Winston Churchill. You can shop on its first two levels, feast on fast food, see a movie, or play sports on the third level. **Café Benneton** here is quite popular. **Plaza Caribe** is at Av. 27 de Febrero and Leopoldo Navarro.

SPECIFIC SMALL SHOPS: At El Conde 153, **El Conde Gift Shop** sells unassembled rocking chairs for export. At Arz. Nouel 151-1, **Musical Padilla** sells a wide variety of traditional musical instruments. **Mercantil Importada** is at El Conde 505. The **Novo Ataranza** is at Ataranza 21. For high-quality crafts check out **Planarte** inside Casa de Bastidas. Sponsored by the Fundación de Desarollo Dominicano (Dominican Development Foundation), crafts found here include rag dolls, birds, and leather items. At C. Nouel 53 (parallel to Conde), **Marialejos** carries ceramics and other crafts. You can have custom designed pottery made by selecting a design from their portfolio. Government-owned-and-operated **Cendarte** (Centro Nacional de Artesania) sells the crafts of its students and local artisans. Goods here include macrame, pottery, furniture, jewelry, and leather items. To get here follow Av. Tiradentes by Plaza Naco and then cross Av. John F. Kennedy, continue to the Public Works Office and turn L. Cendarte is the second structure and is at the corner of C. San Cristóbal. It's open from 8 to 2. **Artessa**, C. Roberto Pastoriza, offers a wide variety of crafts, both local and from Haiti and Latin America. Set on a side street across from Plaza Naco, **Nuebo**, C. Fantino Falco 36, offers Haitian and Dominican crafts including pottery and handpainted birds. Inside Plaza Lincoln, **Habitat**, Av. Abraham Lincoln near 27 de Febrero, sells handicrafts designed exclusively for this store. At C. Cervantes 102, **Tu Espacio** features a wide selection of handicrafts, art, antiques, and furniture. **La Ferreteria Americana**, a hardware store located at San Martin 175 and Av. Mella 413 (near the old town) has a wide variety of local handicrafts as well as items imported from all over the world. On Av. John F. Kennedy, **Casa Hache** sells crafts and housewares. On Av. Romulo Betancourt, between Av. Winston Churchill and Abraham Lincoln, **El Gallo** also sells housewares and other items. Offering high-priced imported items, **Casa Virginia** is at Centro Commercial, and the shops **Mary** and **Alfonso** are at Plaza Naco. On the 2nd F of Plaza Naco, **Triana** offers a wide selection of crafts both local and imported from Central America and Spain. The workshop of craftswoman **Maria del Carmen Ossaye** is at C. Cervantes 52, a street directly opposite the rear exit to the Sheraton's parking lot. Her specialty is handpainted mahogany handbags ranging in design from geometrical patterns to floral pastels. Handcrafted guitars and furniture are also available here. At C. Santiago 405, the **Dpiel** workshop manufactures a high-quality (and high-priced) selection of leather goods; they are sold elsewhere in boutiques. One place to buy them is **La Maleta** on Av. 27 de Febrero near Av. Abraham Lincoln. **Stained glass items** are found at Arte Vitral, C. Hatuey 151, in the Piantini area.

FLEA MARKETS: The **flea market** at Mercado de las Pulgas operates on Sun. at the Centro del los Héroes and at the Mercado de Oportunidades, 27 de Febrero. Another flea market is also sponsored by the office of Cultural Patrimony at the parking lot next to the Atarazana's parking lot. Everything from junk to antiques (including silver and pewter) can be found here.

FURNITURE AND HOME FURNISHING SHOPS: Santo Domingo is renowned for its finely crafted furniture. For budget furniture try **Ambiente Decoraciones**, corner of Independencia and Av. Dr. Delgado, which offers boxes, mirrors, birds, and handpainted cushions; they will also make furniture to your specs. Offering expensive but attractive items are **La Nueva Dimension** (C. Gustavo Mejia Ricart 79 in Plaza Naco), **Hipopotamo** (C. Max Enrique Urena 31), and the **Bonsai** (C. Fantino Falco near Plaza Naco). Featuring modern-style furniture, **D'Arquin** is at Plaza Paraiso. High priced imported furnishings are found at **Domus** on Av. Tiradentes. On the ground level of the San Carlos Bldg., **Artesania Rattan** features a full range of home furnishings (including woven placemats, chests, and baskets). Located at Av. Máximo Gómez 58 just around the corner from the US Consulate, **Delgados** shows wicker and rattan furniture. Offering special orders, **Casa Bibely**, C. Conde, offers wicker and rattan furniture and accessories. **Hogar de Mimbre** ("Home of Wicker"), Romulo Betancourt 1424, offers the same as does **Sauce**, down the street at No. 2056. At Av. 27 de Febrero at the corner of 30 de Marzo, **Gonzales Muebles** offers both a vast array of furniture and furnishings. Also try **Alfonso's**, at Plaza Naco, which produces its own designs under its "mobleart" label. At C. Jose de Jesus Ravelo 81, **Palacios** is an age old name. With a showroom at 27th de Febrero 503 and a factory in the Herrera Industrial Free Zone, **Von** offers original and very contemporary designs in mahogany. Located in Av. Luperón's industrial zone, **Rattan y Decoraciones** has a good selection. Set in the city's Alma Rosa district at C. Costa Rica 136, **Rattan Industrial** is another wicker and rattan furniture exporter.

FABRIC SHOPS: Although much of the fabric found is imported, some cotton and linen is made locally. One of the best places to buy is **Almacenes Doble A** on 19 de Marzo off El Conde. At Galerias Comerciales on 27 de Febrero, **Manikin** is a select and expensive fabric store, as is Plaza Lincoln's **Mundo Modas**.

TAILORS AND MENSWEAR: A few blocks from Av. 27 de Febrero at Av. Winston Churchill, high-priced couturier **La Coruña** has a wide selection. Set on the second floor of Plaza Naco, **Ciprian** offers custom tailoring. At Av. Lope de Vega 18, **Cavalieri** offers a wide variety of high-quality menswear, as does **Solo Para Hombre**, Av. Betancourt 1560. One block from the Merengue Hotel at C. Roberto Pastoriza 152, **Sunny** offers a contemporary selection.

TAILORS AND WOMEN'S WEAR: Ladies can have three piece suits made at **Ciprian** on the second floor of Plaza Naco. Also at Plaza Naco you'll find **Abraxas**, **Marian Cristina Boutique**, and **Cachet Boutique**. **Mercy Jacquez's** boutique is across from the Supermercado Nacional on Av. Abraham Lincoln; tailoring is available upon request. Next to the Salon Rosita at the corner of Av. Pasteur on Av. Independencia, **Mi Boutique** has a wide selection of fabrics and eveningwear. At the corner of C. Charles Sumner at C. Nicolas Ureña 101, **Velka's** workshop and boutique features her line of fashion. At C. Fantino Falcon 59 near Plaza Naco, **Mimosa** has linen goods including blouses. At Centro Comercial Nacional, **Casa Virginia** is another notable boutique. At Plaza Criolla, **Patapoof** offers swimwear, Danskins, shorts, and T-shirts. Another boutique **Babette Butti**, is located in Galeria Comercial on Av. 27 de Febrero. At Plaza Lincoln, **Le Pavilion Boutique** imports Italian shoes and sandals as well as designer clothes. At 71 Gustavo Mejia, **Europa** offers a range of clothes from eveningwear to cottons. Specializing in lingerie, hand-embroidered nightgowns, and infant's clothing, **Natacha** is at C. Sánchez y Sánchez on the corner of

Av. Lope de Vega. For sportswear try **D'Sport** at the corner of Alma Mater and Av. 27 de Febrero. The **Jaez Boutique** in the Sheraton's arcade also has a nice selection. Larger-proportioned women might want to visit **La Dama Elegante**, 47-A C. Manuel de Js. Troncoso.

JEWELRY: El Conde is the center for jewelers, and **Di Carlo** is one of the preeminent dealers. For watches, gold chains, pearls, and other accessories, try **Seiko** in Centro Comercial Nacional. La Ataranza's gift shops have local jewelry incorporating larimar and amber. Try **Amber Tres** here. **Carlos Despradel** and **Eduardo Fiallo** design ceramic jewelery which can be found at select shops; try **Nouveau Gallery** next to the Sheraton on Av. Independencia and also ask at Plazoleta de las Curas's **Plaza Shop** behind the cathedral.

ART GALLERIES: Institute Galerie de Arte Nouveau, cor. of Aves. Independencia and Pasteur, is the best of the modern art galleries. With branches at El Conde 513 and at Av. Abraham Lincoln 904, the **San Ramón Art Gallery** features established artists. With an extensive representation of artists from all over the island, **Galeria de Arte Nader** is at La Ataranza 9. **George Nader's** gallery is at C. Gustavo Mejia Ricart 49, near Plaza Naco. Also while in Gazcue be sure to visit the **Centro de Arte Cándido Bido**, C. Dr. Baez 5, which is run by the renowned painter of the same name. Also visit **Guillo Perez's** gallery and workshop at C. Hatuey 302, just to the W of Av. Winston Churchill. At C. Espaillat 260, **Gallery Paiewonsky** features contemporary work. Finally, the **Casa de Teatro**, Arzobispo Meriño 110, and the **Casa de Francia** also have exhibits. Also try **Arawak** at Pasteur 104, **Auffant** at El Conde 513, **Candido Bido** at Av. Mella 9-B, **Rosa Maria** at La Ataranza 7, **Galeria El Greco** at Av. Tiradentes 16, **Nouveau** at Av. Independencia 354, **Galeria de Arte Sebelén** at Av. Hostos 209, and **Deniel's** at Independencia 120-A.

SERVICES: The **Ministry of Tourism** (tel. 221-4660, fax 682-3806) is open weekdays 9-2:30 at its main office in Santo Domingo . It's located at Av. México at 30 Marzo in a new set of government offices. Unfortunately, they have little or no information available; their function appears to be more in attracting visitors to the island than with providing information. The offices of the **Direccion Nacional de Parques** (tel. 682-7628) are at Av. Independencia 359. They're open Mon. to Fri., 7:30-2:30. It helps if you can speak Spanish, but don't expect much in the way of information! Haiti has a tourist office at 103 C. Arzobispo Meriña. The **American Chamber of Commerce** (tel. 533-7292, 532-7414, PO Box 95-2) operates inside the Hotel Santo Domingo. Large maps are sold in the **Instituto Geografico Universitario** around the corner from the Hostal Nicolas Ovando. A large selection of magazines can be found at **Geyda** in Centro Comerical Naco on Av. Tiradentes.

POST OFFICE: The **Correo Central** (General Post Office) is at C. Emiliano Tejera, opposite Alcázar de Colón. Window services here run from 7-1:30 on weekdays and 7-noon on Sat. Other offices are located nationwide and are generally open weekdays from 7-1:30. You can mail letters only here and at major hotels. Postage is extremely cheap, but your letters and postcards may take a *long* time to arrive. The *Lista de Correo* (post restante) service is on the 2nd F. It keeps mail for two months. If you have their travelers' checks or credit card, you can also have mail sent to **American Express** (tel. 532-2219) at Av. Lincoln 306. Other post offices are on the 2nd F. of El Haucal, a tall government building on Av. Padre Castellanos near Av. Duarte, and in the Hotel Embajador.

TELEPHONE SERVICE: Long distance, international, fax, and telex services are available at **Codetel**, Av. 30 de Marzo 12 near Parque Independencia, and at seven other locations citywide including Av. Abraham Lincoln 1101 and at the airport. **Tricom** has three offices – at Av. Bolivar and Av. Nuñez de Caceres, on Av. Duarte at Santo Cura De Ars, and at Av. Lopé de Vega 95. Another competitor, **Larga Distancia**, is on the old town side of the Malecón. The Palacio de las Communicaciones next to the general post office does not have phone service.

TRAVEL AND TOUR AGENCIES: Bibi Travel (tel. 532-7141), Dilia's Tours (tel. 682-1086), Dimargo Tours (tel. 582-3874), Dorado Travel (tel. 688-6661), Dormitur (tel. 567-5574), Gladys Tours (tel. 688-1069), Halcón Travel (tel. 566-6116), Magna Tours (tel. 532-8267/7141), Merengue Tours (tel. 582-3373), Metro Tours (tel. 567-3138, Av. Winston Churchill), Omni Tours (tel. 566-4228), Pebeco Tours (tel. 567-8636), Portillo SA (tel. 565-3027), Prieto Tours (tel. 688-5715, Av. Francia 125), Santo Domingo Tours (tel. 562-4865/4870), Tanya Tours (tel. 565-5691), Thomas Tours (tel. 687-8645), Turinter (tel. 685-4020, Leopoldo Navarro 4), Viajes Barceló (tel. 685-8411), Viajes Continentes (tel. 532-0825), and Vimenca (tel. 533-9362).

CAR RENTALS: Rent cars from the major hotels, at the airport, or from Avis (tel. 533-9295/3530, 532-2969/2868), Av. Abraham Lincoln at Sarasota; Budget (tel. 567-0173/0174), Av. JF Kennedy at Lope de Vega; Honda (tel. 567-1015/1016, 541-8487), Av. JF Kennedy at Pepillo Salcedo; **Hertz** (tel. 533-9295/3520 or 532-2969/2868), Av. Independencia; **Mc Deal** (tel. 688-6518); **National Car Rental** (tel. 562-1444/1474, 565-5561), Nelly, Av. José Contreras 139; and **Rentauto** (tel.566-7221), Av. 27 de Febrero 247. Check the yellow pages for others. Expect to spend $60 pd on up.

DIVING: For information and reservations contact **Mundo Submarino** (tel. 566-0340), C. Gustavo Mejia Ricart 99. They rent and sell equipment, teach classes, and organize trips. Another is **Buceo Dominicano** (tel. 567-0346), Av. Abraham Lincoln 960, which arranges dive trips, sailing, and snorkelling.

HAIRDRESSERS: All of the major hotels have beauty salons. Other reliable ones include **Salon Rosita** (Av. Independencia at C. Pasteur), **Hermanos Duenas** (Plaza Naco, 2F), **Salon Manolita** (Av. Independencia next to Hotel San Geronimo), **Los Gemelos** (Av. Tiradentes) and **Nolasko's** (Plaza Central).

LANGUAGE SCHOOLS: Offering Spanish classes are **APEC** (tel. 687-1000), Av. Máximo Gómez 55; **Instituto Cultural Dominicano Americano** (tel. 533-4191), Av. Abraham Lincoln 21; and **Instituto Superior de Idiomas** (tel. 688-5336), Av. 27 de Febrero 415. For French, study at the **Casa de Francia** on C. Las Damas in the old town.

HEALTH: Foreigners are recommended to go either to **Clinica Abréu** (tel. 688-4411/687-4922, Beller 42) or **Clinica Gómez Patiño** (tel. 685-9131/9141), at Av. Independencia and Beller, which offer high quality but expensive care on a 24-hr. basis. Also try **Clinica Abel González** on Av. Independencia or **Clinica Yunén** and **Clinica Centro Médico UCE** (tel. 682-0171) at Av. Máximo Gómez 66. Centro **Otorrinolaringología y Especialidades** (tel. 682-0151), Av. 27 de Febrero, specializes in treating eye, ear, and throat ailments.

PHARMACIES: The following offer 24-hr. service and delivery: **Farmacia Tiradentes** (tel. 565-1647), Av. Tiradentes 15 near Hotel Naco; **Farmacia Dr. Camilo** (tel. 566-5575), C. Paseo de los Locutores near Av. Winston Churchill; **Los Hidalgos** (tel. 565-4848), 27 de Febrero 24; and **Farmacia San Judas Tadeo** (tel. 689-6664), Av. Independencia 57. A complete list can be found in the phone book.

BANKS: Banks are open Mon. to Fri. from 8:30 to 2:30. Rates of exchange vary slightly; check the newspapers to find the best rates. Many banks line Isabel La Católica including Banco de la Reserva next to the Palacio de las Communicaciones. At Ataranza and Emiliano Tejera opposite the Alcázar de Colón, Banco Popular has long hours. Citibank is at Av. John F. Kennedy 1, Chase Manhattan at John F. Kennedy and Av. Tiradentes, Banco de Santander Dominicano at John F. Kennedy and at Av. Lope de Vega, Bank of Nova Scotia at Av. Lope de Vega and Av. John F. Kennedy, and the Bank of America is at C. El Conde 103. Exchange counters at the larger hotels are open until 9. Note that some banks do not accept traveler's checks. Changing money on the streets is illegal. In addition to the fact that you will definitely be cheated, there is also the chance that the black marketeer is in cahoots with a policeman who will swoop in and extract a substantial bribe in lieu of carting you off to jail.

LIBRARIES: The **Instituto Cultural Dominicano-Americano**, Av. Abraham Lincoln and C. Antonio de la Maza, has a fine library. (Open Mon. to Fri., 10-noon, and 3-7). Other libraries are in the National Congress, the Pontificia Universidad Católica Madre y Maestra, Universidad Autónoma de Santo Domingo, and the Instituto Tecnológico de Santo Domingo. **bookstores:** At the entrance to the Cathderal on Arz. Nouel, **Linea Studebaker** has a good collection of international newspapers and magazines as well as books. soft drinks and traditional sweets are also available here. **Librería América**, Arz. Nouel at Sánchez in the old town, has a good selection of books. **Librería Avante** is at Arz. Nouel No. 53. Others include **Librería el Estudiante**, Av. Duarte 15; **Librería Pichardo**, Av. Duarte 271; and **Casa Cuello**, El Conde 201.

EMBASSIES: The **American Embassy** (tel. 682-2171) is at the corner of C. César Nicolás Penson and C. Leopoldo Navarro. The **British Embassy** (tel. 682-3128) is at Ave. Independencia 506. The **German Embassy** (tel. 565-8811) is at C. Lic. Juan Tomás Mejia y Cotes 37 at the cor. of Eullides Morillo.

From Santo Domingo

The nation's best (and fastest) bus company, **Metro** (tel. 566-7126/7129) departs from the corner of Av. Winston Churchill and Hatuey daily to Santiago (7, 9, 10, 1:30, 3, 5:30, and 6:30), Nagua (7:30 and 3:30), San Francisco de Macorís (7:30 and 3:30), Castillo (7:30 and 3:30), La Vega (7:30 and 4), Moca (7:30 and 4), and to Puerto Plata (7:30, 1, 4, and 7). The only company running to Sosúa, **Caribe Tours** (tel. 221-5318) also runs a/c buses to Puerto Plata, Santiago, Bonao, Cabrera, Río San Juan, Nagua, Samaná, Dajabón,

Monte Cristi, Jarabacoa, and San Francisco de Macorís. They're located at Av. 27 de Febrero at Leopoldo Navarro, not far from the old town. They also stop at Kilometro 9, Lopé de Vega, and Máximo Gómez. **La Experiencia**, located at C. Los Martires, and Av. Winston Churchill and Hatuey near Av. 27 de Febrero, runs to La Vega, Santiago, Nagua, Azua, San Juan, San Pedro de Macorís, and Puerto Plata. Leaving from Plaza Criolla at Av. 27 de Febrero and Máximo Gómez, **Terra Bus** (tel. 565-2333) uses Mercedes Benz buses and employs uniformed hostesses who dispense free coffee and snacks. It runs to Santiago. Departing from Caracas 69 at Parque Enriquillo (Av. Duarte and Ravelo), **La Covacha** (tel. 686-1533) runs E to Higüey, Nagua, San Pedro de Macorís, Miches, and others. **Transportes de Cibao** (tel. 685-7210, 689-5216), on C. Ravelo at Parque Enriquillo, runs to La Vega, Navarete, Mao, Santiago Rodriguez, Partido, Loma de Cabrera, Monte Cristi, Dajabón, Mamey, La Isabela, Sosúa, Puerto Plata. Located at Av. Independencia 7 near Parque Independencia, **Expreso del Valle** (tel. 686-8985) runs 11 buses daily to La Vega via Bonao from 6:30 AM to 7 PM. They also have a pickup point along Av. Kennedy. Buses for Azua leave from Av. Bolivar near Parque Independencia. **Riviera del Caribe** (tel. 566-1533/5400) runs to points SW from Av. Lincoln 703. Connect in Azua for Barahona, San Juan, and Padre las Casas. **Linea Sunchomiba** (tel. 668-2411) at Av. Duarte and 30 de Marzo, leaves for Barahonas (three hrs.) at 7:30, 10, 2, and 4. For Constanza, **Linea Cobra** (tel. 565-7363/566-8222) leaves from Av. San Martín at 5 AM; get there early as it fills up fast. **note:** Check for times for all of these before traveling.

GUAGUAS: These minibuses leave from Parque Enriquillo at the corner of Av. Duarte and C. Caracas to the N of the old town. Destinations include Higüey, Boca Chica, and Haina. Transportes de Cibao and La Covacha are also located here (see above).

FOR THE AIRPORT: Except for expensive ($20) taxis, it's not easy to get to Las Americas. You must take a *público* from just N of Parque Enriquillo, Av. Duarte and Paris, to Boca Chica. Many of these stop at the airport; if not, you'll have to get off at the gate and walk in. Allow plenty of time if going this route. **departing by air:** In the main lobby you can make last minute phone calls at Codetel or buy ground coffee or other souvenirs if you have leftover *pesos*. Upon checking in you must pay your $10 departure tax ($1.64 for residents and nationals). Foreign visitors must pay in US currency – even if they are British or German! There are some duty free shops after immigration, but if you're planning on buying rum, prices are 35% lower in town, and the selection is far better. Internal flights leave from Herrera Airport which has domestic charters. The airport is located in an area running perpendicular to Av. Luperón at the city's W end. **driving:** To leave the city towards the Cibao or the N, proceed from Parque Independencia heading N on C. 30 de Marzo, then cross 27 de Febrero and head straight ahead to Av. John F. Kennedy, which becomes Duarte Hwy. at the intersection with Av. Luperón. To reach the international airport and the E (Boca Chica, La Romana) you must go across the Río Ozama and keep straight ahead along Las Americas.

BY AIR: Flights depart from Herrera to Santiago, Barahona, Puerto Plata, and La Romana. A new airline, **Bávaro Sunflight** (tel. 320-2202, fax 320-2204) began operating between Las Américas and Herrera airports in Santo Domingo and Punta Cana, Samaná, Santiago, and Puerto Plata. Be sure to allow sufficient time to get to the airport. The major companies operating charter service from Herrera Airport are **Faxa Air Taxi** (tel. 567-1195), **Servicios Aereos Profesionales** (tel. 565-2448), **Servicios Aéreos Turísticos** (tel. 566-1696, 567-7406), **Transporte Aéreo** (tel. 566-2141), and **Uni Charter** (tel. 567-0481, 567-0818). **Prieto Tours** (tel. 685-0102, 688-5715) operates an air taxi service to and from Portillo. **Agencia Portillo** (tel. 565-0832) provides air taxi services to Puerto Plata and Punta Cana for around $35 including transfers and a meal. A division of National Jets, the **Airborne Ambulance Service** (tel. 567-1101/4171), Av. Tiradentes 52, rents executive jets in addition to their 24-hr. ambulance service.

FOR CUBA: Emely Tours (tel. 687-7114/7118; C. San Francisco de Macoris 58) runs package tours to Cuba. Costs run from $400 for three days on up. Call toll free 1-200-3262 or fax 686-0941.

The Southwest

This area outside of Santo Domingo is sparsely populated. Despite Santo Domingo's commanding presence as a center of finance and government, the area in the extreme SW near the Haitian border, which includes Laguna Enriquillo, is semi-desert terrain with few houses and minimal agriculture.

EXPLORING: Carretera Sánchez, the main highway W of Santo Domingo, extends to San Cristóbal and Baní, traversing sugarane fields. Buses going along the S coast will drop you at the entrances to the beaches. Fine beaches are found at or near Las Salinas. Azua, and Barahona, and other beaches, accessible only by car, line the S coast, starting at Barahona. Heading W from Baní, the terrain turns to desert with organ-pipe cacti mingling with acacias and mesquites. Irrigated vegetable farms are found as well. From Cruce de Ocoa, the turnoff for San José de Ocoa, a paved road heads for the Cordillera Central foothills before heading N to Constanza on a dirt track.

HAINA: Santo Domingo's main port, which also contains the world's largest sugarcane mill (built under Trujillo), is located just outside the capital. There's a country club here which has a swimming pool. Stay at the teacher's vacation center which has low budget accommodation. The **Club Náutico Haina** (tel. 532-3961) is on Carr. Sánchez at Km 131.5. Near the village of Nigua, the 17th C. **Capilla de San Gregorio Magno** is the chapel of a ruined 16th C sugar mill. A bust of St. Gregory and a painting of the Virgen de la Altagracia are inside. Curiously, the Virgin is sporting earrings. The junction for the 18th C **Ingenio Boca de Nigua**, a sugar mill, is just past the bridge over the Río Nigua. Also in the area but farther to the S are the ruins of the 16th C **Ingenio de Diego Caballero** and the **Hacienda María** where some of Trujillo's assassins were executed in 1961.

San Cristóbal

Farther to the W some 30 km from Santo Domingo, San Cristóbal, capital of the Province of San Cristóbal, was Trujillo's birthplace; as such it was designated a "Meretorious City" in 1939. First settled at around the end of the 15th C, it is believed that the town got its name after the Spaniards constructed a fortress to safeguard a hoard of gold and placed it under the protection of St. Christopher. Today, it is a small town with an attractive downtown area. **getting there:** Buses, express (D$8.65) and regular (D$5.40) leave from near Parque Independencia. If you take the bus to the terminal, Casa de Caoba and La Toma pools are straight ahead, a few km down a dirt road; you can generally get a ride (D$4.32) on a vehicle. Casa de Caoba is on a hill down the road from the bus terminal outside of town and La Toma is farther down that same road. **sights:** In town, the nation's first constitution was signed in the Palacio del Ayuntamiento (City Hall) in 1844. The 19th C **Iglesia de San Cristóbal** contains Trujillo's mausoleum – although his remains were actually interred in France. A monument across from its entrance marks the spot where the house in which he was born once stood. The **market** is also worth a visit; it's just down the street from the main plaza. The **Casa de Caoba** (Mahogany House), Trujillo's former home, can be reached by Land Rover bus leaving from behind the market. Open 9-5. It's been falling apart but is currently under restoration – a process which will not be complete before the next century. From the road you have to walk up the hill along a very bad road; it's a beautiful, peaceful stroll past gumbo limbo and almond trees rife with Spanish moss and bromeliads. The old caretaker Mario Rodriguez will give you a tour. Trujillo's quarters are under lock and key, but you can see Ramfis's bathroom. Although the original was constructed in mahogany, it's being restored in concrete, and it is intended to serve as a restaurant. Much of the mahogany furniture is still around. **Castillo del Cerro** or El Cerro is the luxurious six-story home he ordered built but never lived in. Both are under restoration. Concrete pools at **Centro Turistico La Toma** are great for swimming. Although concrete and not particularly interesting, there are some water slides and a restaurant. They're open Mon.-Fri., 9-7, and Sat. and Sun., 8-8. Admission is D$10.80 cents. **other sights:** Also be sure to visit **Iglesia de Piedras Vivas**, and the Santa María caves and church which are the site of an African-influenced stick-and-drum festival. Set seven km NW of San Cristóbal, the caves at El Pomier have Taino petroglyphs. Limestone quarrying has been suspended here, and the area has been designated the **Reserva Antorpológica Cuevas de El Pomier**; it is also referred to as the Cuevas de Borbón. The local *fiestas patronales* (San Cristóbal) are held on July 25. It features the *carabiné* dance. While in the area, visit Playas Najayo, Palenque, and Nigua. The mountain town of **Cambita Carabitos** to the NW offers a cooler climate and an overview of the capital.

PRACTICALITIES: Stay at **Hotel Constitución** (tel. 528-3309), Av. Constitución 118, or **Hotel San Cristóbal** (tel. 528-3555/2364), Av.

Libertad 32. Others in town include **Hotel Wing Kit** (tel. 528-3229), M T Sánchez 13; **Hotel Formosa** (tel. 528-3229), María Trinidad Sánchez; and **Hotel El Caminante** (528-3167), M. T. Sánchez 30. **Cafeteria Dulceria Airos, Restaurant Formosa,** and **Cafeteria Pica Pollo la Terraza** are on M. T. Sánchez; the Wing Kit also has a restaurant. *Pasteles en hojas,* a famous local dish, is made with *plátano,* minced meat, and other ingredients. **Codetel** (tel. 528-4196) is at Palo Hincado 14.

FROM SAN CRISTOBAL: Express minibuses to Santo Domingo leave from one corner of the plaza.

Baní

Capital of Peravia province, this town is mainly remarkable for having been the birthplace of 19th C Cuban liberation fighter Máximo Gómez. It is named after Cacique Caonabo's subordinate whose name meant "an abundance of water." Iglesia Nuestra Señora de Regla's *fiestas patronales* is held every Nov. 21. The area is famous for its mangoes. Try the famous goats' milk sweets produced in Paya. In-town hotels include **Hotel Caribaní** (tel. 522-4400), C. Sánchez 12; **Hotel las BBB** (tel. 522-4422), Carr. Sánchez Km 1.5; inexpensive **Hotel Brisas del Sur** (tel. 522-2548), Hotel Alba (tel. 522-3590), C. Billini 13, **Hotel Sylvia** (tel. 522-4674), Carr. Sánchez at Km 2, and **Hotel la Posada** (tel. 522-4551), further down the same road. **Restaurant Heladeria Capri** is at C. Duarte 20. **vicinity of Baní:** The beach at Los Almendros isn't much. Stay at the recently-built 78-rm. **Los Almendros** (tel. 571-3530/3515) which features restaurant, pool, Jacuzzi, water sports, and rooms with a/c and cable TV. **services:** For **information** contact City Hall (tel. 522-3515) and the Governor's Office (tel. 522-3316). **Codetel** is at Padre Billini 3.

PALMAR DE OCOA: There's a grey sand beach here, and a fishing tournament is held annually. Many wealthy Dominicans have built summer homes here.

Azua

Set 121 km W of Santo Domingo, this town was founded as Azua de Compostela in 1504 and named by Diego Velásquez who went on to subdue Cuba. The town was granted a coat of arms by King

Southwestern Dominican Republic

N

Isla Cabritos

To Santo Domingo →

Jimaní

Villa Jaragua

Lago Enriquillo

Neiba

Azua

Duvergé

Tamayo

HAITI

Cabral

Barahona

Pedernales

Paraíso

Parque Nacional Jaragua

Oviedo

Lago de Oviedo

Caribbean Sea

20 MILES

Isla Beata

Ferdinand in 1508, and Azua became a province in 1845. The town has been set on fire numerous times during its history – by French corsairs as well as by invading and retreating Haitian forces. **festivals and events:** The Battle of March 1844, in which Dominicans repelled the invading Haitians, is celebrated Mar. 19. **getting there:** You may wish to change buses for Barahona here. It's two hours here from Santo Domingo, and less than two hours to Barahona from here. Buses also run to San Juan and Padre las Casas.

SIGHTS: The ruins of the colonial town can be seen at **Pueblo Viejo.** Named for the battle that took place here between the Haitians and Dominicans, **El Número** offers a panoramic view. Travel on from here to **Corbanito,** an open cove with a couple of miles of white sand beaches and outlying coral reefs, on the E shore of the Bahia Ocoa. **Playa Chiquita** is a grey sand beach with no waves. **Playa Monte Río** is another beach where rapacious conquistador Hernán Cortés hung out during his formative years. **Playa Blanca** is nearby, and there are also undeveloped **hotsprings**

in the area. **events:** the *fiestas patronales* for Nuestra Señora de los Remedios (Our Lady of Remedies) are held Sept. 8.

PRACTICALITIES: Try inexpensive **Hotel Restaurant San Ramon** (tel. 521-3529), Fco. R Sánchez at Km. 1.5; less expensive **Hotel Brisas del Mar** (tel. 521-3813), C. de Leones; or still cheaper **Hotel Altagracia** (tel. 521-3286), J P Duarte 59, and **Hotel El Familiar** (tel. 521-3556), C. Emilio Prudhomme. **Restaurant Patio Español el Jardin** is at C. Duarte 49, and **Restaurant El Gran Segovia** is at F del R Sánchez 31. **Codetel** is at Av. 19 de Marzo 118 and **Metrobus** (tel. 521-5366) is at Parque 19 de Marzo.

INFORMATION: Contact City Hall at 521-3302 and the Governor's Office at 521-3215. **services: Codetel** is at Av. 19 de Marzo 118. *Metro's* terminal (tel. 521-5366) is at Parque 19 de Marzo.

Barahona

Set on the S coast some 240 km (130 miles) and three hours by car or four hrs. by bus from Santo Domingo, this town was named after one of its earliest colonists. Barahona was founded in 1802 by Haitian General Toussaint L'Ouverture. If it's actually been completed, the "international" airport will have opened up this area a bit, but it still remains largely undeveloped. This will change so get here soon!

SIGHTS: There's not much of specific interest in the town itself. There is a small public beach here, but stinging jelly fish are frequent visitors. Visit the Central Barahona sugar mill in the city. The nearby coffee-producing villages of Platon and Santa Elena are also worth a visit. Barahona may be used as a base to visit Lago Enriquillo and other areas in the SW.

ACCOMMODATION: Simple and inexpensive 22-rm. a/c **Hotel Guarocuya** (tel. 524-2211) is on Av. Enriquillo at Playa Saladilla. It's priced at around $20. The **Hotel Barahona** (tel. 524-3442) is at C. Jaime Mora 5. The **Cacique** (tel. 524-4620), C. Uruguay 2, is less expensive. The **Hotel Victoria** (tel. 524-2392), Padre Billini 15-A (corner Uruguay), features d and s rooms with a/c. Also try the **Hotel Caribe** (tel. 524-2185). Av. Enriquillo; or the **Hotel Palace** (tel. 524-2500), C. Uruguay 18; **Hotel Brasil** (tel. 524-3661), C. Padre Billini 31; the **Hotel Las Magnolias** (tel. 524-2244), C. Anacaona 13, and the **Hotel Bohemia** (tel. 524-2109), C. Sánchez 72. Opened in

1993, the **Riviera Beach Hotel** (tel. 524-5111, fax 524-5798; Av. Enriquillo 6) has 108 a/c rooms with phone and satellite TV; there is a pool, tennis courts, and two restaurants. It's within walking distance of town and is run by the Spanish Continental hotel chain. Located 17 km from Barahona to the SW between the coastal villages of Baoruco and Cienaga, the **Baoruco Beach Club and Resort** (tel. 685-5184) combines an 84-rm. apart-hotel with a 90-suite hotel along with 34 apartments distributed in five blocks. Its features include Jacuzzi, pool, restaurant, bars, satellite TV, horse-back riding, tennis, water sports, and time-shares. **food:** Try the open-air **La Rocca** next door to Hotel Caribe, Av. Enriquillo, the **Restaurant Costa Sur** on the same street, or – for Chinese food – **Restaurant Brisas del Caribe** along Carr. Batey Central. There are also many small restaurants in the town center. **services:** The **Codetel** office is at Nuestra Sra. del Rosario 36.

EVENTS: The town's *fiestas patronales*, in honor of Nuestra Señora del Rosario, are held Oct. 4. They feature the *carabiné* dance which is accompanied by *balsié* (accordion), *güira* (scraper), and *pandero* (tamborine). **services:** For information contact the **tourist office** at C. Anacaona 8 or visit City Hall on C. 30 de Mayo.

FROM BARAHONA: If you have a car, you can explore the rocky but pretty beaches including the spectacular Paraiso. *Públicos* also run. The best scuba and snorkeling is found all along the white sand beaches of the S coast; still undeveloped for tourism, it's an area with beautiful inland scenery. Between Baoruco and Enriquillo wet tropical forest abounds, and the small roadside settlements have fruit stands. From Enriquillo the drier lowlands of the Barahona peninsula begin. From Oviedo to Pedernales, thorny scrub alternates with karst outcrops. Cool freshwater lagoons are found behind several of the beaches, and Limón Lagoon is a flamingo reserve. At **San Rafael** some 40 min. from Barahona, a fresh-water swimming hole is in the river at the beach's end. You can camp here, and there's a small restaurant. **other beaches:** Most of the beaches in the area are rocky but beautiful. **Bahoruco** has large waves and some two km of white sand beach. **El Pato** or Los Patos has smooth white pebbles and is suitable for surfing and swimming. Others are **La Ciénaga**, **Río Caño**, **El Quemaíto** (coconut palms), **El Defiladero de los Amargados**, and **San Rafael** (light brown sand).

SAN JUAN DE LA MAGUANA: On the main road to Haiti, you can visit the **Corral de los Indios**, an indigenous site several km to the N of the town where a large circle of stones is set on a level plain.

OTHER DESTINATIONS: Also visit **Elias Piña**, one of the nation's frontier towns which also has one of the dilapidated old houses built for Trujillo. At **Banica**, visit the church in the **Cerro de San Francisco**. People come here for a ceremony every year on Oct. 3 and 4.

Parks of the Southwest
Reserva Científica Natural Laguna de Rincón

Also known as Laguna de Cabral, Rincón Lagoon is the nation's largest freshwater lagoon and second largest lagoon (after Enriquillo). Set amidst sub-tropical forest, it harbors a large population of *jicotea* (freshwater slider turtles). Notable birds include the *pato espinoso* (ruddy duck), masked duck, flamingo, Louisiana heron, Northern Jacana, and the glossy ibis.

Parque Nacional Sierra de Bahoruco

Rising as high as 7,766 ft. (2,367 m) near El Aguacate next to the Haitian border, Sierra de Bahoruco National Park supports a wide variety of vegetation. **history:** Formed some 50 mllion years ago in the Middle Eocene, the area is of note because Enriquillo (Guarocuya) declared his tribe's independence from its hilltops. **flora and fauna:** Vegetation varies from extensive stretches of pine forest to mixed forests to fields covered with latifoliats (broad-leaved plants). There are 166 species of orchids or over half those found within the country. Trees include the trumpet tree, creolan pine, West Indies laurel, West Indian sumac, and the Hispaniolan mahogany. One of the 49 species of birds present is the white-necked crow which is extinct in neighboring Puerto Rico; others – found in the mountains – include the narrow-billed tody, the white-winged warbler, the Hispaniolan trogon, and the Antillean siskin. The white-crowned and red-necked pidgeons, the Hispaniolan parakeet, the Hispaniolan lizard cuckoo, the Hispaniolan parrot, the white-winged dove, vervain hummingbird, and the stolid flycatcher are found in its dry and humid forests.

Laguna Enriquillo y Parque Nacional Isla Cabritos

Set inside a national park, this 21 mi.-long (12 km) inland saltwater lake is due W of Santo Domingo near the border with Haiti. Plummeting to 130 ft. (40 m) below sea level at its bottom, it is the Caribbean's lowest point. Rising sharply above the lake are two ranges: the Sierra de Neiba on the N and the Sierra de Baoruco (another national park) on the S. **sights:** The largest of the three islands and a reserve to protect the endemic American crocodile, five-mi.-long **Isla Cabritos** (Goat Island) is in the lake's center. Flat with coral beaches, the island lacks fresh water. Currently, crocs are being propagated at the Zoo in Santo Domingo and being introduced; fishermen are also being encouraged not to kill them or steal eggs. The Las Marías sulfur **hot springs** are found in an oak forest by the village of La Descubierta in the lake's vicinity. Cold water baths are at **Las Barias**. A half-mi. before the village of La Descubierta in the lake's NW corner, a remarkable set of petroglyphs are inscribed on cliffs at **Cuevo Las Caritas** (Cave of the Little Faces) – a five min. climb from the road. **history:** Approximately a million years ago, the lake was part of a connecting channel from the Bay of Neiba through to the Bay of Port-au-Prince. Deposits from the Río Yaque del Sur at its mouth served to seal off the lake. Known as Guarizacca by the Indians, Cabrito served as the refuge for the legendary rebellious chief Enriquillo. He and his followers subsisted on dried fish. Between 1822 and 1824, the island and some of the surrounding territory were given to a French family by the occupying Haitians. The area became a national park in 1974.

FLORA AND FAUNA: The islands and surrounding hills are covered with short, dry thorn scrub, cacti, acacias, and mesquites. Some 62 species of birds include greater flamingos, herons, roseate spoonbills, terns, clapper rails, Hispaniolan parrots, village weavers, and burrowing owls. Numerous other species are found in the surrounding hills. Iguanas (rhinoceros and Ricord's) can only be seen on **Isla Cabritos**, which they share with American crocodiles. All three reptile species are endangered. Despite the island's name, goats no longer graze here.

GETTING THERE: From Santo Domingo via Barahona, it takes three hrs. by car to the lake. An additional hr. is required to drive around it. If visiting by bus, it will take you eight hrs. with *La*

Experiencia and *Riviera del Caribe* companies. Get off at Los Ríos or La Descubierta; from there you can walk or catch a ride to the lake. **visiting Goat Island:** Arrangements must be made in advance at the park office in La Descubierta. If the park motorboat is actually running, it takes less than an hour to get here; a rowboat requires two hrs. To get to the park, drive four km SE of town to La Zofrada. Arrangements are made in a building below the road (around $15 for four). Bathe in the sulfur hot springs here. Bring water and expect high temperatures. Aside from a small shop in Descubierta, the nearest facilities are in Barahona.

PRACTICALITIES: At Jimaní, stay at low budget **Hotel Jimaní**, **Hotel Quisqueya**, **Mellitzos** (facing the park), or others. You can also stay in one of several *dormitorios*. One is on the corner opposite the disco in the central square. There's also a fine *balneario* (swimming hole). It's possible to cross the Haitian border here and visit **Laguna del Fundo**, a saltwater lagoon inhabited by American crocodiles. **tours: Delia's Tours** (tel.682-1086 in Santo Domingo) offers tours to this region.

Parque Nacional Jaragua

Set in the nation's SW and named after a Taino chieftain, this park extends W from Oviedo to Cabo Rojo, covering the S portion of Pedernales Province along with the small islands of Alto Velo and Beata. Extending over 520 sq. mi. (1,350 sq. km) including 270 sq. mi. (700 sq. km) of sea, this extremely arid park is generally hot. Covered with heavily weathered and sharp "dogtooth" limestone, cacti, and other rough vegetation, it can be a difficult place to walk around in. The several beaches along its coast can only be reached by long hikes or by boat. Set E of the town of Oviedo, **Lago Oviedo**, a six mi. long saltwater lake, is separated from the Caribbean by a sandy barrier. **history:** Although the mainland was created in the Oligocene some 50 million years ago when land masses rose from the sea, the Laguna Oviedo and the outlying islands of Beata and Alto Vela surfaced only a comparatively recent million years in the past. Archaeological remains have been unearthed in the park from a settlement dating back to 2950 BC. The park's name is taken from that of the SW's *cacique*, Xaragua. The **caves** of Guanal, Mongó, and La Poza contain pre-Columbian pictographs and petroglyphs. **flora and fauna:** Cacti and other vegetation adapted to a hot, dry climate predominate. The forest contains trees like copey, Hispaniolan mahogany, lignum vitae, gumbo-limbo, and wild frangipani. Seagrapes are found at the beach and red, button, and white mangroves line the swamps. Solenodons and hutias reside here as do 11 of the nation's 18 species of bats. The 130 species of birds, half of which are aquatic, represent 60% of the nation's total number. The nation's largest population of flamingos reside at the Oviedo Lagoon while the common potoo lives around the coastal mangroves. Boobies and brown pelicans are found around the beach where turtles also nest. Greater flamingos, pearly-eyed thrashers, the willet, the endemic green-tailed warbler, Antillean palm swifts, burrowing owls, and Ridgway's hawk all live on Island Beata off the park's S tip. You might also see great egrets, sooty terns, little blue herons, roseate spoonbills, and frigate birds. All four species of sea turtles (hawksbill, leatherback, green, and loggerhead) are found here. The rhinocerous iguana and Ricord's iguana also live in the area.

PRACTICALITIES: The road from Barahona to Pedernales passes by the park. You must have a truck or a jeep to get there, and you must bring whatever food and water you require. Pedernales has some small shops.

Onward to Haiti

Conditions in Haiti are such that visits are not now advised. However, conditions may improve. For travel information on Haiti consult the current edition of *Caribbean Islands Handbook*. A great book to read before traveling is *The Rainy Season* by Amy Wilentz. It deals with Aristide and the political situation.

PRACTICALITIES: Check to see if you need a visa from the Haitian Embassy (tel. 562-3519), C. Scout 11, Santo Domingo.

GETTING THERE: If the border is open, buses run from the Hotel San Tomé, Calle Santomé (next to the Mercado Modelo). Call 688-5100 and ask for Alejandro. Also call *Linea Sur* (tel. 682-1414). It's a six-hr. drive from Santo Domingo to Port-au-Prince. **by air:** When and if conditions improve, there will be flights. **Aerolink** (tel. 567-0819, 320-0627) has offered air tours.

The Cordillera Central Region

The nearest thing the Dominican Republic has to an unexploited frontier, this mountainous area, containing the nation's largest mountain range, is reached via roads intersecting with Carretara Duarte, the main highway running between Santo Domingo and Santiago. Its two contiguous national parks have the nation's highest peaks, numerous waterfalls, the endangered *cotorra*, and the headwaters of its rivers. The gateway towns to this area are Bonao and La Vega. **note:** If hiking in the mountains around this region, watch out for Mayas, miniature biting black flies. If you're allergic, your bites will swell up and last for weeks!

Bonao

Halfway between Santo Domingo and Santiago along Carr. Duarte, Bonao (pop. 30,000) has been transformed from village to sizeable town by the discovery of mineral wealth and the arrival of the mining industry. Rich deposits of nickel, bauxite, silver, and gold were discovered here in the early 1970s. Note the contrast between the shanties of the miners – who work long hours under dangerous conditions for low wages – and the transplanted suburban lifestyle of the American expatriate community in Barrio Gringo. The town is also known as Villa de las Hortensias, and the nation's most famous bus stop is at the entrance to town.

PRACTICALITIES: Hotels here include **Hotel Bonao Inn** (tel. 525-2727), Aut. Duarte at Km 85; **Hotel Viejo Madrid** (tel. 525-3558), just before it; **Hotel Restaurant Yaravi** (525-3267), C. Duarte 153; and **Hotel Plaza Nouel** (tel. 525-3518/2909), C. Duarte 128. Also try the **Elizabeth**, **Mi Provincia**, and **San Juan** (near market). Eat at **Restaurant Tipico Bonao**, Aut. Duarte at Km 83, **Restaurant San Rafael**, C. Duarte 182, or **Restaurant San Rafael**, C. Duarte 182. The **Codetel** office is at 27 de Febrero 69.

La Vega

Centered in the heart of the Cibao, this quiet valley town (pop. 200,000) stands near the junction of the road to Jabaracoa to the W. Although nothing remains of the original, the town's history dates back to the 15th C when Columbus ordered a fort to be built here. Sugarcane was first planted commercially in the surrounding area, the New World's first mint was set up here, and the first royally sanctioned brothel was opened in this town. Diego Columbus summered here, and the famous monk Bartolomé de las Casas also lived here. The original town's prosperity was shattered when it was destroyed by a hurricane in 1562; it was moved to the present location the next year. Neither extraordinarily pedestrian nor enthralling, the town is best used as a transit point or as a base to explore the surrounding area. **getting there:** On G. Godoy, *Expreso del Valle* (tel. 573-0722) has a number of runs. *Metro* (573-7099) runs twice daily at 7:30 and 4; they return at the same times from Santo Domingo.

SIGHTS: There's not much of note in the town itself. From La Vega on the R is the road to **Santa Cerro** and its convent where the Virgen de las Mercedes (Virgin of Mercy) is worshipped. Legend has it that Columbus placed the first cross here, one of which had been a bon voyage gift from Queen Isabella. During a bloody battle between the Spanish and Tainos led by Cacique Guarionex, the Indians attempted to burn the cross. It failed to catch fire and the Virgen de las Mercedes miraculously appeared on one of its arms; the Indians fled in terror. A piece of the cross has been preserved but is not on display. You may, however, see the "Santo Hoyo" – the "Sacred Hole" where Columbus is said to have planted a cross to mark the spot where the Virgin appeared. Situated inside **Iglesia Las Mercedes** (1860), it's covered with a square wire grill and is illuminated. There's a fine view from the multi-level terrace outside; see it in Jan. when thousands of coffee-shading *amapola* trees bloom and the vast valley turns coral pink. The festival of Nuestra Señora de las Mercedes is celebrated here around Sept. 24. From here the entire Vega Real (Royal Valley) is unveiled. The road continues over the hill and into the valley where the ruins of **La Vega Vieja** – a small church and fort – stand. Founded by Columbus and destroyed by the 1564 earthquake, it has been undergoing restoration. The turnoff for Jarabacoa is straight ahead to the L from here. Backtracking a bit towards La Vega, you will find the ruins of the **San Francisco monastery**. A number of skeletal remains have been unearthed here, and locals may lift the covers for your viewing pleasure.

ACCOMMODATION: Hotel America (tel. 573-2909), **Hotel Del Valle** (tel. 573-3974), and **Hotel Guariano** (tel. 573-2632) are all on Aut. Duarte. Others include **Hotel Astral** (tel. 573-3535), C. N de Cáceres 18; **Hotel Real** (tel. 573-6487) nearby; **Hotel San Pedro** (tel. 573-2884), C. N de Cáceres 33; **Hotel Santa Clara** (tel. 573-2878), C. N de Cáceres 91; **Hotel Bello** (tel. 573-5282), Av. Rivas 67; **Hotel Cafeteria Genao** (tel. 573-4878), Av. Rivas 64; **Hotel Nueva Imagen** (tel. 573-7351), C. Restauración 3; and **Hotel Restaurant Royal Palace** (tel. 573-2738), C. Padre Adolfo. Cheapest (less than $5) are the **Hotel Comedor** and the **Hotel Buenos Aires** (tel. 573-5120) next door; they're at Las Carreras and Ubaldo Gómez, not far from the bus stop. More expensive ($11) but superior is the **Hotel Restaurant "Quinto Patio"** (tel. 573-6842) at C. Restauración 48.

FOOD: Eat at **Hotel Restaurant "Quinto Patio"** (tel. 573-6842) at C. Restauración 48; **Restaurant Maturijere** and **El Coche** on Aut. Duarte; **Restaurant Malecón** on Av. Imbert; **Restaurant Frito Lindo** on 18 de Abril; **Restaurant Cafeteria La Casona** at C. J Gómez 127; and **Restaurant La Cocina** at C. Mella 29.

ENTERTAINMENT: Astromundo, Autopista Duarte, is the town's major disco. **Codetel** is on Juan Rodriguez at the corner of Duvergé.

EVENTS: The best time to visit the town is every Sun. afternoon in Feb. when colorfully costumed *diablos cojuelos* take to the streets in celebration of *carnával*. On Aug. 15, the *fiestas patronales* of Nuestra Señora de Antigua are held.

FROM LA VEGA: *Públicos* leave for Santiago and Jabaracoa from the center of town. *Moto Saad* (tel. 573-2103) departs for Santo Domingo from Colón 37.

Jarabacoa

This popular resort town flowers during the summer when locals arrive to beat the heat. The rest of the year it's pleasant, laid back, and very low key. And the presence of the nearby hydroelectric plant means that there's power practically all the time. The Río Jimenoa edges the town, which has only a few main streets and is surrounded by mountains. Jabaracoa may be used as a kickoff point for the trip up Pico Duarte, a base to explore the area's waterfalls, or as just a pleasant place to kick back and relax in for a few days.

GETTING THERE: Take a *público* from La Vega or a Caribe Tours bus from Santo Domingo. From La Vega, it's an attractive ride along a two-lane asphalt road. As you climb higher, young pines line the road.

SIGHTS: Balneario La Poza is a short walk from town. Its beautiful ambience is marred by the Brugal Rum ads thoughtlessly painted on the huge boulders in the river. More attractive but much less accessible, the *balneario* at "La Confluencia" on the Río Jimenoa offers somewhat dangerous swimming and a restaurant. To get here you must follow a road lined with the houses of the elite. It's about an hour's pleasant walk. **waterfalls:** Most accessible of the three waterfalls is **Salto de Biguate**. It's about a half-hour walk to the entrance, which is marked by a sign. Visit, if you can, between excursion groups of Germans on horseback. Allow an hour or two from the road both ways. Visit the upper and lower Río Jimenoa falls; the upper falls is five km or so farther up the same road and down a steep slope. To get there, travel six mi. (9.6 km) to the village of El Salto, where an unmarked trail from the road's edge leads to the falls. Look for the parking area on the R. While it's easy to get down, coming back up is a bit steep. The "lower" falls is some km out of town along the road to Monabao and a suspension bridge is also in its vicinity. Hire *motoconchas*.

ACCOMMODATION: Set about one km from town on the road towards Constanza, inexpensive **Pinar Dorado** (tel. 574-2820) features a small pool and restaurant. Very popular with Germans and other Europeans, its rooms have double beds and a balcony. Although aging, it's the plushest hotel within walking distance of town, and from here it's possible to walk to the Salto Biguate waterfall. Rooms here start from from around $25 with fan; a/c is more expensive. In the US call (800) 843-3311. Heading towards town along the road from la Vega, **Centro Turistico Alpos Dominicanos** is the first establishment you pass. Alpos Dominicanos features 132 rooms distributed in 11 villas and 66 apartments with more on the way. **La Montaña** (tel. 682-8181), **Piños del Puerto**, and **Hotel Nacional** are also on the way. Charging around $12 s or d, **Hotel Hogar** (tel. 574-2739) has rooms with a bath and fan. There is a nice courtyard and friendly management. A way out of town on the road towards La Confluencia, **Anacaona Villas** (tel. 574-

2686) offers concrete bungalows complete with fan and kitchen for around $120/wk. Farther on to the L down the same road, **Jabaracoa River Resort** (tel. 574-2772/2161) has units for around $20 pn with TV and kitchen. **low budget:** A cheap but unmarked hotel is on the cor. of Independencia. The **Dormitorio** is basic but clean and has a good *comedor*. **Hotel El Carmen** stands near it. Out of town, the Hotel Continental is for short time sex. You can also **camp** at La Confluencia.

FOOD: Cafeteria Angel, Av. Independencia, has good coffee and is run by a sweet lady. **De Paolo Restaurant** has Italian food, as does **Restaurante Pizzeria El Cofre** which offers Dominican-style pizza. **Restaurant Brasilia**, C. Colón 26, has one of the nicest atmospheres. **Restaurant Sandy** is also good, but you can expect a large contingent of affluent Germans to arrive around 12:30 PM. A small market in town sells fruits and vegetables.

ENTERTAINMENT: You can play billiards at **Club Deportiv El Dugout**, next to the ballfield on the way to the Confluencia.

SERVICES: Codetel is on the upper part of Av. Independencia to the R in the direction of La Vega.

Constanza

Set in a 4,000-ft (1,219-m) high mountain valley, this is one of the nation's most pleasant towns – one virtually undeveloped for tourism. Fresh vegetables (such as mushrooms, potatoes, and garlic), fruits (strawberries, raspberries, peaches, and pears) and flowers for export are grown in the area. There's also a Japanese emigrant farming community here who are descendants of some 30 Japanese families brought in during the 1950s at the behest of Trujillo. On June 14, 1959, a C-46 twin-engine transport landed here with 56 rebels on board. The plane was loaned by Venezuela, but it came from Cuba. Trujillo's forces swiftly defeated the rebels and later sunk two ships off the coast of Puerto Plata. This marked the end of Castro's one attempt to overthrow Trujillo. UFOs were sighted here during the mid-1970s; the latest was seen in 1991. This pleasant if nondescript town, which boasts a giant camouflage-painted military base, shows the dramatic contrasts between affluence and squalor. Frequently if somewhat misleadingly billed as a bit of Japan or Switzerland in the tropics, the surrounding area is one of the nation's prettiest, with verdant forests, cool mountain air, and brisk streams and waterfalls. Reasonably pleasant during the days, temperatures may drop to freezing during the winter. View the cloud-covered peaks of the Cordillera Central from the high escarpment on the valley's S side. **getting there:** Constanza can be reached from Bonao by two *públicos. Linea Cobra* also runs. (See "From Santo Domingo" in the Santo Domingo section). Direct transport between Constanza and Jarabacoa is only available in the morning. The alternative at other times is to go via the Santo Domingo-Santiago Hwy. **from Neiba:** A time-consuming, difficult, but adventurous route is take a *guagua* to Cruce de Ocoa from Neiba (in the SW) and then take another from there to San José de Ocoa (NE of Azua). In **San José de Ocoa**, you can stay at low-budget **Hotel Marien** or at 10-bungalow **Rancho Francisco** (tel. 558-2291 or 565-7637/562-1930 in Santo Domingo) just outside the village. Its facilities include an Olympic-sized pool and a restaurant. From here there is only regularly scheduled transport three times per week (Mon., Wed., and Fri.). If you can get to Rancho Arriba by bus, it's possible to hire a motorcyclist to take you along an awful road to Piedra Blanca on the Santo Domingo-Santiago Hwy. From there you can get to Constanza. **by car:** The road between Jarabacoa and San José de Ocoa passes through Constanza and Valle Nuevo. From Bonao, it's a more direct one-hour drive from the Carretera Duarte. The road's first part climbs into the mountains plying a ridge above Laguna Rincón, one of a chain of six man-made lakes found in the area.

ACCOMMODATION: Low-budget ($4) **Hotel Margarita** is on C. Luperón, the main street. Located on a sidestreet, pleasant **Hotel Brisas del Valle** (tel. 539-2365), C. Gratereaux 76, offers rooms for $7.50 and up. Also try **Hotel El Gran Restaurant** (tel. 539-2675). C. G Luperón 70. The **Hotel Restaurant Mi Cabaña** (539-2472), R. Espinosa 60, has rooms with shared bath for $8; rooms with private baths are $10. **Hotel Restaurant Sobeyda** (tel. 539-2498), 16 de Agosto 22, offers very basic rooms for around $4. **Lorenzo's**, down the street, has pleasant rooms for around $7; rooms with private bath are higher. It also has a restaurant.

FOOD: There are a number of small restaurants, but some run out of food later on so eat dinner early. A number of places are near the plaza including a pizza place and the **Anacaona** bakery. **Restaurant Pizzeria y Heladeria Rey**, S Ureña 22, has pizza and a wide selection of other goods. The **De Clase Restaurant** is next door to the Margarita. Located down a side street from Banco Mercantil and near the Texaco Station, the **Acosta Restaurant** has reasonable prices. The **market** on Av. Gratereux has a good assortment of fruits and vegetables. Many other shops are in the vicinity.

ENTERTAINMENT: Evaldra is the local disco.

FESTIVALS AND EVENTS: The *fiestas patronales* of Nuestra Señora de las Mercedes is celebrated here around Sept. 24.

FROM CONSTANZA: A bus leaves in the pre-dawn hours to Santiago via the Bonao road. They'll pick you up; ask your hotel about it or call 573-2793. *Linea Cobra* (tel. 539-2415) runs to Santo Domingo; their offices are at C. Sánchez 37. There's regular but quite slow transport to San José de Ocoa three times per week (generally Mon., Wed., and Fri.) along a very rough road; ask around. In any event, if you have the opportunity, travel the road towards Bonao which has truly spectacular scenery.

Aguas Blancas

About six mi. (9.6 km) S of town, **White Water Falls** is a two-staged waterfall with a chilly pool. Birdwatchers should keep an eye peeled for the Hispaniolan trogon, the gray-headed quail-dove, and the sharp-shinned hawk. **getting there:** From Constanza, take a dirt road S to Valle Nuevo along the Rio Grande river valley. The turnoff is a hillside named El Convento. The steep, narrow, and winding track requires a four-wheel-drive vehicle, but it's less than a mile on foot.

Reserva Científica Valle Nuevo

One of several areas in the country designated as a scientific reserve in 1983, Valle Nuevo extends from near the Valle Nuevo Military Post to the Pyramids, a local monument some 24 mi. (39 km) S of Constanza. One of the nation's true virgin areas, the woods, at 7,000 ft. (2,134 m) elevation, offer cool temperatures and solitary hiking trails. Two of the nation's major rivers, the Yuna and the Nizao, have their headwaters here. **flora and fauna:** Thought to have been sown by migrating birds, lyonia and holly are found only here in the Caribbean and flourish in the area's temperate climate. Dominican magnolia covers some western parts of the reserve. Of the 249 plant species, 97 are endemic. Unfortunately, a full third of the reserve burned during a 1983 forest fire and is just now recovering. **getting around:** Follow old logging roads into the forests. Some are driveable, but all deteriorate during the wet. Zigzagging through thick pine forest and fields of pine savannah, the route S climbs up to 8,000 ft. (2,438 m) before the province of Peravia. On the way, the road traverses rocky crags and bluffs, the remains of what was once an extensive montane cloud forest, and then drops down to the Valle de Río Ocoa before ending at San José de Ocoa. A forest of acacia, mesquite, and mahogany lies to the S of town. Although the road is bad and rain is frequent here, this is one of the nation's loveliest areas. It takes about two hours by car to Santo Domingo. Allow a full day from Constanza for the trip.

Parque Nacional Armando Bermúdez & Parque Nacional José del Carmen Ramírez

With a combined area of 380,514 acres (153,994 ha), these parks contain the northern and southern slopes of the Cordillera Central. Here are the highest mountains in the Caribbean: Pico Duarte, 10,417 ft. (3,175 m); Pico La Pelona, 10,393 ft. (3,168 m); Pico La Rucilla, 10,003 ft. (3,049 m); Pico de Yaque del Norte, 9,826 ft. (2,995 m); and Pico del Gallo, 8,694 ft. (2,650 m), among others. This area forms the gigantic watershed from which most of the rivers originate, including Yaque del Norte and a dozen or so others. Hydroelectric dams have been built at Taveras, Sabaneta, Sabana Yegu, and Bao. Dominated by pines, forests are found mostly in the regions surrounding Pico La Pelona up to Pico Duarte and from La Mediania hill in the S. Human life in this region scrapes by at bare-bones subsistence level. Illegal squatting is an increasing problem here. If you wish to get an overview, check out the wonderful mural in Manobao highlighting the park; it also shows the location of all the nation's national parks.

HISTORY: This area began forming some 60 million years ago during the Cretaceus period; a series of volcanoes erupted, and the lava blended with the earth's crust and solidified. The underlying rock is predominately igneous: volcanic limestone, slate, diorite, and marble. Armando Bermúdez was declared a protected area in 1956; Carmen Ramirez followed two years later.

FLORA AND FAUNA: Subtropical mountainous humid forest and rain forest predominate here. West Indian cedar, wild mountain olive, wild cane, palo amargo, and West Indian walnut are found at elevations up to 3,600 ft.; lirio, copey, sierra palm, and fiddlewood occur from 3,600 to 4,500 ft.; palo de viento, wild brazilleto wild avocado and tree ferns are found from 4,500 ft. to 5,100 ft.; and creolan pine and a variety of bushes flourish at 5,100 ft. and above. Wild boars are abundant in Tetero Valley. Hutias also reside within the park. Birds include the Hispaniolan parrot, Hispaniolan woodpecker, the Hispaniolan trogon, the white-necked crow, palm chat, ruddy quail dove, mourning dove, and red-tailed hawk.

GETTING THERE: Access to the park is via the 32-km road from Jarabacoa (500 m) to La Ciénaga (1,000 m).

SIGHTS: The main activity here is climbing Pico Duarte. Pre-Columbian rock carvings are found in the Tetero Valley area of José del Carmen Ramírez National Park.

Pico Duarte

The brilliant Swedish botanist Erik Ekman ascertained that Pico Duarte was the highest mountain in the Antilles. Taking him at his word, Trujillo renamed it Pico Trujillo – replacing the former name of Pico La Pelona ("Baldy," for the treeless plain on its top). After Trujillo's fall, the mountain was renamed after the 19th C revolutionary elder and founding father. The peak was not climbed until 1944, as part of the independence centennial celebrations. **climbing Pico Duarte:** The dry season is a good time to undertake this venture. Begin at Jarabacoa and hitch to Manabao, and then hitch or hike along the poor road to La Ciénaga (no public transportation) – stocking up on food along the way – and Casa Tabalone, at the entrance to the Parque Nacional Armando Bermúdez where the trail begins. Follow the L bank of the Río Yaque del Norte for a few km before turning up a steep mule track which winds its way around a series of ridges. Palms give way to coarse bracken ferns and *palo de cotorra* ("parrot tree"), a thin-stemmed tree with feathery leaves. At 5,900 ft (1,800 m), the vegetation changes to jungle, congested with a variety of ferns, bromeliads, orchids, epiphytes, mosses, lichens, tree ferns, and conifers. Pine forest takes over near the crude bush shelter and spring at 2,650 m (7,900 ft.). From here follow a trail to the incredibly desolate summit. Allow two days from Casa Tabalone for this hike.

PRACTICALITIES: You must be in excellent physical condition for this demanding trek. In addition to all of your own food, you must bring warm clothing for the cold nights when temperatures may drop to freezing or below. Entrance fee to the park is around $10. Local guides and mules can be hired either in Monabao or in La Ciénaga; a guide is required for entry, and the National Park staff will help you locate them. Mules are not necessary no matter what you may be told, but they will take the burden off your back; in any case you will have to pay for at least one mule for your guide. You should arrive in La Ciénaga the day before to make preparations and ensure an early start the next day. You should purchase the majority of your supplies and provisions in Jabaracoa; in Manabao only things such as rice, beans, and spaghetti are available. The only accommodations here are the very reasonably priced rooms offered at Doña Patria's. She'll help you find a guide; you may also camp in fields outside the park, and there's a river for water and bathing. Otherwise, the nearest hotels and restaurants are at Jarabacoa, about an hour's drive on a rotten road. The park entrance is four km walk from La Ciénaga. At La Compartación, about nine mi. (14.4 km) up the slopes from La Ciénaga (Boca del Río), there's a cabin. From there, it's a minimum of two hours (at a fast pace) to the top. Trekkers generally overnight at La Compartación again. The mostly downhill return trip from there takes seven hours or so. You should overnight at Los Tablones on the first night. You can make it all the way down on the fourth day; it's possible to sleep at the park office. The last *camioneta* (pickup truck) departs from Manabao to Jarabacoa at around 2:30. **note:** Try to inquire about current information in Santo Domingo with the park service before undertaking this expedition. This is not an easy trip and is not for everyone. You should note that it's 23 km from La Ciénaga (1,000 m) to the top of Pico Duarte (3,175 m).

The Cibao

Set between the Cordillera Central and the Septentrional, the Cibao is the nation's largest agricultural valley. It comprises the provinces of Santiago, Monsignor Nouel, Duarte, Espaillat, Sánchez Ramirez, and Salcedo. Famed for its coffee, cattle, rice, and bananas, this "food basket" has long attracted farmers and ranchers. Late in the 1800s, Cuban refugee *independentistas* settled in the region. Intermarrying with local landowners, they built up the export tobacco industry. The region's folk are so prideful that other Dominicans refer to it as the "Republic of the Cibao." Its largest city, Santiago de los Caballeros, is Santo Domingo's main rival which once played kingmaker in national politics. The nation's most Castillian Spanish is spoken here, locals use words common in the 16th-18th C, and they often subsititute the consonant "r" for "l" or "i" when speaking.

Santiago de los Treinta Caballeros

Once the nation's largest city, "Santiago of the Thirty Noblemen" (pop. 500,000) has been relegated to a distant second place. Located in the N-central part of the country in the heart of the lush and fertile Cibao, the local economy runs on rum and tobacco. Santiago is often regarded as Santo Domingo's alter ego. Unlike the capital, with its urban sprawl and frenzied pace, the pace here remains a bit slower. It has a reputation as a city of refinement where many of the most aristocratic and historic families live, but today Santiago appears to be losing its special character as "development" has razed many of the old houses and others are deteriorating through neglect. Still ladies on mules compete for road space with taxicabs, and there are enough old gems around to make for some attractive pictures. Santiago may also be used as a base to visit the beautiful town of San José de las Matas to the SW, the town of Moca with its faceless dolls, and the national park of El Morro.

GETTING THERE: Santiago may be reached by express and regular bus from Santo Domingo. *Metro* runs seven times daily and also runs from Puerto Plata.

HISTORY: Legend has it that Santiago was founded by 30 noblemen who named it after St. James, their patron saint. In fact the suffix "of the 30 noblemen" was probably added during the second

Central Santiago

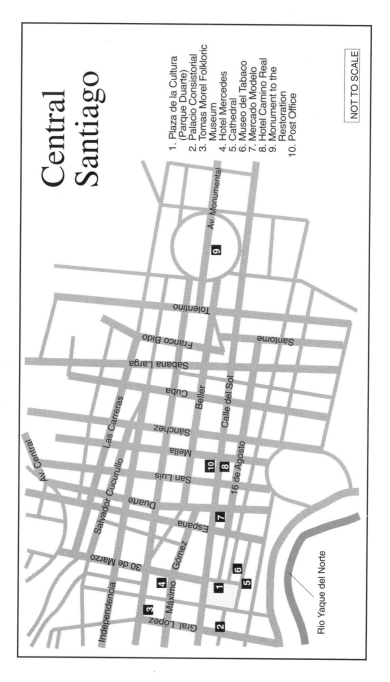

1. Plaza de la Cultura (Parque Duarte)
2. Palacio Consistorial
3. Tomas Morel Folkloric Museum
4. Hotel Mercedes
5. Cathedral
6. Museo del Tabaco
7. Mercado Modelo
8. Hotel Camino Real
9. Monument to the Restoration
10. Post Office

NOT TO SCALE

Av. Monumental

Tolentino

Franco Bido

Sabana Larga

Cuba

Beller

Calle del Sol

Santome

Sánchez

Mella

San Luis

16 de Agosto

Duarte

España

Gómez

Máximo

Las Carreras

Salvador Cucurullo

30 de Marzo

Independencia

Av. Central

Gral. López

Rio Yaque del Norte

half of the 16th C. There are conflicting stories as to who exactly founded the town and when. One holds that the brother of the notorious Christopher, Bartolomew Columbus founded Santiago on the Rio Yaque in 1495; another holds that Columbus himself did so in 1498 or 1499. This settlement disappeared, and the second Santiago was founded by Santo Domingo Gov. Frey Nicólas de Ovando who granted land to recently arriving settlers from Spain and others relocating from La Isabela. This settlement was known as Jacagua. It was destroyed by the 1562 earthquake and rebuilt the next year on its present site. It then became known as Villa de Santiago. In 1970, at the behest of the Dominican Academy of History, the Spanish Royal Academy renamed the city's residents. They are now known as *santiaguenses*; formerly they were known as *santiagueros* or *santiagueses* which caused confusion with Santiago de Cuba and Santiago de Compostela. However, despite the Academy's dictum, locals still use the latter two terms.

ORIENTATION: The major thoroughfares are Av. Salvador Estrella Sadhala which cuts through the city's E side; Carr. Duarte which becomes Av. Central as it enters the city from the W and becomes Av. Franco Bido before it leaves to the E; Av. Central which heads into the city from the NW and turns into C. 30 de Marzo; C. Del Sol, the crowded main street which runs between the main plaza and the Restoration Monument (where it becomes Av. Monumental before turning into Autopista Duarte); and C. Restauración which runs parallel and a few blocks to the N of C. Del Sol. The Av. Circunavalación runs parallel to the Río Yaque del Norte which defines the city's SE perimeters. Finally, crossing the Río Yaque del Norte is the Puento de Hermanos Patino, a monstrous bridge and another Trujillo production.

GETTING AROUND: There's a large network of private shared taxis and public buses, but you'll have to ask locals which ones to take. It's easy enough to walk everywhere around the central part of town, but the blackouts make everything very gloomy at night. Taxis start from a bit less than $5.

SIGHTS: The best place to start a tour of Santiago is at the centrally located **Plaza de Cultura** also known as Parque Duarte. Located at the intersection of crosstreets C. Del Sol and 30 de Marzo, it's bordered by *frio frio* (ice cone) vendors and aspiring shoe shiners. You might see an old lady with a hair net sitting on a bench searching to see if she has a winning lottery ticket, a guy chasing his puppy, or a mother holding her unruly child. Built with a combination of Neoclassical and Gothic styles between 1868-1895, the **Catedral de Santiago Apóstol**, at one side of the plaza, features an elaborate carved mahogany altar. It also contains the tomb of dictator Ulises Heureux, stained glass windows by Rincón Mora, as well as some heroes of the "Restoration," a revolt which re-established independence from Spain in 1865. It was renovated in 1991. Another interesting old building in the plaza is the **Edificio del Centro de Recreo** (Recreational Center Building), an exclusive private club, which is built in Mudejar-style. The 19th C **Palacio Consistorial**, which stands next door, is the former town hall which now has been incorporated into the cultural center. A small museum of city history is inside. Across from the cathedral on C. 30 de Marzo, the **Instituto de Tabaco** illustrates the harvest and production of the noxious carcinogenic weed that figures so prominently in the region's economy. Negotiate at this plaza for a carriage ride around the city – the drivers will find you – or head down bustling C. Del Sol where you might see local lovelies window shopping, a guy selling puppies, men selling old coins, and cassette and other vendors plying their wares. Set in a Victorian-style home, the **Museo de Artes Folkloricos Tomás Morel** contains a collection of carnival masks and other folk art. Note the masks of the *lechones*, mischievous imps from the town's *carnaval*. It's on C. Gen. Lopez, less than a 10-min. walk from the main plaza. A sort of Dominican Eiffel Tower or Statue of Liberty, the aesthetically unappealing 67-m-high **Monumento a los Héroes de la Restauración** is the city's highest point. Its interiors are adorned with murals by Spaniard Vela Zanetti. It was originally constructed by Trujillo in his own honor and named the Monumento a la Paz de Trujillo. You may or may not be able to enter depending upon the current state of restoration of this monument which now commemorates the Restoration, the nation's second independence from Spain. While no one would term it one of the great architectural wonders of the world, it certainly is imposing enough and provides a useful beacon for bearings. Shaped something like a glassed-in high school gymnasium, the motley **Mercado Central** at the end of C. 6 de Septiembre (follow 30 de Marzo and cross the road) features a shop selling amber and a few small restaurants. Founded in 1962, the **Universidad Católica Madre y Maestra** is on Aut. Duarte at Km 1.5. Although nothing spectacular, colonial ruins are found at Jacagua. The **Camp David Ranch** (tel. 583-5230/1543) has a number of old cars belonging to Trujillo. **tours:** You can visit **La Aurora Tabaclero** (tel. 582-1131), 27 de Febrero, and the **Brugal Distillery** (tel. 575-1427), Av. 27 de Febrero 130.

GETTING AROUND: The central area with the sights is compact enough to easily walk around. Local buses have limited service.

Carros de concho are the same price. Expensive *carreras* are also available. For a bit of local color, try a carriage ride.

ACCOMMODATIONS: Located at C. del Sol and Mella, one of the best places to stay is the 72-rm. a/c **Hotel Camino Real** (tel. 581-7000, fax 582-4566; Apdo. 459, Santiago). Its comfortable rooms are equipped with cable TV and private bath. Up on the top floor is the Olympus Restaurant, and the hotel's plush bar, which features entertainment nightly, is in the basement. On Restauración just down from 30 de Marzo, there are a number of less expensive places including the white **Hotel Colonial** (tel. 583-3422) which has rooms with a TV and balcony for around $15; the **Hotel Monte Rey** (tel. 582-4558) and **Hotel Dorado** (tel. 582-7563) are nearby on C. Cucurullo. **Av. Estrella Sadhalá:** A number of hotels are located on this important street. The 40-rm. a/c **Don Diego** (tel. 575-4186; Apdo. 27, Santiago) features color TV, pool, tennis court, disco, and a Chinese-Creole-International restaurant. Also on Av. Estrella Sadhala, 36-rm. a/c **Hotel Ambar** (tel. 575-1957/4811) offers TV, bar, and restaurant. Newest and largest, the **Hotel El Gran Almirante** is also on Av. Estrellas Sadhalá. It also has a restaurant. **low budget:** If it hasn't been restored and boosted in price, the 40-rm. **Hotel Mercedes** (tel. 583-1171) on 30 de Marzo at Máximo Gómez charges about $20 for rooms with fans; a/c rooms are double the price. This hotel, built in the 1920s, features an incredible spiralling marble staircase and balconies in each of its small rooms. It's truly like entering another era. If that's full try the unmarked *pensión* on C. Restauracion, the **Hotel Alaska** (tel. 582-2764) at 16 de Augusto 129 at Benito Moncion, or search for other cheap hotels around Plaza Valerio. Another alternative is the **Hotel Dorado** (tel. 582-7563), Cucurallo 88. There are innumerable other small hotels in town. **outlying accommodation:** A Dominican-style hotel built by Trujillo, the 52-rm. a/c **Matum** (tel. 581-3107) is at Las Carreras (altos) and features cable TV, pool, disco, and casino. **Hotel Cananas "La Posada"** (tel. 583-3291) is at Km 4.5 on the Aut. Duarte (Carr. Moca). The 35-unit **Cabañas Palmar** (tel. 583-7247/7248) is at Km 5 on Aut. Duarte (Carr. Canabacoa); it features a/c, TV, and an AM-FM stereo.

FOOD: There are many sandwich and pizza places in town as well as local restaurants. Good but not inexpensive, the **El Dragón** on Av. Estrellas Sadhalá serves Chinese food. **Don Miguel**, on the Autopista Duarte opp. the Catholic University, has good food, including Cuban and *Norteamericano* dishes. In Parque Duarte, **Las Antillas** has meals from $4. In Ensanche El Ensueño, **El Mexicano** has Mexican food. **Restaurant Yaque** is at Restauración 115. **Olé,**

Juan Pablo Duarte and Independencia, has pizza. On Juan Pablo Duarte just past the Instituto de Tobaco, the **Roma** has good Italian food and pizza. Also try the **Oriente**, C. 30 de Marzo 57. *Chimi* stands (esp. the *arepa* stands) behind the monument, are good for cheap dinners.

FORMAL DINING: Try the **Restaurant Pez Dorado**, C. El Sol 43, which has Chinese and international cuisine including seafood. One of the town's most exclusive restaurants, **Restaurant Osteria**, Av. 27 de Febrero, specializes in Italian food. Set atop the Hotel Camino Real on C. El Sol, fancy **Restaurant Olympus** specializes in international cuisine. It has moderate prices, with some of the nation's best food and most attentive service.

ENTERTAINMENT: All the discos are high tech, but the Hotel Matum's **La Nuit** is that rare beast – a laser-equipped disco. Popular with locals, the **Hotel Camino Real**'s glitzy basement club features live bands nightly. Also try **La Mansión** in outlying San Jose de las Matas, **La Antorcha** (at Av. 27 de Febrero 58), and Las Vegas. For information about events at the **Centro de la Cultura** call 971-5460. If you crave the sight of spilled blood, you can visit the **Gallera Municipal**, the local cockfighting venue. **El Baturro**, Av. Franco Bido 147 (Nibaje), has live nude shows from 9-4 nightly.

FESTIVALS AND EVENTS: Santiago has a reputation for putting on the best *carnavál* celebration in Feb., and another takes place in Aug. Representing a mischievous devil, the pig-like *lechones* are the highlights of the celebration. Donning multicolored costumes adorned with mirrors and other ornamentation, these participants wear paper maché masks which, according to the shape of the horns, identify them as inhabitants of rival neighborhoods, Los Pepines and La Joya. The local *fiestas patronales* of Santiago Apostol are held around July 22.

INFORMATION: The **tourist office** is on the second floor of the *Ayuntamiento* (Town Hall) on Av. Juan Pablo Duarte. **services:** **Codetel** (tel. 582-8918) is on Estrella Sadhalá. The **PO** is on C. del Sol near the Mercado Modelo. **car rental:** Cars may be rented from Budget (tel. 575-2158), Av. 27 de Febrero; Honda, Av. Estrella Sadhalá at Av. Bartolomé Colón, Nelly (tel. 583-6695), Av. Duarte 106; and Rentauto (tel. 582-3139/3130), Av. Bartolomé Colón 4.

SHOPPING: There are rattan and wicker factories including **Artesania Rattan** on Carr. Duarte at Km. 4.5. **El Gallo**, Máximo Gómez

14, and **Casa Hache**, Av. Estrellas Sadhalá, sell housewares, and **Sirena** on C. Del Sol sells personal goods.

FROM SANTIAGO: Probably the best company to take, a/c *Metro* (tel. 582-9111/4611) runs to frequently Puerto Plata and to Santo Domingo (7, 8:15, 10, 12:45, 3, 4:30, 5:30, 6, and 7:30). To get here take a carro marked "A" heading away from the park and ask to be let off at "frente de la Metro Bus." The exact location is on C. Maimón at Duarte. At C. Restauración and Av. Juan Pablo Duarte, *Terrabus* (tel. 587-3000/5060/4554) serves Santo Domingo. Also in the vicinity, *Transporte de Cibao* has buses to Dajabón near the Haitian border. *Caribe Tours* (tel. 583-9198/9197) runs from Av. Sadhalá at C. 10 to Santo Domingo, Puerto Plata, Monte Cristi, and Dajabón. For buses to Constanza call *Lydia Jr.* at 582-5709. If driving to Puerto Plata, you should note that the reconstructed old Santiago-Puerto Plata highway has been closed to heavy vehicles in order to make it more attractive to tourists.

Vicinity of Santiago

Moca

Set to the E of Santiago, this coffee and *cacao* center makes an intriguing day trip. Be sure to see the splendid organ in the **Iglesia Corazón de Jesus**. The only other one of its ilk is in Brazil. The tourist office is located in the Ayuntamiento (Town Hall) on Av. Independencia and Antonio de la Maza. Outside the town on the road towards the Autopista Duarte, **El Higuero** is a center for the *muñeca sin rostro,* the popular "faceless" dolls portraying Dominican working women or flower or fruit vendors. Practically every building here is a cottage industry. Bargain hard.

practicalities: Stay at **Hotel Panorama** (tel. 578-2252), Av. Independencia 27, **Hotel El Dorado** (tel. 578-2113), **Hotel La Casona** (tel. 578-3465), C. Imbert 77, and **Hotel L'Niza** (tel. 578-2248), Carr. Santiago. **from Moca:** There's a beautiful road which winds through verdant hills to Caspar Hernández on the coast. You can also go from here to Sosúa by bus: change at Cruce de Veragua/Sabaneta. This is another beautiful trip with attractive views. *Metro* (tel. 578-2641) departs from Moca for Santo Domingo daily at 7 and 3:30 from C. Morillo.

San José de las Matas

Located to the SW, this attractive mountain town is near Santiago. **Hotel La Mansión** (tel. 581-0395/0393) has 20 d rooms and 50 two-bedroom villas with a/c and phones. There is a restaurant, pool, horseback riding, stables and full spa facilities. Stay at **Las Samanes** (tel. 578-8316), Av. Santiago 16, or at the cheaper **Hotel Restaurant Oasis** (tel. 578-8298), 30 de Marzo 51, or at **Hotel La Modenza**.

Puerto Plata and the North

The N Coast has become one of the top the tourist attractions of the the Dominican Republic. Nearby is the upscale tourist mecca of Playa Dorada. Sosúa is another major tourist town.

EXPLORING: Puerto Plata is connected by bus with Santiago and Santo Domingo. Destinations such as Samaná, Nagua, Las Terrenas, and Sosúa can be reached directly by bus from Santo Domingo. If traveling between points on the N coast, you must take either small minibuses, crowded vans, or pickup trucks.

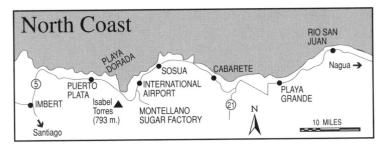

Puerto Plata

As with all Spanish colonial towns in the Americas, this old port – the major town on the Atlantic or "Amber" coast – centers around a plaza whose houses sport gingerbread trim. The most prominent town in the N coast, Puerto Plata has become the island's major tourist resort town – the Ocho Rios of the Dominican Republic. Unlike the former, however, there is a comparative lack of hassle, and it's still a relatively laid back place. Although a number of attractive 19th C homes with overhanging balconies still stand, the majority have been torn down and replaced by specimens from the concrete box school of architecture. The second largest port in the nation, it handles 12% of exports and 2% of imports.

HISTORY: Puerto Plata was discovered by Columbus on his first voyage. Seeing a high mountain capped by a snowlike mist resembling silver, he dubbed the spot "Silver Port." He commissioned Fray Nicolás de Ovando to establish a settlement here in 1502.

Becoming a leading port on the Spanish Main, it soon lived up to its name. By 1605, however, it had turned into a haven for smugglers and pirates and was destroyed by Spain. Bartolomé de las Casas, the celebrated monk of the Dominican order, began his epic tome *Apologética Historia de las Indias (Historical Apology for the Indies)* in a monastery here. Las Casas is considered to be the spiritual father of the once-trendy historical fashion known as *indigenismo* (Indianism) in which the pre-conquest Indian civilization was portrayed as a golden age. Re-established in 1750, Puerto Plata became a free port shortly afterwards. Infratur, a department of the Central Bank, began building tourist development in Sept. 1971. Today, with the arrival of cruise ships and the completion of a major tourism village at Playa Dorada, tourism is the major "industry" and with it have come the usual problems. The provincial economy is based on factories manufacturing alcohol, chocolate, and shoes, as well as production of dairy products, refined sugar, and sausages.

GETTING THERE: Puerto Plata can be reached by bus or *público* from Santo Domingo. Highly recommended *Metro Bus* (tel. 554-4580) runs via Santiago. *Caribe Tours* also runs. *Públicos* run from Sosúa and Cabarete. If you're driving, the approach from Santiago or Sosúa, along the old road, has superior scenery.

ARRIVING BY AIR: Union International Airport lies midway between Puerto Plata and Sosúa. It's easy to get into town: just walk out to the main road and board a *público*. However, be sure you have the current fare. You may rent a car here or take a taxi. From the airport to Playa Dorada or to town it costs around $11.

ORIENTATION: Unlike its congested cousin in Santo Domingo, Puerto Plata's Malecón is virtually free of traffic and is graced by a gentle sea breeze. Its most notable feature is the bronze statue of Neptune poised on an offshore rock – an aesthetic ad for the Puerto Plata Beach Resort. At the E corner of town is Long Beach, a long stretch of sand popular with locals as well as tourists. Near its entrance is a plaza area with a concrete tower you can climb, a number of shops, and a few hotels.

GETTING AROUND: Nowhere in town is too far to walk. Otherwise, the best way to get around is by bus. Often painted white with blue or red markings, the small city buses have two routes. Both "A" and "B" run with variations from the main entrance to the Playa Dorada complex, down Av. Circunvalación, though Av. 27 de Febrero, up 12 de Julio, pass through downtown, loop through the

W side, head S along Separación, pass through downtown again, and then head back to Playa Dorada. Buses run from 6 to 6, but some run as late as 7. Taxis can be found around the gazebo or you can call 586-3454 (day) or 586-3458 (evening). A ubiquitous feature on the landscape (and awfully annoying at times), *motoconchos* run out to Playa Dorada and will take you anywhere else you want to go. Expect to pay around 25 cents for a short ride inside the city; prices double at night when the buses are asleep.

SIGHTS: In **Parque Luperón** (Parque Central), the main square – bordered on its four sides by C. Del Castillo, C. John F. Kennedy, C. Separación, and C. Beller – stands the **gazebo** which was recreated from period drawings of the original. Other buildings bordering the park include the Victorian-style **Sociedad Fe en el Porvenir**, the art deco-style Iglesia de San Felipe, and the Club de Comercio. Set on the Malecón (waterfront) and surrounded by persistent hordes of salesmen, **Fortaleza de San Felipe** features a moat of sharp coral, and a variety of poorly-annotated artifacts and pictures – from coins to cannonballs – are displayed inside its cramped three rooms. It's mainly worth a visit just for the views from its plazas. When construction began in 1541, the fortress was intended to defend against French buccaneers or other intruders. By the time it was completed in 1577, the town's strategic importance had been undermined by events. The nation's George Washington, Juan Pablo Duarte, was once held in one of its cells. Depicted forever frozen in bronze and on horseback out in the middle of the parking area, Gen. Gregorio Luperón fought to overthrow the Spanish from 1860 to 1865. This museum-park honors Juan Pablo Duarte. The fort is open daily from 9-noon and 2-5 except Wed. A small admission fee is charged, and you should tip your guide if you use one. Located near the *plaza* at 61 C. Duarte, the compact **El Museo de Amber** (tel. 586-2848) houses one of the nation's largest collections of amber. It's a big draw with the tour buses, and downstairs is a large shop packed with every type of souvenir. Admission is charged to the upstairs museum. A leaf, fly, mammalian hair, mating chinch bugs, a miniature walking stick, a cricket, and a centipede are all entombed in pieces of amber here. If you can get here between tour buses, you might have the museum to yourself. Reached by the only *teleférico* (suspended cable car) in the Caribbean, **Loma Isabel de Torres** (2,565 ft., 789 m) is cooler by 30° F on top. Like its cousin at Rio de Janeiro, Christ the Redeemer spreads his arms above a fort built by Trujillo. Sip an expresso at the café and savor the view. This small park and scientific reserve (formally titled Reserva Científica Isabel de Torres) is surrounded by the heavily forested mountains of the Cordillera Septentrional. While in the area watch for 32 species of birds including the rufous-tailed solitaire, the Hispaniolan trogon, the Caribbean martin, the Hispaniolan parrot, the sparrow and red-tailed hawks, and the smooth-billed ani. The teleférico (around $3) takes Wed. off and may be running less frequently in the off-season; it also has a history of being out of order. You can also ride a horse up, and the road has been improved. Visit the ruins of the Vieja Logia and the Parque Central. Cool winds and fog are frequent here during the winter months. **tours:** Set to the E of town on Av. Luis Ginegra in the front of Plaza Turisol, **Brugal** offers distillery tours with free daiquiris from Mon. to Fri. 9-noon and 2 to 5. Drinks are on the house. There isn't much to see on the tour (only the bottling, which you watch from an overhead viewpoint), and it appears to be designed mainly to sell rum and overpriced Brugal souvenirs. **beaches:** Playa de Long Beach is at the E end of the oceanside avenue. It's crowded on weekends and not exactly the most spotless beach in the world. Watch your possessions here! Much better but further W is Punta Rucia where **La Orquidea de Sol** ("Sun Orchid") beach resort is located. Boat trips can be arranged from here to some of the more secluded beaches such as Playa Goya and La Encenada or to "La Laguna," a mangrove swamp. No buses run out here. **events:** The fiestas patronales of San Felipe take place around July 5.

Puerto Plata Accommodations

The tourist area known as Puerto Plata includes not only the town itself but also the tourist village of Playa Dorada and the smaller developments at Costambar, Cofresí, and Punta Rucia. The best value accommodation is in the town itself; the disadvantage is that Long Beach, the town's beach, is far from the greatest. But staying in town allows increased access to Dominican life and culture – a distinct advantage in itself.

IN TOWN ACCOMMODATIONS: Just a block from the main plaza, 22-rm. a/c **Hostal Jimesson** (tel. 586-2137/5131), C. John F. Kennedy 41, is modern – yet its antiques and old furniture give it the feel of an old home. The old house (1875) is attached to a more conventional and modern building in the back. Rooms are quite comfortable and have attached bath; some have cable TV. Write Cafemba, C. Separación 12, Puerto Plata. In Plaza Anacaona, **Hotel Restaurante El Indio** (tel./fax 586-1201) is at 30 de Marzo 94-98. Owned and run by Wolf Wirth, an outgoing and extremely helpful German expatriate who is one of the founders of the Dominican Red Cross, the hotel is one of the best places to stay for the price.

Rooms are clean and have bath and fans, and the restaurant is an attractive place to dine. It's very popular with Germans. The water comes from a spring and is specially filtered. Wolf knows the nation well and can make arrangements and offer suggestions. **Hotel El Condado** (tel. 586-3255) is on Av. Circunavalación Sur (M T Juto 45). The inexpensive ($13 pp), centrally-located **Hotel Castilla** (tel. 586-3736) is at J.F. Kennedy 36 at José del Carmen Ariza. On Av. J.E. Kundhardt, 22-rm a/c **Mountain View Hotel** (tel. 586-5757/4093) features a pool, piano bar, and restaurant. A bit out of town on the way to Long Beach and along the Malecón, **Hotel Puerto Plata Latin Quarter** (tel. 586-2770/3858, fax 586-1828) has comfortable rooms, a restaurant, and a pool. Rates are around $35 s and $42 d.

LONG BEACH ACCOMMODATIONS: Managed by AMHSA (tel. 562-7475, Los Piños 7, Santo Domingo). **Puerto Plata Beach Resort and Casino** (tel. 586-4243) is on Av. Malecón, a short walk from Long Beach. It features 152 one-bedroom suites, 24 standard rooms, and 40 deluxe Victorian Club Suites. Its proximity to town makes it a much more desirable destination than other resorts at Playa Dorada for those who want to experience Dominican life. The resort features two restaurants, convention bar, a disco, jazz bar, a café, water sports, Jacuzzi, a pool, and a pool bar. It's presided over by personable and friendly English-speaking hostesses. Across the Malecón are its Neptuno restaurant, a mini-beach, and water sports facilities. In the DR, call (800) 752-9326 or fax 320-4858. In the US, call (800) 472-3985. Across from Long Beach, the moderately-priced 104-rm. **Hotel Montemar** (tel. 586-2800; Box 38, Puerto Plata), Av. Hermanas Mirabal, offers rooms, suites, and bungalows. Facilities include a conference room, disco, restaurant, and a shuttle bus to Playa Mara Pica where there's a bar and a range of water sports. Conveniently located on the Malecón, 34-rm. a/c **Hotel Caracol** (tel. 586-2588) has cable TV, restaurant, terrace, piano bar, disco, nightclub, and a pool. Right near the beach, **Hotel Beach** (tel. 586-2551/2565/2403) offers a/c rooms and bungalows. Also ask in **Adolfo's Wienerwald Restaurant**, Long Beach, about rooms for rent.

LOW BUDGET: Possibly the best value is **Hotel Atlantico** near Caribe Tours and on 12 de Julio. Rooms start as cheap as $7 d with a fan and bath; a/c rooms are $10 and up. Call 586-6108/2503 and ask for sweet natured Anabella. **Hotel llra** (tel. 586-2337) is at Villanueva 25. Low budget **Alfa** (tel. 586-2684) is at C. Padre Castellanos 20. **Hotel Comedor Glenn** (tel. 586-4644) is at Ortega 5 near C. Beller. **Hotel Doña Julia** (tel. 586-6640) is at San Felipe 11

Hotel Guaronia (tel. 586-2109) is at 12 de Julio 76. Hotel Martin (tel. 586-4616) is at 30 de Marzo 40. **Hotel Boutique Dilone** (tel. 586-4525) is at 30 de Marzo 100. **Hotel Cafeteria La 41** (tel. 586-4828), C. 6 No. 41, is in the Dubeau neighborhhod to the W of town. Finally, **Hotel España**, Duarte 13, is a "motel" used for short time sex.

PLAYA DORADA ACCOMMODATIONS: This highly-developed resort complex of the same name is E of town and four km from the airport. Sugarcane fields have given way here to resort development with thousands of hotel rooms and an 18-hole championship golf course. It all began with a World Bank loan in the 1970s, and Infratur (the Tourism Infrastructure Department of the Central Bank) supervised construction. Horse-drawn carriages supply transportation within the complex. All the properties here are luxury class; the average price is over $100 pn for two. For value, it's best to get a package tour here. The complex is for people who wish to insulate themselves rather than become involved in realities of the Dominican Republic. For more information on accommodations here, write Asociación de Proprietarios de Hoteles y Condominios de Playa Dorada (tel. 586-3132, telex ITT 346-0360, fax 586-5301). The first project to be finished, 250-unit **Jack Tar Village** (tel. 586-3800, Box 368) is an all-inclusive resort with a/c apartments and cable TV. Its facilities include casino, restaurant, bar, tennis court, golf course, horseback riding, sauna, and a variety of water sports. In the US, call (800) 527-9299. With some 254 rms. and suites by the beach, **Playa Dorada Hotel** (tel. 320-3988, 586-3988, 562-5616, fax 320-1190; Box 272), offers a/c, cable TV, restaurant, nightclub, disco, golf, tennis, horseback riding, pool, water sports, convention facilities, and secretarial services. The Club Playa snack bar next door is cheaper for food. The 150-unit **Dorado Naco** (tel. 586-2019, PO Box 56) features urban-style sophisticated apartments with wall-to-wall carpeting, complete kitchenette, and cable TV. Its facilities include pool and deck, golf course, and horseback riding. Next door stands the recently completed **Dorado Naco II**. Also nearby and under the same management, the 428-rm. and 250-unit **Playa Naco Golf & Tennis Resort** opened in 1992. In the US call (800) 223-6510 and in Canada call (800) 424-5500. With a total of 207 rms. ranging from standard to villas, **Villas Doradas Resort Hotel** (tel. 320-3000, 586-3000, fax 320-4790) offers a/c, cable TV, pool, restaurant, and water sports. It was remodeled in 1993. Larger and with a greater variety of sports, 282-room **Flamenco Beach Resort** (tel. 320-5084, 586-3660, fax 320-6319), its sister hotel, stands next door. It has double, jr., and suites with a/c, phone, cable TV, and minibar. Its Club Miguel Angel, designed for business executives, has pool, solarium, Jacuzzi, and other services. Uniquely designed 420-unit **Eurotel** (tel. 567-5159) features eight different models of apartments ranging from studios to one- and two-bedroom suites. The property features murals by Dominican artist Ada Balcacer, and other touches include a Japanese-style garden with waterfall, and fantastic architectural design. **Villa Caraibe** (tel. 562-8494) offers 200 well-appointed a/c apartments, with TV, and also provides tennis, horseback riding, water sports, and golf. The 336-unit **Radisson Puerto Plata** offers fully-equipped two-bedroom villas and apartments with a/c, kitchenettes, and TV. Facilities include eight tennis courts, pool, restaurant, bars, extensive convention facilities, a supervised playground for children along with organized activities, a health spa, horseback riding, golf, and water sports. Call (800) 228-9822 in the US. The 118-unit **Costa Dorada** features one bedroom apartments with two double beds, a/c, TV, kitchenettes, and private balcony. Facilities include pool, golf, tennis, horseback riding, and a "Lagoon Club" set at the edge of a lagoon. The 488-unit **Puerto Plata Village** (tel. 586-4012) offers two-rm. apartments and three-rm. villas done up Victorian-style. Its setting has a pseudo-plaza with gazebo, clock tower, and a town hall housing shops and services. There's also a concert and convention hall, golf course, horseback riding, spa, five tennis courts, two pools, disco, numerous restaurants, bars, and watersports. A Caribbean Villages resort, the **Club on the Green** (tel. 320-5350) is spread over 16 acres and has 336 rooms, three restaurants, three bars, beach club with complimentary shuttle, scuba, horseback riding, and water sports. A second Caribbean Villages resort, the **Fun Royale** (tel. 586-4054) has 168 rooms, three restaurants, five bars, beach club with complimentary shuttle, two pools, disco, two tennis courts, and special children's programs. Rooms have a/c, cable TV, and phone; all-inclusive packages are available for both resorts. Managed by AMHSA, 150-rm. and suite **Heavens** (Box 576, tel. 320-5250, 586-4739) is an all inclusive which offers a/c, cable TV, an Olympic-sized pool, gym and spa, watersports, disco, and access to Playa Dorada's facilities. Another AMHSA property, the **Paradise Beach Club and Casino** (tel. 686-3663) has 436 rooms, three restaurants, three bars, pool. two tennis courts, shopping arcade, horseback riding, and water sports. Its a/c rooms have phone and TV. In the DR, call (800) 752-9326 or fax 320-4858. In the US, call (800) 472-3985.

COSTAMBAR: Set near the cable car station for Isabel de Torres, this new resort area features cottages and hotels as well as sports facilities. Featuring 100 condos, **Costambar** (tel. 568-3828) also has vacation homes for rent and residential sites for sale. Horseback

Puerto Plata

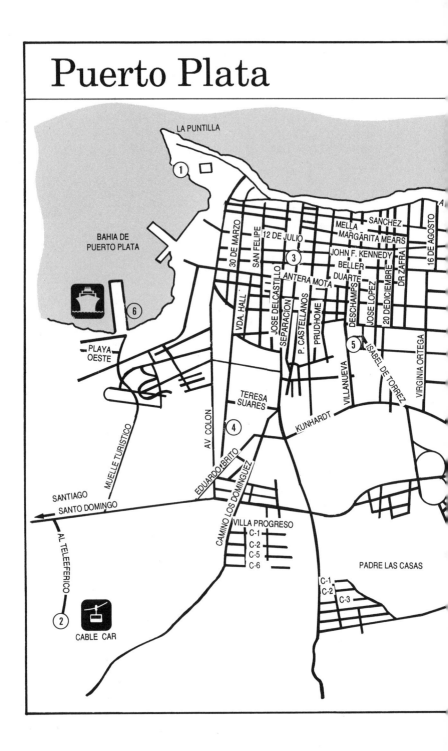

LA PUNTILLA

BAHIA DE
PUERTO PLATA

PLAYA
OESTE

MUELLE TURISTICO

SANTIAGO
SANTO DOMINGO

AL TELEFERICO

CABLE CAR

30 DE MARZO
SAN FELIPE
12 DE JULIO
MELLA
MARGARITA MEARS
SANCHEZ
JOHN F. KENNEDY
BELLER
DUARTE
16 DE AGOSTO
DR ZAFRA
20 DEDICIEMBRE
JOSE LOPEZ
DESCHAMPS
VIRGINIA ORTEGA

VDA. HALL
JOSE DELCASTILLO
SEPARACION
ANTERA MOTA
P. CASTELLANOS
PRUDHOME
VILLANUEVA
ISABEL DE TORREZ

TERESA
SUARES

AV. COLON

KUNHARDT

EDUARDO BRITO
CAMINO LOS DOMINGUEZ

VILLA PROGRESO
C-1
C-2
C-5
C-6

PADRE LAS CASAS
C-1
C-2
C-3

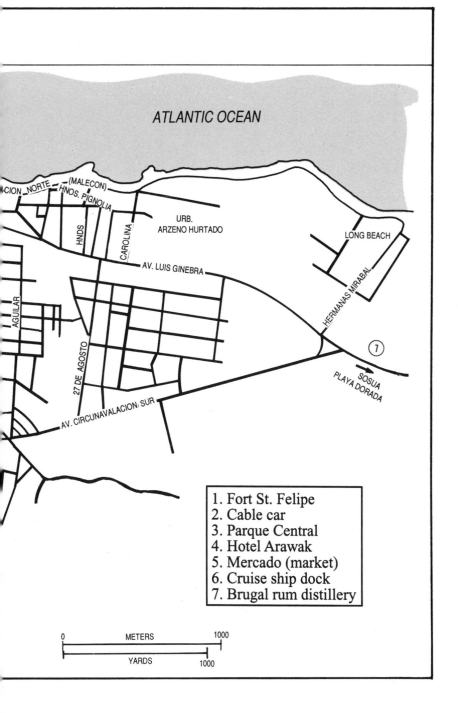

ATLANTIC OCEAN

CION NORTE (MALECON)
HNOS. PIGNOLIA
HNDS
CAROLINA
URB.
ARZENO HURTADO
LONG BEACH
AV. LUIS GINEBRA
AGUILAR
27 DE AGOSTO
HERMANAS MIRABAL
①
SOSUA
PLAYA DORADA
AV. CIRCUNAVALACION, SUR

1. Fort St. Felipe
2. Cable car
3. Parque Central
4. Hotel Arawak
5. Mercado (market)
6. Cruise ship dock
7. Brugal rum distillery

0   METERS   1000
             YARDS   1000

riding is available. **Los Mangos** golf course is here as well as a club house with swimming pool and tennis. **Bayside Hill Resort & Tennis Resort** here (tel. 320-3503, fax 320-6225) offers all-inclusive packages, two pools, restaurant, and – of course – golf courses. In the US call (800) 223-6510 and in Canada call (800) 424-5500. Less than 200 ft. from the beach, 40-rm. a/c **Apart-Hotel Las Caobas** (tel. 562-4171/7461 in Santo Domingo) offers tennis and water sports. The 33-unit **Apart-Hotel Marlena** (tel. 586-3692) has studios, one- and two-bedroom apts. The **Apart-Hotel Atlantis** (tel. 586-3828/1353) also rents villas and houses.

AT PLAYA COFRESI: This area is named after the 19th C pirate. Featuring functional cottages facing the sea, the 100-unit a/c **Cofresí Hotel and Club** (tel. 586-2898, fax 586-1828) offers cable TV, tennis, archery, spa, miniature golf, restaurants, and fresh and salt water pools bordering the sea. Consisting of 12 one- and two-bedroom condos done up Spanish-style, the **Cofresí Cove Hideaway** (tel. 586-6882; Box 598, Puerto Plata) provides pools and is near the beach. In Montreal call (514) 292-4408 or fax (514) 292-3797. An intimate 18-room inn, **Club Paradise** (tel. 586-5551, fax 586-5552; Box 675, Puerto Plata) has gardens, pool, Jacuzzi, and a restaurant. The 66-room **Club Hacienda-Cofresí** (tel. 586-6879, fax 686-6099) has rooms with phones, a/c, and TV as well as a pool, tennis courts, horseback riding, and live entertainment. An all-inclusive three km from Puerto Plata and five min. by car from Cofresí and Costambar, **Club Las Rocas** (tel. 586-5303, fax 586-8533) has 52 units which have ceiling fan, cable TV, refrigerator, and balcony. The resort also has two pools, a restaurant, bars, water sports and horseback riding. In Montreal, call (514) 922-3252 or fax (514) 922-3253.

PUNTA RUCIA: Right on the beach, 28-rm. **La Orquidia del Sol** (tel. 583-2825) features a choice of a/c or fans, restaurant, and water sports. It also has a family house on the beach. Managed by AM-HSA (tel. 562-7475, Los Piños 7, Santo Domingo), the 27-rm. **Discovery Bay Club** (tel. 586-5656) offers a/c rooms with cable TV, water sports, horseback riding, and nightly video movies.

LUPERÓN: An hour's drive E by car from Puerta Plata, the 310-room and -suite **Luperón Beach Resort** (tel. 457-3211/9628) offers a/c, cable TV, four restaurants, bar, disco, conference room, video theater, adult and children's pool, golf course, horseback riding, jogging paths, heliport, and car and motorbike rentals. The beach here is wide and has beautiful golden sand. Historically, its claim to fame is that an invading force intent on overthrowing Trujillo disembarked here in 1959.

Food

DINING OUT: There's plenty of fine dining here. The more expensive restaurants may require a jacket. At Av. Mota 23 near the park, renowned restaurant **De Armando's** (tel. 586-3418/1131) offers splendid seafood including lobster in sauce as well as nine soups, paella, and steak. Entrees are around $10. **Restaurant Café Galeria**, near the former on C. Separacíon, has good prices and desserts. At C. Diagonal 11, **Mamis Kneipe's** (Café Margarita) offers family-style Austrian cuisine. Tea with marble cake and other pastries is served between 3 and 5. Call 586-4030 for mandatory reservations. In another gingerbread-style house with a verdant garden in back, **Valter's**, C. Hermanas Mirabal, has seafood and Italian specialties. On C. Luperón, Hotel Montemar's **La Isabella** offers fine dining. On Hermanas Mirabal, **Los Piños** features creole and international cuisine. Near C. Separación on the Malecón, **Oceanico** features Italian-style seafood. On C. Hermanas Mirabal, **Orient Express** serves French and Chinese style seafood. Featuring *comida criolla* in an old house, **La Carreta** is on C. Separación. At C. Separación 9, the romantic **Victorian Pub** serves seafood and international cuisine in an outdoor garden. Up the street from the movie theater of the same name, the **Roma II**, C. Beller at C. Emilio Prudhomme, serves local food in an attractive, formal atmosphere.

OTHER DINING: Popular with foreigners, the **No Name Pub** is near the waterfront. Follow the road around from the Hotel Castillo. Overlooking the Parque Central and popular with locals, **Pizzeria Roma II** serves up dishes ranging from pizza to paella. The Restaurant Central on the main plaza is reasonably priced; try the stewed conch. The **Star Café** is at C. Beller 87 serves seafood, omelettes, and other dishes. On the main road, **Pizzeria Internacional** serves seafood and other dishes. Featuring local cuisine, **El Chef Tipik** is at Luis Ginebra and Hnas. Mirabal. Two blocks N from the main square, **La Canasta** serves good lunches. An inexpensive place is **Plaza Los Messones**, off the side of Parque Luperón, which has lunch specials for less than $2.

SNACKS: Branches of **Pepe Postre**, a pastry chain, are on 27 de Febrero and at Av. Colón 24. **El Sombrero** is on Playa Cofresí along the Autopista Santiago-Puerto Plata. **El Dorado**, a bakery, is at Duarte and San Felipe. Unusual sweets are sold at a shop opposite the Listin Diario office on C. J.F. Kennedy.

SUPERMARKETS: Bellers Liquor, C. Beller and Emilio Prud-homme, is right near Parque Luperón and has a good selection. Pick up a beer or soft drink here and go out to the park. **Supermercado Italiano** is at Beller 110. **Supermercado Central** and **Supermercado José Luis** are on C. Monolo Travares Justo. Both the old market and the **Mercado Nuevo** (on C. Imbert two blocks NW of the main plaza) are good places to buy fruits and vegetables. **Erika**, C. Separación near the park and just down from the PO, sells cheese, meat, and other dairy products.

DINING NEAR LONG BEACH: If you're staying or visiting near Long Beach, you can dine at European-oriented **Don Pedro** or at **Restaurant Mozart. Adolfo's Wienerwald Restaurant**, right by Long Beach, serves a hearty breakfast. In this area you'll also find **Café Terminus** (inq. about horseback safaris), **Tex Mex**, **El Cable**, **La Paella**, **Wienerwald**, **Orient Express**, **Swiss Garden**, and the Beach Club Restaurant. **Marie Andres** here specializes in Spanish and Italian food. Up the next side road to the N, the very affordable **Portofino Restaurant** is run by affable Máximo Almondez Portofino. Right on the beach at Puerto Plata Beach Resort, expensive **Neptuno Bar & Grill** specializes in seafood. Waves crash on its windows and a statue of the sea god on an outlying outcrop; a wide variety of seafood dishes are served.

DINING AT PLAYA DORADA: Most of the gourmet restaurants here are open exclusively for evening dining. The Radisson Puerto Plata's **La Condesa** serves continental food; a jacket is required. Eurotel's **America Restaurant** offers "light gourmet" dishes; a pianist plays evenings. **Porto Dorado** here offers seafood dining to the accompaniment of a guitar trio. At Villas Dorada Beach Resort, **El Pescador** offers fresh seafood dishes. **Jardin de Jade** here serves Chinese food including Peking Duck. Dorado Naco's **Flamingo**, Playa Dorada's oldest restaurant, specializes in dishes such as lobster and sea bass. **Valentino's Italian Restaurant and Pizzeria** is in the Playa Dorada complex near the Dorado Naco. Serving dishes ranging from risotto to grilled chicken, the Flamingo Beach Resort's **El Cortijo** offers Spanish-style cuisine including exotic seafood dishes and desserts. At Jack Tar Village, **Elaine's** serves up imported lamb chops and other US and Dominican style dishes. Set on the upper floor of Victoria Resort's main building, **Jardin Victoria** offers international cuisine. At the Puerto Plata Club on the Green, **La Condesa** serves Caribbean-accented gourmet food. Playa Dorada Hotel's **La Palma** specializes in steak and lobster. The Swiss-oriented **Blue Marlin** is at Aparthotel Elisabeth in Cofresi. Near Playa Dorada is **"Otro Mundo"** (tel. 543-8116/8019: toll free), a restaurant set in a 120-yr.-old farmhouse. It features a small zoo as well as exotic dishes such as tempura frog legs and squid stuffed with shrimp. **dining at Costambar:** At Costambar, Bayside Hill Resort features **Cafemba**, a Victorian-style restaurant specializing in French and other seafood cuisines. **Restaurant Primrose** is in Apart-Hotel Barlovento.

ENTERTAINMENT: The only movie theater, the **Roma Cine**, is on C. Beller just up from the park. The **Rock Café**, an expatriate hangout, is on Av. Circunvalación, as is **Willy's Sports Center Restaurant**. Dominican males like to frequent the bar/restaurant above the **JR Car Wash**. The only formal nightclub, the Orion is on 16 de Julio at 30 de Marzo. It has live music (cover charged) on weekends. Merengue players arrive most evenings at **Cafeteria Los Bonilla** at Las Javillas. Featuring a mix of merengue, salsa, disco, and rock, **Studio Vivaldi** is on C. Hermanas Mirabal, as is **Los Piños** bar. **Yellow Beard Pub** on 30 de Marzo offers more than its share of scurrilous graffiti on its walls; you're welcome to add your own comments. Check out the "Obituary to Cap Kenny" on the wall. Nearby on Av. Colón and perpendicular to the watefront, the **Hard Rock Café** (no connection to the chain) is popular with Canadian males down for the winter; it also serves food. Up on Av. Hnas. Mirabal and off to the W from the Long Beach shop/restaurant area, **Paco's Bananas** is open 24 hrs. For the bloodthirsty who thrive on cruelty to animals – or for those simply curious about a not-so-quaint aspect of Dominican life – cockfights are held Thurs. and Sat. from 1-6 and on Sun. from 2:30-6; the location is a small coliseum on C. Ramón Hernandez, a side street which connects to the Malecón. An afternoon may see as many as 30 feather-flying skirmishes. **discos:** Puerto Plata Beach Resort features **Bogart's Disco**. Down the road towards town, the **Mermaid** is open all night. **Playa Dorada nightlife:** Offering a range of music – from merengue to salsa to international pop, **Andromeda** disco is in the Heavens Hotel. Playa Dorada Hotel also has a disco; Jack Tar's has **Charlie's Discotheque**; Eurotel has **Crazy Moon**; and Playa Dorada Village has the **Disco Village**. Out at Costambar, the Bayside Hill Resort has **Lips**, a "laser ray"-equipped disco which can hold 1,200.

FESTIVALS AND EVENTS: The town's patron saint festival (for San Felipe) takes place July 5. Similar to Santo Domingo's Merengue Festival, the **Puerto Plata Festival**, held here in Oct., includes live bands, food tents, parades, and the like.

SERVICES: Set above the plaza at Long Beach, the **tourist office** (tel. 586-3676) doesn't appear to welcome visitors or be prepared to serve them. You may be able to pry a photocopy of a map out of them. Near the park, **Libreria Fenix** sells imported newspapers. It's open Mon. to Fri. from 9-2:30. **Codetel** has its offices at Beller 58, at Plaza Turisol, and at the airport. **Tricom** is on San Felipe at Beller. A third long distance company, **All America** (fax 586-6930), is at J. F. Kennedy 40. Mail may also be dispatched from the front desk of the large hotels. Open Mon. through Sat. from 8 to 5, the post office is at the corner of Separacíon and 12 de Julio. The **US Consulate** (tel. 686-3143) is at 12 de Julio 55. **Canadian citizens** can contact Tim Hall (tel. 586-5761); British can call on David Salem (tel. 586-4244). **Immigration** (tel. 586-2364) is at 12 de Julio 33. **tourguides:** Unfortunately, there are a large number of unqualified and unscrupulous "guides" – including small boys, taxi drivers, and others – who are willing to steer you towards a certain shop or restaurant with whom they have established a commission arrangement. Taxi drivers will go so far as to maintain falsely that a restaurant is closed or insist that they've never even heard of it. It's always preferable to go shopping on your own. However, should you want a guide, the **Association of Tour Guides** (tel. 586-2866) will show you around. They operate on a "tip" basis, but they expect a decent one. Their offices (open 8-noon and 2-5) are at Av. J. F. Kennedy 45. Even if you don't want a guide, they'll answer questions – a valuable service given the incompetence of the local tourist bureau. The best person to meet is affable Association President, Ramón Cabrera. **tours:** Most agencies offer the same variety of trips. Standard excursions are around Puerto Plata, to Santo Domingo, Santiago and the Cibao, to Samaná, to the Gri Gri Lagoon, and to Jarabacoa. **Agencia de Viajes Cafemba** (Cafemba Tours, 586-2177, C. Separación 12) is one of the island's premier travel agencies. **Go Dominican Tours** (tel. 586-6277/1101; fax 586-6652/4310), Av. J. F. Kennedy 47, is another. Other travel and tour agencies include **Prieto Tours** (tel. 586-3988, C. Marginal), **Puerto Plata Tours** (tel. 586-3858, Av. Beller 70), **Agencia de Viajes Victoria Tours** (tel. 586-3744/3773, C. Duarte 59) and **Vimenca Tours** (tel. 586-3883). Typical offerings include city tours ($25), Santo Domingo tours ($60), trips to Sosúa ($15), Río San Juan and Playa Grande, and to Santiago. **Columbus Air** (tel. 586-6991) offers daylong tours of Santo Domingo. At Plaza José Augusto Puig, **Turinter** (tel. 586-3911, fax 586-4755) has the usual range of tours. **Go Caribic** (tel. 586-4075, fax 586-4073) deals with German tourists. **Aerolink** (tel. 567-0819, 320-0627) has air tours to Samaná, Santo Domingo, and (when conditions permit) to Haiti. If you want something out of the ordinary, **Wolf Wirth** at the Hotel Restaurante El Indio (tel./fax 586-1201), 30 de Marzo 94-98, can put you in touch with trips ranging from Pater Pedro Brunschwiler's unique 14-day trips around the island in jeeps to boat trips to Los Haitises. **rentals:** Cars can be rented at the airport or in town from Puerto Plata Rent Car (tel. 586-0215); Rentauto Puerta Plata at 568-0240 or (800) 631-0058; Abby (tel. 586-2516/3995) on Av. J. F. Kennedy; and Budget (tel. 586-4433) on Av. L. Ginebra. Weekly rentals of 80cc motorbikes are available at the port. Trixxy Rent-A-Car rents motorcycles at reasonable cost. Yuyo (tel. 585-5440), 12 de Julio opposite Cosme Restaurant, rents scooters and "motorcicles." If renting scooters you should note that there is no insurance, and stealing scooters is a popular crime. **health:** Clínica Dr. Brugal (tel. 586-2519), is at C. José del Carmen Ariza 15. Grupo Medico Dr. Bournigal (tel. 586-2342/3542) is on Av. Mota. Farmacia Deleyte (tel. 586-2583), Av. J. F. Kennedy 89 in front of Parque Luperón, is open 24 hrs. Others include Farmacia Josefina at C. Separación 62, Farmacia Popular at C. Beller 27, and Farmacia Socorro at C. Beller 41. A complete list can be found in the phone book.

SHOPPING: On C. Duarte, **Rancier Boutique** is a small department store featuring Dominican manufactured goods. The **Rainbow Gift shop** is at C. Duarte 22. Featuring jewelry, hand-knitted blouses, ceramics, and dresses, **The Mine** is at C. San Felipe 32 at C. Duarte. Located at C. J. F. Kennedy 14, **Harrison's** specializes in gold jewelry, larimar, amber, and crystal. Distastefully, it also advertises black coral jewelry; don't buy any! At C. Duarte 32, **Macaluso** offers crafts and jewelry as well as rocking chairs. At C Duarte 23 and C. J. F. Kennedy 27, the **Grand Factory Gift Shop** features amber and larimar. At C. J. F. Kennedy 3 at 30 de Marzo, **Centro Artesenal** offers jewelry by its students, handmade dolls, domino and chess sets, and wooden trays. Also try **Planarte** on C. Las Damas. For beauty-related items, **Casa Leonel** has two shops: one is on C. Beller and the other is across from the PO on 12 de Julio. The **Libreria Fenix** has imported newspapers as well as postcards. The **Tourist Bazaar** is at C. Duarte 6. On C. Separación, **Casa Nelson** offers a wide variety of goods. **Casa Colón** nearby has tee shirts and related clothing items. Near Playa Dorada on the road from Puerto Plata, **Plaza Isabela** offers a selection of gift shops and a small supermarket. **Plaza Turisol** is a small shopping mall.

FROM PUERTO PLATA: For Santiago and Santo Domingo, *Metro* (tel. 586-6063) runs from C. Beller, and *Caribe Tours* (tel. 586-0282) departs from C. 12 de Julio at José Carmen Ariza. Caribe also runs to Sosúa, Mao, Dajabón, and Manzanillo. *Transportes de Cibao* (tel. 586-9408) has regular departures from a gravel lot next to Casa

Criolla across from the Hotel Atlantico. *Carreras* (chartered) run to Playa Dorado for $7, to Sosúa, $11. From Playa Dorada to the airport, it costs $11, and around $7 to town. *Voladoras*, smaller minibuses, run all over and leave from La Javilla, the hospital, and from near Parque Luperón. If heading towards Sosúa, don't stand on the road but go to the terminal (near the hospital) or to Parque Luperón; most buses are packed when they pass, and every other vehicle will be offering itself up as a charter – even the city buses. These charge about 65¢ to Sosúa, Playa Dorada, and the airport, and about 80¢ to Cabarete; ask a local to get the current price in *pesos* before boarding because many specialize in overcharging. *Motoconchos* will also take you anywere you want to go. **heading west:** To get to Monte Cristi, you have to take a *público* from La Javilla (at the NW end of town on the main road) to the outskirts of Navarete and then one on to Monte Cristi. **note:** No matter where you are heading be sure to get an early start. It takes four hrs. to Nagua, and (allowing for frequent transfers) will take you a full day to get to Las Terrenas or Samaná. There are no big buses heading out this way, and the overload can be horrendous.

Heading West From Puerto Plata

Well worthy of exploration, the nation's NW is still undervisited and undeservedly neglected. Some of the country's best and most extensive coral reefs lie offshore between Monte Cristi and Punta Rucia. In addition, there is the major town of Monte Cristi as well as Monte Cristi National Park and Villa Elisa Scientific Reserve.

La Isabela

An archaeological site, thought to be La Isabela where a settlement was founded in 1493, lies to the W of Puerto Plata near the village of El Castillo. The site has generated great excitement among the archaeological community because it is believed that the settlement may be the site of Columbus's first landfall in the New World on Oct. 12, 1492. On the other hand, it is no more certain that this in fact is the settlement of Columbus than that Columbus's ashes are buried in his tomb in the lighthouse. If it was Columbus's settlement, then this is the spot where he began his transformation from master mariner to bungling administrator and rapacious imperialist. In a misguided attempt to commence restoration during the 1960s, the site was bulldozed and countless artifacts were swept along with the topsoil into the sea. Despite this, the foundations of homes grouped around a central plaza have been unearthed along with numerous potshards executed in the Moorish style common to 15th C Spain and glazed a pink salmon color. Two ancillary sites, El Castillo and Los Coles, have been unearthed, but their exact connection with La Isabela is uncertain.

Monte Cristi

Set to the NW and reached via the Valle del Norte, this dusty coastal town's highlights are its unusual town clock and the home of patriot Máximo Gómez, who played a key role in the Cuban independence struggle and in the Dominican Restoration. Destroyed in 1605-1606, this small town – whose name is also sometimes spelled Montecristy – was resettled in the 18th C by Germans, Spaniards, Italians, and English immigrants. It prospered during the 19th C and into the beginning of the 20th when it exported wood and agricultural products to Europe. Owing to its windswept, desert-like setting, it's known as *Estamosmoriendo de sed* ("We die of thirst"). A *balneario* is at Loma de Cabrera on the Haitian border.

ACCOMMODATION: Montechico (tel. 579-2441) is on Playa Bolaños; **Roalex** (tel. 579-2405) is on PJ Bolaños, and **Hotel El Chic** (tel. 579-2316), is at C. B. Monción 44. Italian-run and attractive **Las Carabelas** (tel./fax 579-2682) is near Playa Paroli on Carr. El Morro. It is the only hotel near the park and charges from around $20 on up including breakfast. In the town of **Mao** to the SE, try inexpensive **Hotel Cahoba** (tel. 572-3357), E Reyes, **Hotel Céntrico** (tel. 572-5253), **San Pedro** (tel. 572-3134), and **Marién** (tel. 525-3558).

FOOD: El Parada is an inexpensive Italian restaurant right on the main road before town. There are a number of places to eat in town. **Heladeria and Pizzeria Kendy** is at C. Duarte 92. **Restaurant Coco Mar** is on PJ de Bolaños. **La Taberna de Rafua** is at Duarte 84. **Panifacadora Vitamina** is at S Fernando 18. Capped by a satellite dish, the **Restaurant Rabel** is on the main road to Dajabon.

SIGHTS AND ENTERTAINMENT: There's little to do in town which appears to have no true center. You may visit the **Casa Museo Generalisimo Máximo Gómez** – the house of patriot Máximo Gómez, which is now a small museum. Along with José Marti, Gómez penned the *Manifesto de Montecristi* here in March 25, 1895; it called for Cuban independence. Or view the **clock tower** – a sort of cuckoo clock meets the Eiffel Tower construction. Or hang out at one of the underpopulated and over-volumed discos. There's also a generator-powered movie theater, as well as the Academia de Music which has the remains of old saxophones and tubas hanging on the walls. **services: Codetel** is at Av. Duarte 85. **Alianza Francesa** is also on C. Duarte. **festivals and events:** The town's patron saint festivities (for San Fernando Rey) take place around May 30.

FROM MONTE CRISTI: *Caribe Tours* runs to Puerto Plata via Dajaban. Be sure to get an early start. There is no easy way to head S along here paralleling the Haitian border unless you have your own vehicle; a *carro* heads through to Pedro Santana a few times per week from Dajaban. You can get to Lomas de Cabrera (visit Balneario El Salto) and then take a truck to Restauracíon past breathtaking mountain scenery. Here you may get stuck. The road to Dajaban passes through cactus tree forests and by herds of goats. You might see a young boy herding cows followed by his even younger companion sporting a Batman tee shirt.

Parque Nacional Monte Cristi

Located in the NE near the border with Haiti, this park is also known as "El Morro" after its principal feature – a 900-ft.-high mesa overlooking the sea. Along with a nearby small hill called La Granja, El Morro is covered with windblown trees and shrubs on the ocean side which turn to desert scrub inland. Reachable by swimming in many places, the park's inner portion lies in water 7-10 ft. deep, and its outer reaches range from 10 to 40 ft. deep. So far, 10 wrecks have been discovered here. There are also a number of small islands offshore known as the **Cayos Siete Hermanos** (Cayes of the Seven Brothers). **getting there:** A road runs from Monte Cristi via commercially exploited salt flats to the coast and up the mesa's side. You pass some restaurants along the way. The Club Naútico is adorned with red, white, and blue Brugal rum and red and white Marlboro posters aplenty. A huge imitation bottle of Presidente adorns the roof. A rusting sign denotes Villa del Morro, a tourist complex that – judging by the rust – will never come to fruition. Along the road, you might see legions of dragonflies suddenly pop out of bushes or fishermen casting their nets in the water. **Las Carabelas Hotel** is near the park. There are a number of expensive homes, some only partially constructed, which have been built within the park boundaries. Illegally built without by the rich from Santiago, construction has been halted. **exploring:** The area has been defaced with hideous white-painted metal crosses. If you follow the path to the L all the way to the top, there's an absolutely magnificent view which, in and of itself, makes the park worth visiting. The visibility in the water is incredible. Back down the hill, you find more crosses and a sort of roadside altar with a set of stones like those of the ten commandments. Follow this road to a small yet beautiful beach. If you branch off to the R, the road passes by a lagoon with mangroves aplenty. **flora and fauna:** Subtropical dry forest predominates here. Plant species include poisonwood, West Indian boxwood, wild frangipani, and waterlilies. The 163 species of birds include the magnificent frigatebird, great egret, yellow-crowned night heron, American kestrel, wood stork, American oystercatcher, gulls, five species of terns, plovers, willet, osprey, and brown noddy. There are 11 reptilian species including the American crocodile, and three amphibians. **practicalities:** Stay and eat in Monte Cristi or at the **Las Carabelas Hotel**.

RESERVA CIENTIFICA NATURAL DE VILLA ELISA: Established in 1986, Villa Elisa Scientific Reserve is in Guayubín municipality near the village of Villa Elisa. The small stretch of subtropical forest features birds like the *cotorra* (parrot) and the *carpintero de sierra*. The 138 species of vegetation include a number of orchids and bromeliads.

Sosúa

Featuring a small beach on a bay, this very European town is five mi. (8 km) from the airport and around 16 mi. (25 km) E of Puerto Plata. It is divided into two areas: El Batey is the resort area featuring the majority of the area's tourist-oriented bars, restaurants, and hotels. Much of it has sprung up recently and continues to expand. Connected both by beach and road, Las Charamicos is at the W end. Tin-roofed shacks predominate here, and the atmosphere is the same as you'll find elsewhere in the nation. El Batey's special character originally derived from the 600 Jewish refugees who settled here in 1940. Although only 100 actually sunk down roots, they developed the dairy and sausage plants. The synagogue still stands, and English, French, and German are commonly spoken in town. **getting there:** Take a *público* from Puerto Plata. *Caribe Tours* (tel. 221-4422) runs here via Puerto Plata. A taxi from the airport is around $7. Or you can walk to the road and take local transport for much less if you don't have much baggage.

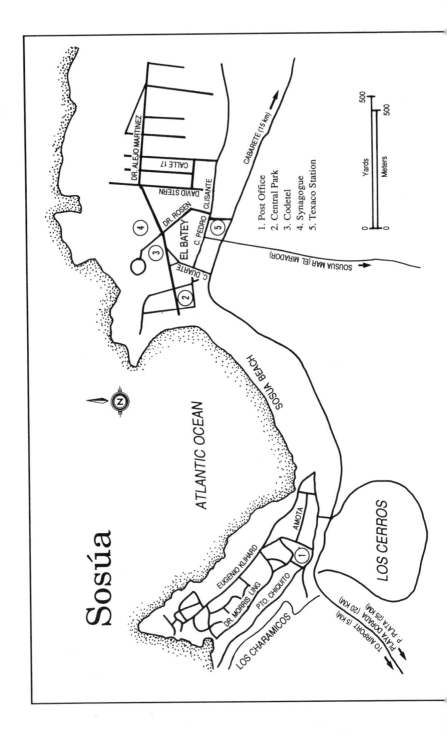

Sosúa

ATLANTIC OCEAN

1. Post Office
2. Central Park
3. Codetel
4. Synagogue
5. Texaco Station

DR. ALEJO MARTINEZ

CALLE 17

DAVID STERN

DR. ROSEN

C. PEDRO CLISANTE

EL BATEY

C. DUARTE

CABARETE (15 km)

SOSUA MAR (EL MIRADOR)

SOSUA BEACH

LOS CERROS

AMOTA

EUGENIO KLIHARD

DR. MORRIS LING

P'TO. CHIQUITO

LOS CHARAMICOS

TO AIRPORT (5 KM)
PLAYA DORADA (20 KM)
P. PLATA (25 KM)

Yards 500

Meters 500

BEACHES AND SIGHTS: There are three beaches. To get to the main beach, follow the main drag and turn L at the end. Nearly the entire stretch is a huge outdoor market filled with vendors selling typical souvenirs – ranging from imitation Haitian paintings to tee shirts. They'll rent you beach chairs, braid your hair and add a bead on the end, sell you trips on glass bottomed boats, or take you on tours. They can get to be a nuisance; the best solution is to walk along the edge of the water. However, you'll soon find jewelry sellers and the like accosting you when you sit down. Give them a firm "no" if you're not interested and hope they go away.

There's also the smaller **Casa Marina Beach** between the Casa Marina Hotel and Sosúa by the Sea. It's less spectacular but also has fewer vendors. A third beach is in front of the Larimar. Located perpendicular to the Codetel on C. Martinez near C. Dr. Rosen, the synagogue holds services every two weeks on Fri. at 7 PM. **events:** The town's *fiestas patronales* of San Antonio is held in Sosúa June 13, but the biggest time of the year is Easter weekend.

ACCOMMODATIONS: There are innumerable guest houses, hotels, and villas in the area with well over 2,000 rooms available. The town's borders are expanding rapidly, and new construction is everywhere. By the time of your arrival, there will undoubtedly be a number of new additions so ask around. None of the hotels here border the main beach, but most are only a short walk away. One of the best places to stay is the 8-rm. **Auberge/Village Inn of Sosua** (tel. 571-2569/3030, fax 571-2865/3750) run by semi-retired expatriate American lawyer J.J. O'Connell. At C. Dr. Rosen 8, just five min. or so on foot from the three beaches, it has a small pool. This inn features a restaurant, free ice and purified drinking water, and the rooms are equipped with your choice of a/c or ceiling fan. You can also watch satellite TV with J.J.; he is well informed about the DR and will be happy to talk to you. For reservations write Auberge/Village Inn of Sosúa, c/o Comet Couriers, Box 679, Puerto Plata. Situated next to the Village Inn, expensive 66-rm. **Woody's Hotel** is also on C. Dr. Rosen. It has a pool. Located near the beach, 32-rm. a/c **Hostal de Lora** (tel. 571-3939, 867-9690), Av. Dr. A. Martínez, offers executive and junior suites as well as a pool. and is decorated with beautiful stained glass and other artwork. Part of the Dormitel chain, 116-rm. **Casa Marina Beach Club** (tel. 571-3690, fax 571-3110) offers pool, three restaurants, Jacuzzi, and access to a small beach. Windsurfing and sunfish sailing are available. On C. Pedro Clisante, the 210-room **La Esplanada Hotel-Sosúa** (tel. 571-3333, fax 571-3922) has a/c rooms with satellite TV, minibars, and phones. It also has a pool. At C. Alejo Martinez 1, 18-rm. **Nino's Hostal Colonial** (tel. 571-2655) offers a pool and reasonable rates. Also on C. Alejo Martinez, a/c **Hotel Sosúa** (tel. 571-2683) features a pool. Set on a cliff, expensive but simple and functional **Villa Coralillios** (tel. 571-2645) has a pool, restaurant, and nightclub. It offers direct access to the sea. Peaceful and relaxed Canadian-run **Hotel Jardín Del Sol** (tel. 571-3553, fax 571-3485) has one- and two-bedroom villas, studios, restaurant, bar, and pool. Write EPS-D-224, PO Box 02-5548, Miami, FL 33102. Rooms are around $30 s and $50 d. Featuring nine cabañas and four rooms, **Koch's Ocean Front Guest House** (tel. 571-2234) has two rooms (8 and 9) with ocean views. The 28-rm. **Hotel Sosúa** (tel. 571-2683, Av. Martinez) features a pool and kitchenettes in some rooms. You can have your choice of either ceiling fans or a/c rooms. Featuring 28 a/c rooms, the **North Shore Hotel** (tel. 571-3830) has a pool. Offering your choice of a/c or fan-equipped rooms, 24-rm. a/c **Hotel Yaroa** (tel. 571-2578), C. Pedro Clisante, features a rooftop deck, French restaurant, and swimming pool. With a/c studios, two- and three-bedroom apartments and villas, there is **Los Charamicos Resort Hotel**. The **Tourist Studio** has 12 one- or two- bedroom a/c furnished apartments in a convenient location. Moderately-priced 27-unit **Charlie's Cabañas** (tel. 571-2690) offers simple rooms with fans and refrigerators. **On the Waterfront**, a steak and seafood restaurant, is next door. At Av. Martinez 1, is **Villas Larimar** (tel. 571-2645). Facing a small beach, **Sosúa-by-the-Sea** (tel. 571-3222, fax 571-3020) offers a/c rooms with cable TV and refrigerator. Its facilities include pool, Jacuzzi, massage parlor, restaurant, and bar. In the US, call (800) 531-7043. The **Tiburón Blanco** (tel. 571-3471), Dr. Rosen 3, features a swimming pool and has a BBQ. **Villas Carolina** (tel. 571-36260) offers 55 junior and six senior suites as well as two pools, bar, and restaurant. **Palm Village Hotel** (tel. 571-3188) features two pools, a/c, cable TV, and other facilities. For those who appreciate condo-style digs, **Club Residential Aparthotel** (tel. 571-3675, fax 571-1143), Pedro Clisante, offers attractive units for weekly and monthly rent. In the US, call (800) 831-1795. In its second decade of operation, the **Hotel Tropix** is a 10-cabaña resort which borders a swimming pool and gardens; inexpensive meals are served. Rates are around $35 s and $40 d; rooms are $20 off-season. **Los Charamicos acccommodations:** The only hotels within the pocketbook of low budget travelers are found in this lively area. On C. Carmen, **Pension Gómez** (tel. 571-5159) has rooms for $9 which include bath and fan. Similarly priced and a bit superior, **Hotel El Bambú** (tel. 571-2379) has a nice sitting room and balcony; enter from the building's side. About half that price are **Pension La Cancilleria** (tel. 571-3594 – ask for Odé) at C. Charles Kinder #15, and **Pensión Tata**. For a more luxurious stay, try **Charamicos Beach Resort** (tel. 571-2675) or the

Sosúa **"Sun Bay Club,"** (tel. 571-0704) which has three bars, restaurant, disco, pool, and other facilities. This 68-rm. resort is exclusively for singles. A hole in the wall set across from the Sun Bay Club and on the main road, **Chupi** offers chicken served on a cutting board with fries or yucca. Set on a hill behind the Club and recommended by reader Madeleine Hope, the **Vista Mar Hotel** charges around $30 d; it has a swimming pool and ping pong table. **apart-hotels:** On C. Dr. Alejo Martinez, the **Sea Breeze Hotel** (tel. 571-3858, 586-4132 in Puerto Plata) has 30 a/c rooms with balcony and kitchenette. Facilities include tour desk, pool, live entertainment, pool table and cable TV in an a/c game room, plus complimentary water sports and horseback riding. Prices are around $32 s or d. The 55-unit **One Ocean Place** (tel. 571-3131) is an a/c apart-hotel with cable TV, phone, balconies, kitchenettes, pool, children's pool, and 24-hr. security. **Condos Sosúa** (tel. 571-2504), C. Garcia, offers 15 one-bedroom apartments for short- or long-term rental. Inexpensive 16-unit **Sosúa Sol** (tel. 571-2334, fax 571-2416; Box 55, Sosúa) offers one- and two- bedroom bungalows with kitchenettes and ceiling fans. It has a pool. At Pedro Clisante 11, **Apartotel Nuevosol** (tel. 571-2124) offers fully equipped apartments with a/c or fans, and private balcony. Restaurant and laundry facilities are also available. Constructed with colonial arches, 12-unit **Apart-Hotel Alcázar** (tel. 571-2321) has a pool. **Condos Dominicanos Apart-Hotel** (tel. 571-2504) offers 12 studios, four one-bedrooms, and four two-bedrooms. It also has a pool and is not far from the beach. Located near the beach and eating and drinking spots, modern-style **Las Palmas Apart-Hotel** (tel. 571-2545) has two-bedroom apartments, a boutique, and a kiosk. The 78-rm. **Los Almendros Beach Resort** (tel. 562-7461/3921/4171) is a fully-equipped apart-hotel. At La Puntilla in El Batey, **El Neptuno** (tel. 571-2664) offers 18 luxury two-bedroom apartments overlooking the ocean. Facilities include pool, Jacuzzi, and snack bar. With one- and two-bedroom apartments, **Don Andres Apart-Hotel** (tel. 571-3103) offers pool, bar, and restaurant. At Av Martinez 1, **Villas Larimar** (tel. 571-2645) is another alternative.

OUTLYING ACCOMMODATION: On a beach just outside Sosúa, the 240-rm. **Sand Castle** (tel. 571-2420) is designed in pink Moorish style. It has three restaurants, shops, and water sports. On the town's outskirts, the 180-rm. a/c **Hotel Playa Chiquita** (tel. 571-2800) has a pool, restaurant, and conference center. All rooms have kitchenettes. At Puerto Chiquito, **Coral Beach Resort** (tel. 571-2577, Box 711, Sosúa) is a four star resort with a split-level Victorian design. Facilities include carpeted suites and cable TV. The **Sosúa Paradise Resort** (tel. 571-3438/3539) offers 28 a/c rooms with cable TV, balcony; junior suites offer a refrigerator. The 72-room **Hotel Colina Sol y Mar** (tel. 571-3250, fax 571-3540) is just minutes away from the airport. Facilities include shuttle to the beach, pool, restaurant, disco, billiards, and an 18-hole mini-golf course. With 209 rooms and all-inclusive (including booze), **Club Escapade** (tel. 571-5852/5854/5856), is in the hills. It features restaurants, pool, tennis, and a shuttle to the beach every 30 min. The six **Villas Balearas** (tel. 562-7461/3921/4171) overlook Sosúa. Set between Sosúa and Cabarete, the **LTI Sol de Plata** (tel. 571-3600, fax 571-3389) is a four-star hotel with 216 a/c rooms in six three-story bldgs. and 134 rooms and 20 suites in 28 villas. All are equipped with phone, minibar, and satellite TV. The resort has three pools, four tennis courts, nearby golf courses, and shuttlebus to Sosúa. **others:** An exclusive private development fronting 250 acres of seafront, pasture, and woods, **Sea Horse Ranch** (tel. 571-3880, fax 571-2374) includes homes, tennis courts, and a riding center.

EL BATEY DINING AND FOOD: There are a large number of gourmet and aspiring gourmet restaurants here; most are in the vicinity of C. Pedro Clisante. The best thing to do is to stroll along, look at menus and specials, and take your pick. The **Auberge/Village Inn's restaurant** is on C. Dr. Rosen; it's a good breakfast spot. At C. Pedro Clisante No. 13, **Don Juan's Restaurant** offers good food and tries to please. **Restaurante Amigos**, Pedro Clisante 7, offers international and seafood dishes. **Pollo Rico**, Pedro Clisante, serves Dominican food. Compact **Café Mama Juana** is open from breakfast on. At the town entrance, **Café Sosúa** offers snacks and light food. **PJ's International**, Pedro Clisante 5, serves US-style food including soups and salads. Featuring reggae and other Caribbean music, **Casablanca Bar & Grill**, Pedro Clisante 12, is a bar-eatery. **Mauricio's** also serves seafood. Sosúa-by-the-Sea's **Sunset Place** offers buffet on Wed. nights as well as all-you-can-eat breakfast buffets. Set inside the Hotel Yaroa, **Sonya's** (tel. 571-2651) offers French food in an elegant setting; reservations required. Serving steak and seafood, **On the Waterfront** also has live entertainment. Set on the main drag, **Cyrano's Café** serves French, German, English, European, and Caribbean cuisine amidst a Mediterranean atmosphere. **Hotel Sosúa Sol** serves European gourmet cuisine in a garden setting. At No. 28 on C. Pedro Clisante, **Restaurant Spaguetti House** (tel. 571-3301) operates a wood-fired pizza oven. Farther down Pedro Clisante away from the beach and off by itself, **Restaurante Tipico Morena** offers Dominican food at very reasonable prices. A gourmet Victorian-style restaurant perched on a cliff, **La Puntilla de Piergiorgio** is the former summer home of an

American diplomat. **Caribae** (tel. 571-3138) is an organic restaurant off the main road towards the Club Escapade Hotel. **Lorenzo's** on C. Pedro Clisante serves pizza and Italian and Dominican specialties. Overlooking the beach, **Pizzeria-by-the-Sea** also serves mixed drinks. On the way to Los Charamicos on the beach, **La Hispaniola** offers evening dining by candlelight.

FOOD SHOPPING: One supermarket is on C. Dr. Rosen, another is on the main road, and a third is at the corner of C. Pedro Clisante and C. Ayuntamiento. **Aleman Panaderia** is a German bakery offering baked goods at US prices. **Supermercado El Batey**, C. Pedro Clisante, offers a good selection of items such as mosquito coils, cassava bread, and imported newspapers ($3). **Messón Liquor Store** is at Av. Pedro Clisante 14. **Super Super** on Ayuntamiento has an excellent booze selection including wines (note that rum is cheaper than Gatorade!).

LOS CHARAMICOS DINING AND FOOD: Set right next to Molinos Dominicanos, **"La Deportiva"** offers local food at reasonable prices; it's often packed with locals. Right in town, **La Peto** offers gourmet dining. **Restaurant Tortuga** serves local food at reasonable prices. Set atop a cliff on the Charamicos end, **Atlántico** offers great views and seafood. **El Oasis** serves *comida criolla*. **Molinos Dominicanos** is the area's best local-style bakery.

ENTERTAINMENT: The chief activity here is at the discos. There are two in the same building: **La Pyramide** and **Barrock**. Touts compete to get you to visit their disco. High season attracts hordes of prostitutes – both male and female. Known as "Sanky Pankies," the male versions are often basically homosexual: they just service the German women for the added income. Forced into prostituting themselves because of economics, the females send their profits back home to mother and their babies. The classier **Moby Dick** down and across the street charges cover. The **Merengue Bar**, across the street from the Moby Dick, features two pneumatic young gals playing *güiro* and laying down some mean steps in formation. A quieter place to have a drink is at the **Tree Tops International Bar** down the street which has an attractive atmosphere. **gambling:** Over in Los Charamicos, you can catch **cockfights** on Sat. Opened in 1992, the **Casino Playa Chiquita** is the only casino in the area. Every type of gambling can be found here.

SHOPPING: The most unusual shop is **Toe Rings**, C. Pedro Clisante, which offers an abundance of gems, fossils, crystals, and – you guessed it – toe rings. It's worth a visit just to window shop.

Coconuts Botique offers female casual apparel. Visit the **Viva Art Gallery** on C. Alejo Martinez in El Batey. Saddles and other leather items are available at the workshop of **Juan Francisco de los Santos** near the Gran Parada on the Sosúa road. Heading towards Sosúa, it's on the R by the fork.

INFORMATION AND TOURS: Headquartered in the Jardín Del Sol Hotel, **Paradise Safaris** (tel. 571-3090) offers unusual tours of the outback in jeeps. It is one of the few organized opportunities to see the real Dominican Republic. You will see sugarcane processing, how the Haitians live, stop at a swimming hole, and visit with *campesinos* who seldom see a vehicle let alone a foreigner. Enroute you pass legions of cheering children, cross rivers, all on rough backroad tracks which are generally used only by donkeys. Drinks, box lunch, and BBQ dinner at the hotel are included. Guides are multilingual. German-owned and friendly **Melissa Tours** (tel. 571-2567) is on C. Duarte near C. Pedro Clisante. They offer a variety of tours and have a very useful map of the town on their flier. Despite the name, **Camping Tours** (tel. 571-2810) offers little in the way of camping. Located on C. Alejo Martinez, they offer trips to Los Haitises and Cabarete's caves long with the standard stuff. **Servitur Travel** (tel. 571-3500), C. Pedro Clisante 2, runs similar trips. **Turinter** (tel. 571-2635, fax 571-2402) is in the Edificio Bommarito across from the Hotel Los Almendros.

SERVICES: Open Mon. to Fri. from 8:30-3:30, the **Banco de Reservas** is at Ayuntamiento and Pedro Clisante. A **Codetel** office is also on the main drag in Los Charamicos; there's another in Sosúa on C. Dr. Rosen at Av. Martinez. You can also try **Tricom** which offers overseas calls and internal faxes at discounted prices. With information and services ranging from messages, mail, and fax to translations, typing and photocopying, **Comet Couriers** (tel. 571-3030, fax 571-3750) is at C. Dr. Rosen #2, upstairs in Ste. 5. Offering a whole range of facilities, the German-oriented **Plaza Tropical Club** is on the town's outskirts. Rent cars from **Honda** (tel. 571-3280) in the Hotel Los Almendros. **Elba Rent-A Bicycle** can be contacted at 571-2050/2824.

SPORTS: Northern Coast Aquasports (tel. 571-1028/3883), Hotel Los Almendros, offers diving as well as snorkeling, kayaking, water skiing, and other activities. For miniature golf ($4 pp) or to work out, visit the **18 Hoyos** which combines the course with a health club ($4 for one-time use). It has a sauna and Jacuzzi.

FROM SOSÚA: Taxis depart from the North Shore office, Av. Martinez, in El Batey. *Caribe Tours* (tel. 571-3808) is located at the entrance to Charamicos. They run a number of buses (around $5) to Santo Domingo via Puerto Plata. To leave town, go out on the main road and ignore the persistent and obnoxious taxi drivers. Be sure you stand on the correct side of the road for the direction you're heading; Río San Juan-bound transport departs on the opposite side.

Vicinity of Sosúa

Although, along with Puerto Plata, Sosúa is the chief tourist draw for the N Coast, there are a number of other attractions worth a day trip or even an extended stay.

Cabarete

Set around 15 mi. (23 km) E of Sosúa and some 15 min. by taxi from the airport, this unpretentious village, running along a two km curving bay, has been dubbed the windsurfing capital of the world. Once offering only bare-bones accommodation, it is swiftly evolving into a resort town. Originally popular with Quebecquois, it now attracts lots of Germans; many women sunbathe topless here. Besides the beach, another attraction is the lagoon where you can rent a rowboat and birdwatch. Along the main road (which doubles as the main street), you can still see authentic slices of Dominican life – from clucking chickens to the man on his donkey transporting clanking metal milk cans tied to the sides. You might see children eating in front of the evangelical church or dogs frolicking in the dust.

GETTING THERE: Take a *público* from Puerto Plata or Sosúa. Determine the correct fare in advance and have change available. This *is* a tourist area! Charters are also available, but be sure to bargain.

ACCOMMODATION: Hostal Maria Bonita has a pool and offers rooms from around $25. The 28-rm. Swiss-run **Cabarete Beach Hotel** (tel. 751-0755/0832, fax 571-0831) features rooms with a/c or fan, two restaurants, a disco, and a gift shop. In Switzerland write Maria Bieri, Schoren 9, 3653 Oberhofen; call 43-3040, or fax 43-5064. Rooms start from $37 off-season and rise to $87 for the best room in season. Offering 24 fully equipped studios, one- and two-bedroom apartments, **Los Orquídias de Cabarete** (tel. 571-0787, fax 571-0853) has a restaurant and a pool; it's near the beach. A few km. before the town, 132-rm., 100-acre **Punta Goleta Beach Resort** (tel. 571-0700, 581-4222, Box 272, Puerto Plata) caters to package tours. Its features include a pool, two tennis courts, two Jacuzzis, sauna, gym, jogging track, bicycle rental, and horseback riding. The 20-unit luxury **Nanny Estate** (tel. 571-0744, fax 571-0655) features a pool, Jacuzzi, two-story, two-bedroom beach house condos, and a restaurant. **Camino del Sol** (tel. 571-2858) faces the beach and has Jacuzzis and a tennis court. The **Cita del Sol** (tel. 751-0720, fax 571-0795) has 48 one-bedroom units and is in the town's center. Features include kitchenette, pool, and restaurant/bar. With "jungle" gardens surrounding its 30 *bohio*-style bungalows, the **Hotel Ka-O-Ba** has a pool, restaurant, and bar. The 48-unit **Casa Laguna Hotel & Resort** (tel. 571-0725) also offers a pool, bar, and restaurant. With 42 one- and two-bedroom units, **Villas del Atlántico** (tel. 571-0730, fax 571-0740) offers a restaurant, BBQ, bar, pool, and Jacuzzi. Rooms at the intimate **Ocean Breeze Inn** (tel. 282-40260) include a poolside breakfast. At Bahía de Arena, the 21-rm. luxury **Hotel Condos Albatros** (tel. 571-0841, fax 571-0704) offers a pool, restaurant, babysitters, and other facilities. Set a few minutes from town by a complimentary shuttle, the 36-rm. **Hotel Bella Vista** (tel. 571-0759) features cafeteria, pool, and watersports. Also outside of town the 56-unit luxury **Coconut Palms** (tel. 571-1625, fax 571-1725) features one- and two-bedrooms with kitchens, bar, restaurants, tennis, and a pool. A beachside European-style condo hotel, luxury **Terrasas Las Palmas** (tel. 571-0780, fax 571-0781) has 78 rooms. The **Banana Boat Hotel** (tel. 771-0690) is another option. At Vista del Caribe, 24-studio **Condos Val Maré** (tel. 571-3904, fax 571-3346) is 15 min. from the airport. The remote and secluded luxury **Royal Larimar Beach Resort** (tel./fax 571-0940) offers 72 deluxe a/c rooms with color TV, phones, and balconies. On the premises are three restaurants, two bars, a pool, disco, game room, and fitness center. The luxury **Tropic Breeze Apartments** (tel. 571-0748, fax 571-3346) offer one- and two-person studios with large balconies and a three-bedroom house (available by the week or month). Right on the beach, the **Cabarete Beach Studio Apartments** (tel. 571-0772, fax 571-3346) has rooms with kitchenettes; an attached restaurant serves German food. Rates are around $30. The 16-unit **Cabarete Palm Beach Condos** (tel. 571-0758, fax 571-0752) has two-bedroom apartments with kitchens and large patios. Rates are about $160 for one to four occupants during the high season. Write c/o Comet Couriers, Box 679, Puerto Plata. Other hotels include the 30-rm. **Hotel Auberge du Roi** (tel. 571-0770), **Elsy's**

Apartamentos (tel. 571-0717), **Gigi Beach Hotel** (tel. 571-0722), **Hotel El Magnifico** (tel. 571-0686, C. del Cemeterio), **Hotel El Toro** (tel. 571-0878, C. Deportivos), **Hotel Playa De Oro** (tel. 571-0880), **Windsurf Apartment Hotel** (tel. 571-0710), and **Villa Tranquila** (tel. 571-0751). Finally, the **Costa Verde Beach Resort**, on the road between Cabarete and Río San Juan, will open in 1994 or 1995.

FOOD: Set right on the beach, **La Louisiane** serves delicious Cajun food and other dishes. **Leandro's** is the only Dominican-owned restaurant. **L'Italiano** serves authentic Italian cuisine including pizza baked in a brick oven; a buffet is served all day Fri. Steak-house and creperie **El Pirata** is in Plaza Don Pepe on the main road. **Le Jasmin** (tel. 571-0725) is set in the Casa Laguna Hotel; it offers nightly buffets including lobster on Wed. For pizza try **La Pizzeria de Cabarete**, which also features a happy hour, or **Island Pizzería Restaurant**, with seafood and other dishes. Los Orquídias de Cabarete has **Le Café Flore** (tel. 571-0787). In Villas del Atlantico, **El Taino** offers everything from pancakes stuffed with shrimp to mero filet and other delicacies. Set in the Coconut Palms Resort, **The Palm Room** offers cuisine ranging from Creole to Cajun to continental. Offering free transport to and from Cabarete, the **Chez Cabarete** (tel. 571-0744) specializes in fondues. Other restaurants include **El Toco** inside Casa Laguna, **El Patio**, **Lucy Mar**, **Cita del Sol**, and **La Casa Del Pescador**. The two **supermarkets** are La Casa Rosada and Albertico.

ENTERTAINMENT: The town is pretty dead at night. The liveli-est spot is **Las Brisas**. A **jazz festival** is held in Dec.

INFORMATION: Check out the current copy of *Cabarete Winds* for info on what's going on where. **services: Cabarete Sail & Board Repair** will fix your board. All of the places listed under "Windsur-fing" below also offer courses, rent boards, and rent boogie boards. **Massage** therapist Isabelle Prince is at Los Orquídias de Cabarete (tel. 571-0787). **Motorbike and auto rentals** are offered by Mauri (tel. 571-0660), El Gitano (tel. 571-0951), and Pivi (tel. 571-0653). Cars can be rented at Puerto Plata airport. Call Thrifty (tel. 586-0242), Avis (tel. 586-0214), National (tel. 586-0285), or Nelly (tel. 586-0505). For a **taxi** call 571-0767. **Banks** are in Sosúa. A money-changer operates in town.

WINDSURFING: Although there are few waves in summer, con-stant trade winds blow. In winter, some days may be windless, but on the days the wind does blow, the waves are humongous. The Cabarete Highwind Classic is held in May. Expect to spend a hefty

$40 pd or $165 pw to rent a board. **Happy Surf & Ski Tours** (tel./fax 571-0784) is one option. Managed by Udo Jansen, **Spin-Out Cabarete** (tel. 571-0805) is a high tech windsurfing center. The **Carib BIC Windsurfing Center** (tel. 586-9519, 571-0640, fax 586-9529, 571-0649) is on the beach. Write EPS C-114 2898 NW, 79 Av., Miami, FL 33122. In the US call (800) 635-1155/243-9675. The **MB Funboard Center** (tel./fax 571-0957) is affiliated with the Hotel Auberge du Roi. **Happy Surf** (tel./fax 571-0784) also offers lessons as well as sales and rentals.

BIKING: The *norteamericano* **Iguana Mama** (tel. 57-0640/0649, fax 571-0649) offers mountain bike tours and rentals; the office is at the Carib BIC windsurfing center.

SHOPPING: Containing 31 businesses, **Plaza Commercial Laguna D'Don Pepe** is the largest shopping complex. On the main road, **Librería Daniela** (tel. 571-0775) sells books.

TOURS: The **Islabon Boat Tour** (tel. 571-0624) charges from $8 pp. Tours go from the river to the ocean. **Dive, Dive, Dive** (tel. 224-3534) offer a variety of dives. For horseback riding, contact the **Rancho Sol y Mar** (tel. 571-3346, fax 571-3346) or the **Hacienda Alto Grande** (fax 571-3346). Set 1.3 km from the main road to Río San Juan, the **Cabarete Adventure Park and Caves** offers complete tours for around $15 pp.

GOLF: Try the **Costa Azul Golf and Beach Resort** which features nine holes amidst 45 acres of greenery.

Río San Juan

Located in the heart of the dairy industry, this small, ordinary town borders the **Gri-Grí Lagoon**, and a popular tourist excursion here is an hour in the lagoon cruising past mangroves, *grí grí* trees, flocks of seabirds, and bizarrely shaped rocks. The tour's highlight is a visit to the Cueva de las Golondrinas, a cave containing swallows. Located beyond the river's mouth and several miles along the rocky coast, it was created by an 1846 rockslide. Tidal conditions have to be right for you to enter. If chartering your own boat, expect to spend around $24 per boatload; each boat can hold 20. Reservations are unnecessary. **nearby beaches:** Caleton and Playa Grande are also nearby. Playa la Preciosa lies at the headland of Parque Nacional Cabo Francés Viejo, as does Playa El Breton; Playa

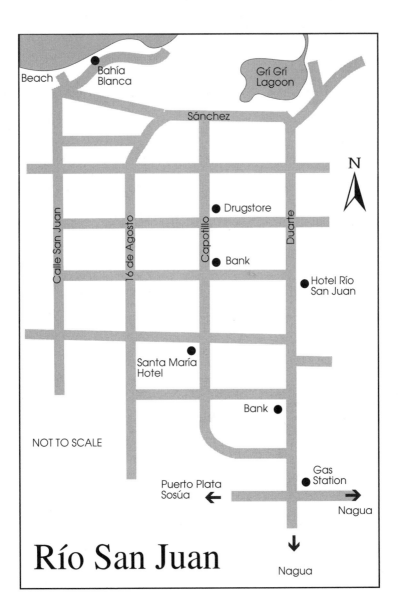

Beach

Bahía Blanca

Grí Grí Lagoon

N

Sánchez

Calle San Juan

16 de Agosto

Capotillo

Duarte

Drugstore

Bank

Hotel Río San Juan

Santa María Hotel

Bank

NOT TO SCALE

Gas Station

Puerto Plata Sosúa ←

Nagua →

Nagua ↓

Nagua

Río San Juan

Diamante and Playa Boba are farther on. La Entrada is another unspoiled beach in the area. Another attraction is la Virgen de la Cueva, a rock formation in a cave just off the road which is said to resemble the Virgin Mary.

PRACTICALITIES: On the main street, family run 38-rm. **Río San Juan Hotel** (tel. 589-2379/2211) resembles a country inn; it has a restaurant, bar, lounge, tennis court, pool, nightclub, and disco. They can also arrange the boat trip. In Santo Domingo call 567-3325. Set right on a bluff overlooking the sea, the **Bahía Blanca** (tel. 589-2562/2563, fax 589-2528), Gaston F. Deligne, is another alternative. The ambitious project of Quebec-born Lise Peineau, it has attractively-furnished rooms. Its restaurant has both good food and ambience. Also try the less expensive **San José** and **Santa Clara** hotels. Less expensive still are the **San Martín** and the **Caridad**. There are a few restaurants along the street that has the Río San Juan Hotel. The otherwise attractive **Cheo's Café Bar** should be boycotted because it serves sea turtles on the menu.

Playa Grande

Set 60 km W of Puerto Plata and an hour's drive from the airport, this new resort is being developed in conjunction with Playa Dorada. Scheduled facilities at this mile-long beach – some of which are still under development – include mammoth luxury villa hotels, apartment hotels, tennis courts, horseback riding stables, and an 18-hole, $3.2 million dollar golf course. Hotels here will include the **Playa Grande Beach Resort** and the **Punta Preciosa Beach Resort**; each will have 300 rooms and may have been completed by the time of your arrival. Scheduled to open in 1995, the **Caribbean Village Playa Grande** will have 300 rooms; another 540 rooms will be added on later. Also scheduled for 1995 is a new $3.2 million 18-hole golf course designed by Robert Trent Jones. It will be the only course in the world with 10 tees overlooking the sea. Nearby are the lighthouse at Cabo Frances Viejo and the cliffs and bay of Cabo Breton, an area which contains vacation homes of the elite, some of which are for rent. Set 5 km to the E of Playa Grande, **Club Paradise** (Box 750, Land O'Lakes, FL 34639) is a naturist (nudist) resort on 120 acres and includes 190 rooms and cottages, four tennis courts, pool, fitness center, snorkeling, and diving. In the US, call (800) 237-2226, (813) 949-9327, or fax (813) 949-1008.

Nagua

This beach-lined fishing village stands on the shores of the Bahia Escocesa. Get here before it's developed! It takes three buses and some 3.5 hrs. to get here from Puerto Plata or 3.5 hrs. from Santo Domingo. If changing buses here, the two terminals are in different locations so you may need to take a *motoconcho*; ask your driver. Stay at low budget **Hotel San Carlos** ($7 with bath, fan and power plant) **Hotel Familiar** ($8, may not have electricity) or **Hotel Corazón de Jesús**. In Cabrera, you can stay at the **Hostal Catalina**, the **Hotel Julissa** (tel. 589-6355), or the **Hotel Naranjo**. **Hotel Condo La Palmeral** (tel. 437-8389) is also here. Outside of town on the way to Río San Juan are **Las Brisas** and **Casa Blanca**. At C. Duarte 81-A, friendly and unpretentious **La Escocesa** offers seafood, delicious fruit juices, and other local specialties.

Samaná Peninsula

This beautiful 30-mile (48-km) peninsula, 120 km NE of Santo
Domingo, is characterized by heavy rainfall and by a range of lush,
forested hills as well as coconut and banana plantations. Houses of
locals are painted in pink and purple pastel washes, and fishermen
in the bay cast for snapper from flat-bottomed boats. There are a
wealth of activities for the adventurous here: you can snorkel at
Cayo de Lavantado in Samaná Bay, at Rincón Bay, and at other
locations.

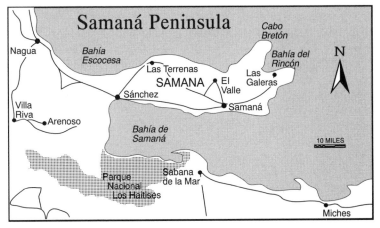

FAUNA: Along the coast, you can expect to see wood storks,
brown boobies, and white-tailed tropicbirds. Plovers, rails, sandpi-
pers, roseate spoonbills, terns, purple gallinules, and ibises are
found in the marshy areas near beaches. **whale watching:** Whales
may be seen along the mouth of the Samaná Bay during Jan. to late
Feb. If you obtain advance permission from the Samaná Naval
Station, you can negotiate whale-watching trips with the boatmen
in Samaná town harbor. A humpback whale sanctuary, Sanctuario
de Ballenas Jorobadas del Banco de la Plata, lies 50 mi. (80 km) from
the coast, due N of Cabrera. This "Silver Bank," a 100-ft.-deep
lagoon, attracts some 2,000 to 3,000 migrating humpbacks from late
Dec. to early March. Giving birth to their offspring here, the young
are nurtured before taking off together for points unknown. Sea
turtles also congregate here. Scientists may make trips out here
during the mating season. For information on joining the expedi-
tions – which take 7-12 hrs. each way – contact the National Parks

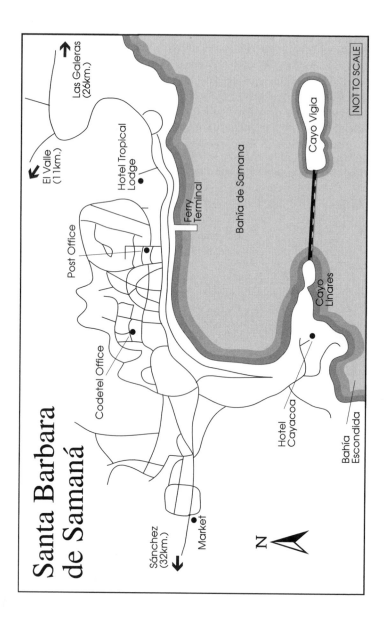

Santa Barbara de Samaná

El Valle
(11km.)

Las Galeras
(26km.)

Hotel Tropical
Lodge

Post Office

Ferry
Terminal

Codetel Office

Bahía de Samana

Cayo Vigia

Cayo
Linares

Hotel
Cayacoa

Bahía
Escondida

Sánchez
(32km.)

Market

N

NOT TO SCALE

Office in Santo Domingo (tel. 682-7628), the Centro de Investigaciones de Biología Marina (CIBINA) at the University of Santo Domingo (tel. 668-8633), or the Fundación Dominicana Pro-Investigación y Conservación de los Recursos Marinos, Inc. (MAMMA) at Av. Anacoana No. 77, Apdo. C-4 or at Apdo. 21449 in Santo Domingo. MAMMA can assist in planning trips from Puerto Plata and Samaná.

GETTING THERE: It's a 4.5-hr. trip from Santo Domingo to Samaná via San Francisco de Macorís, Nagua, and Sánchez. Take a return bus from Caribe Tours or take a bus or *público* to San Pedro de Macorís and then another to Sabana La Mar (stay at low-budget Hotel Sabana la Mar), and then cross by one of three often crowded boats per day (7, 10, and 3) from Sabana to Samaná. You should note that black marketeers have been known to buy up tickets on this route and motorcyclists have been ripped off by boatmen who load the bike from the ferry. A 25-min. flight from Santo Domingo, brings you to out-of-the-way Arroyo Barril airport. The bay is also popular with cruise ships.

GETTING AROUND: The entire peninsula can be explored by boat but the local boatmen charge an arm, a leg, and a rudder. Not all the roads are paved. In the peninsula's NE, Rincón Bay can be reached by road from Samaná town as can Limón village in the peninsula's center. Las Terrenas and Portillo beaches can be reached by paved road from Sánchez or by a much worse road from Limón.

Santa Bárbara de Samaná

Birthplace of Balaguer, Samaná's main town is a popular honeymoon spot for rich Dominicans. Overlooking a bay speckled with tiny islands, the town is located on the peninsula's S side. Big things were planned here, but they never developed. Once-beautiful narrow streets overhung by wrought-iron balconies were destroyed under Balaguer's first 12 years and replaced with ugly concrete buildings and broad asphalt boulevards. Used primarily by pedestrians and horses, a four-lane highway borders the waterfront; it's the closest thing to a main street that the town has. The planned airport was never built, and the railroad, which once ran across the peninsula to Sánchez, has been shut down. A high bridge runs from a point near the town to an offshore island, where a restaurant was planned but never constructed. Still remaining is the small evangelist "*churcha*." It dates back to 1823 when it was inaugurated by an English Methodist missionary with the wonderful name of Narcissus Miller; today it serves as the Dominican Evangelical Church. All in all, there's little reason to visit the town except to use it as a base for visiting the peninsula's beaches by car.

HISTORY: On Jan. 12, 1493 Columbus arrived here but was repulsed by the Ciguayos; he named it the Golfo de las Flechas (the Gulf of Arrows). The remains of his fort still stand here. The town was founded in 1756 by Gov. Francisco Rubio Peñaranda and populated by families brought from the Canary Islands in order to stave off conquest by French buccaneers from Tortuga, an island off Haiti's N coast. After Haitian independence, fleeing French planters arrived with their slaves. English-speaking blacks are a prominent if suprising feature of the town. There are conflicting stories as to how they got there. One maintains that Samaná was founded during the 1824 Haitian occupation when the *Turtle Dove*, a sloop carrying escaped American slaves wrecked in Samaná Bay. Swimming ashore, they founded a settlement. Another maintains that Haiti's leader at the time, Jean Pierre Boyer, made contact with abolitionist groups in Philadelphia and financed passage and resettlement of as many as they could send down. Of the 6,000 sent, some died, while others were unable to adapt. Some 2,000 chose to remain. Under Trujillo, anyone heard speaking English publicly was beaten, and today all are bilingual. In any case, the language and culture of America's Old South are still very much intact here, and Browns, Joneses, Kings, Smiths, and Greens abound. They still have a rich cultural tradition – including tales of werewolves and vampires – although this is fading. In the 1870s, the town and the entire peninsula narrowly escaped annexation by the US.

THINGS TO DO: Samaná has a dramatic backdrop, but the town isn't what you would call wildly exciting. Given the extensive urban renewal, it lacks atmosphere, and persistent touts can make life unpleasant. The most interesting thing to do is to walk out along the **bridge to nowhere**. There are actually a chain of three connecting small islands. As you can see, it would've been quite a walk to dinner if the restaurant had actually been constructed. The structure might be considered Zen statement on the futility of life or a comment on the insanity of unplanned development. In any case, there is definitely nothing like it anywhere else in the world. Allow an hour for the walk both ways. Also in the vicinity, but farther away from town at the bottom of the hill, is a small beach at Puerto Escondido. If you have your own wheels (or rent a scooter or bike) the town can be used as a base. A **waterfall** is on the Río Coco, about a 15 min. walk from Km 7. Be sure to keep walking past the brook: it's not the waterfall! Finally, you can also visit Cayo Levantado (see below).

ACCOMMODATIONS: One unfortunate aspect of town are the hordes of otherwise unemployed English-speaking young gentlemen who wish to show you a hotel and to collect a commission. The best way to defeat them is to feign deafness and ignore them. Formerly named the Bahía Beach Resort and now run by Occidental Hotels, the 66-rm. **Cayacoa** (tel. 538-3131/3139, fax 538-2985) is dramatically set on a hill overlooking the bay; it was remodeled in 1992. Newly opened in 1992, the **Hotel Gran Bahía** (tel. 538-3111, fax 562-5232; Apdo. 2024, Santo Domingo) is a large British-owned luxury resort set some 8 km E of town. It has a small beach, and shuttle service is provided to Cayo Levantado. In Santo Domingo call 562-6271, fax 562-5232. In the US call (800) 221-4542, and in Germany call (06196) 48 38 18 or fax (06196) 48 38 16. Dominicans are offered special low rates. Right in town, **Tropical-Lodge Hotel** (tel. 538-2480) overlooks the bay and is right on the Malecón. Out on Cayo Levantado, Occidental Hotels has remodeled **Cayo Levantado Resort**. (There have been reports that both of the two Occidental Hotels here are less than superbly run). **inexpensive:** On the way out of town and across from Captain Morgan's, family-run **King's** (tel. 538-2352) offers rooms with fan and bath from $10. At Santa Bárbara and Colón, the inexpensive and hospitable **Nilka** (tel. 583-2245) has 10 rooms. Only the ones upstairs have a/c. There are also a number of others including **Hotel Kiko** (tel. 588-2565), C. La Logia 4; **Hotel Docia**, C. Santa Barbara; or the more expensive (around $20) **Hotel Ecu de France** (tel. 538-2579) and the **Hotel Tropical Lodge** (tel. 538-2480, fax 538-2046), which charges about $35. Owned by a teacher, the **Casa de Huéspedes Tete de Casado**, C. Duarte 4, is good value if you bargain. **low budget:** There's really nothing basic here except the **Fortuna**, which is next to King's.

FOOD: Typical dishes here include *pescado con coco* (fish cooked in coconut milk), gingerbread, and Johnnycakes. Heading E along the Malecón, you come to **Tipico El Coco** and **La Hacienda**. Next, **Le Café de Paris** offers crepes, pizza, and cocktails. Set on the corner of Parque Central, **La Mata Rosada** and **Camilo** have local food. **Quioli**, **Le Belge**, and **Salt and Pepper** are between the Malecón and the market. Reasonably priced **Captain Morgan's** is across from King's Hotel on the way out of town. It sports American-style food and a menagerie of knicknacks. The Captain himself frequently turns up in his jeep and plays backgammon with his friends.

ENTERTAINMENT AND BARS: Yachtie types hang at **L'Hacienda**. **El Cielo**, **El Coco**, and the **Naomi Nightclub** are the two discos. The latter is on the waterfront.

SERVICES: For information, try the **Samaná Information Service** (531-2541/2740), on Av. la Marina; it's closed out of season. The **Banco Hispano Dominicano** is on the Malecón. A gas station is along the dock. A **post office** is behind the Camilo just off of the Parque Central. Open from 8 AM to 10 PM daily, **Codetel** is at C. Santa Bárbara 6. Rent cars from **Xamana Rent A Motor** (tel. 538-2556/2066), Av. Malecón 3 and 5.

FESTIVALS: The *bambúla* and the mildly erotic *chivo florete*, traditional dances, may be seen at the local festivals such as the *fiestas patronales* of Santa Bárbara held on Dec. 4 and the one for St. Raphael on Oct. 24. The *oli oli* is a men's dance which is seen in *carnavál* parades.

FROM SAMANÁ: *Caribe Tours* departs from its offices on the Malecón for Santo Domingo three times daily. A direct road between Samaná and Las Terrenas is under construction and scheduled for completion in 1994 or 1995; the current one is poor. Roads also lead to Las Galeras on the coast (see below). A ferry runs to and from Sabana La Mar.

Vicinity of Santa Bárbara de Samaná

Cayo Levantado

This is the most popular of the offshore islands and has a white sand beach. **practicalities:** The cheapest way to arrive is by public boat from the Samaná dock. The other alternative is to take a *público* from town to the point where Transportes José and Simi Báez (also fishing, whale spotting) run boats to the island. They'll also pick you up later. Bring your own food and drink. Planned excursions cost $40 pd and up. Lunch is served by vendors, but is not especially cheap. The island is suffering under the impact of pollution. It is often overcrowded with visitors. Watch out if purchasing jewelry here; peddlars are notorious for selling fakes. Hotel accommodation is at the luxurious **Cayo Levantado Beach Hotel** (tel. 221-2131, fax 532-5306).

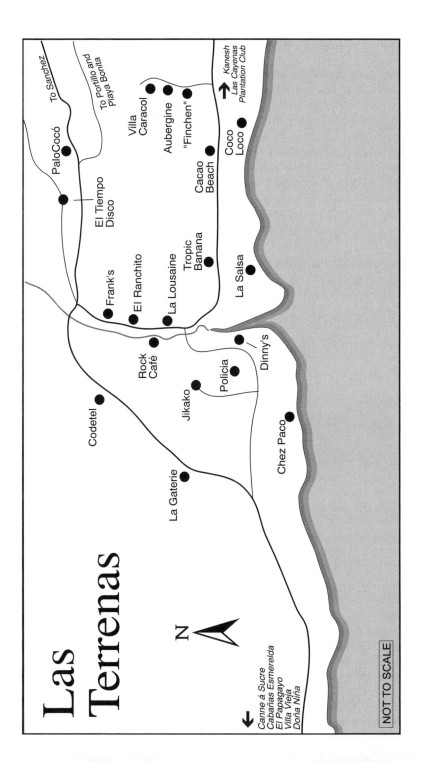

Sánchez

Once a prosperous seaport, this little town has 19th C architecture and basic accommodation. It once had the nation's only railroad which ran from San Francisco de Macorís and La Vega. This is the first town visitors will come to upon entering the peninsula. If you should need or wish to stay here, try **Hotel Restaurant La Costa** (tel. 552-7275), C. Libertad 44 (doors lock at 10!), or the less expensive **Hotel La Gran Parada**. Another alternative is to take a room in the aging yellow Victorian house. Eat at **Restaurant Las Malvinas** or other bistros.

Playa Las Galeras

Set at the E end of the peninsula some 26 km from Samaná town, this half-mile beach is in a lovely setting. There's no electricity or telephone here. Only two two restaurants are in town, along with two hotels , the French-owned **Marea Beach** and the **Villa Serena** (tel. 223-8703, fax 538-2545; Apdo. 51-1, Samaná). The latter has 11 a/c and fan rooms with private terraces. More are planned, and this could become a major tourist center in the future.

Playa Rincón

This deserted beach is 20 min. away from Galeras by boat or 40 min. by jeep along a rough track. Cliffs of the 2,000-ft.-high (600 m) Cape Cabrón flank its rear.

Limón

This town on the river of the same name has a wonderful 165 ft. waterfall. To get a guide for the falls and to rent horses, inquire at the navy guard post in Limón. The trip takes an hour along a steep one-mile trail. You'll have to wade two rivers; the water comes up to your knees. Needless to say, it's not an easy trip, and it's not advisable to bring children.

Las Terrenas

This long stretch of the N coast offers some of the nation's finest beaches. At low tide you can walk right out to the coral reefs. Although it lacks Sosúa's glamour, it also has less noise and hassle.

The area is becoming more and more developed, but it still has the informality of a small village and remains highly recommended as a place to go and relax. Secluded Playa Bonita is situated around the headland to the W, and Portillo lies to the E. Humpbacked whales can sometimes be spotted off of the coast in season. **getting there:** A number of *carreras* run from Sánchez. Expect to wait a long time for the back of the pickup truck to fill up. The 11 mi (17 km) paved road from Sánchez offers fantastic views – passing rolling hills covered with palms and marvelous overlooks – as you rise and then descend. A new direct road to Samaná is under construction. **by car:** It would be difficult to find a better use for a rental car than take it on this road. Although there are no gas stations after Sánchez until Las Terrenas, some homes sell it in gallon jugs.

ORIENTATION: The layout is pretty simple. A main road stretches all the way from Sánchez to Limón via Portillo. As you enter Las Terrenas, a side road leads off L to Punta Bonita, several km away. Pickup trucks terminate at the end of the village; the road straight ahead continues to Portillo. A branched loop road heads off to the L; the bulk of the guesthouses are down here along the beach and on the way. A few others are towards Portillo. As you head towards Portillo, the beach becomes more and more beautiful and less frequented.

GETTING AROUND: You can generally get everywhere on foot, and there are no safety problems at present. **Motoconchos** charge five *pesos* (40¢) during the day and ten *pesos* (80¢) at night. Locals are charged only three pesos so pestering foreigners is an obsession. These guys work so hard and so late because they've bought the bikes on credit and have to make payments or face repossession.

ACCOMMODATION ON THE MAIN ROAD: Attractive **Palococo** (tel. 240-6068, fax 240-6151) charges from around $40 d. It has a pool and Jacuzzi. Dinners at its international restaurant are around $12. **Mami** (tel. 240-6074) on the main road, also has rooms for under $5; it can be noisy. **Dinnys** has plain but breezy rooms near the sea for around $9.

BEACHSIDE ACCOMMODATION: A number of small hotels/guest houses including **Espinal**, **La Selva**, **Habitaciones**, and **Louisiane** are off the loop road and near the beach. Most guesthouses and hotels have backup generators; public electrical power is a recent development here. On the road to the beach, **Supercolmado Frank** has rooms for around $12. **Hotel Tropic Banana** (tel.

240-6110, fax 240-6112; Apdo. 25, Sánchez, Samaná) has a pool and attractive rooms from around $30 on up. In Montreal, Canada, call (819) 546-7010 or fax (819) 564-8191. With 190 rooms, **Cacao Beach** (tel. 240-6000) is the largest hotel and seems larger than the village. Call 565-2097 in Santo Domingo for information. Off the main road past Cacao Beach near Coco Loco, attractively designed **L'Aubergine** (tel. 240-6167, fax 240-6070) charges around $16 off season and $28 during the season. Kursten and Josefina Kramer have three rooms above their **Finchen Restaurant** (tel. 240-6116, fax 240-0670). While the rooms are low priced and very attractive, they're best suited to nightowls because the restaurant stays open late. Farther up the same road, **Hotel Villa Caracol** has rooms without bath starting at about $9. Its best suites are around $36. In Germany, contact DER Resie-Center Lippstatdt GmbH, Markstrasse 3, 4780 Lippstradt; call (02941) 3185 u. 51 18; or fax (02941) 59685. Another good place to stay is the seaside **Kanesh Beach** (tel. 240-6187, fax 240-6070). Rates start from $25 for rooms with overhead ceiling fans. **Coralitos**, which has villas for rent, is next. Atmospheric **Las Cayenas Hotel** (fax 240-6070), which resembles an old Caribbean great house, is the brainchild of Marie-Antoinette Piguet, a French-woman who visited here on vacation. It's powered by solar panels. Rates (which include breakfast and taxes) are $45 s and $60 d. Farther down this same road on the way to Punta Bonita, the very expensive **Plantation Club** (tel. 240-6008, fax 240-6009) is the product of financing by Domincan fat cats from La Romana. **to the W:** There are three hotels at Punta Bonita, the German-run 19-rm. **Atlantis** (tel. 240-6111, fax 240-6101), the **Acaya** (tel. 240-6161, fax 240-6166) and the **Punta Bonita** (tel. 240-6082). For information and reservations at the 10-unit **Apartamentos El Atlantico**, contact Hotel Palacio (tel. 682-4730, fax 800-687-5535). They rent for $35 pn and sleep up to four.

ACCOMMODATION ON THE PORTILLO ROAD: Opposite El 28 on the road towards Portillo and run by a very hospitable and outgoing Swiss couple, **Los Piños** offers very attractive bungalows ($36) and room ($20) rentals. Designed for Europeans who are used to youth hostel accommodation, their very clean but compact dorm rooms rent for $6 s and $9 d (two in one larger bed). Breakfasts are served on the attractive patio. Contact Marlene and Hans Fretz (tel. 240-6168, fax 240-6070). **Cabañas Esmeralda** is some 150 ft. from the road. Modest rooms with shower and mosquito net cost $20/d. Bargain during the slow season or if you're staying for a few nights. Owned by a Venezuelan, **El Papagayo** (tel. 240-6095) is right on the road to Portillo as well; it has a very pleasant atmosphere. Rooms start from around $20-$25. It has a restaurant and snack bar.

Nearby, **Villa Vieja** rents a furnished two-bedroom apartment with kitchen for about $25/night. Popular with Peace Corps volunteers, the lowest priced place is run by **Doña Niña** off the road to Portillo; ask around for directions. An old Dominican lady, she almost seems to have stepped straight out of a historical photo. Her place also seems to be a historical relic as well. She charges $2 for a full breakfast and $4 for a room. Doña charges standard rates for soft drinks as opposed to the extortionate D$10 (80¢) charged by most restaurants. Her favorite but rather suspect phrase is *"mi es pobre."* Whatever money she garners does not go back into maintenance, and stories are told about her wealth. There's an outdoor shower, and a manually flushed toilet. Be certain not to kill any tadpoles while flushing, or you might find yourself reincarnated as a frog. A large condo project (Villas las Flores) is planned for this stretch of road; it may or may have not materialized by the time of your arrival.

EL PORTILLO ACCOMMODATION: Head straight from Las Terrenas and follow a potholed road for four km to find the simple but attractive **El Portillo Beach Resort** (tel. 240-6100, fax 240-6104) which has 171 rooms and cabañas, pool, two tennis courts, scuba clinics, volleyball, and horseback riding. It's popular with European package tourists and has its own airstrip. It's a 30-min flight. Make arrangements with Prieto Tours (tel. 685-0102, 688-5715) in Santo Domingo. El Limón is 10 km farther.

FOOD: If cooking for yourself, there's a small market and other vendors along the main road. Possibly the best bread in the nation if not the entire Caribbean is baked at **Panaderia Francesa** in front of Disco El Tiempo. The Dominican baker learned his chops from his French brother-in-law when he came for a visit. Some of the nation's finest seafood dining is in this vicinity. **Posada Chez Paco** is a good restaurant for seafood and French cuisine. French-owned **La Salsa** is a thatched roof beach restaurant. **main road food and dining:** High priced **La Gateria** offers deli type food and take out items. **Cafeteria des Artes** is an attractive French-run place offering local food and atmosphere. **El Capitan** (tel. 552-7593) is a bar and restaurant near Sánchez. **Portillo road dining:** Excellent places to eat breakfast are at **Los Piños** and at (lower budget) **Doña Nina's**. **El 28** is a small Spanish restaurant on the beach near the beginning of the El Portillo road; it has fish and paella. **Comedor La Escala** is on the road towards Portillo. **La Canne á Sucre** serves pasta, salad, and crepes at inexpensive prices (starting at $1.75 for crepes). **Casablanca** is an attractive bar which has a restaurant in season. **enroute to and near the beach:** La Chicha serves inexpensive creole food. **Rincón de Fleur** is on the water. Near La Louisiane, **La Orquidea** serves moderately-priced French food. **La Tita** is another Italian restaurant. Specializing in Basque and French food, **Restaurante Jikako** is off the road to the beach. Near the beach, **Dinny's** is a reasonably priced restaurant. **Zuni's** has good seafood. The French-owned **Tropic Banana** features gourmet cuisine. **Finchen Restaurant** serves Dominican and German food; it's also a very popular watering hole. Down the road, you can also dine at **Kanesh** or the attractive **Las Cayenas Hotel**. Palococo's **Los Canarios** is the classiest place on the main road. There are a large number of local restaurants on this road as well as some low budget eating stalls where you can really revel in atmosphere.

ENTERTAINMENT: Out on the main road, the roar of *motoconchos* conflicts with that of blaring generators. The singing in the Iglesia Biblica clashes with disco coming from the pub across the street. The night market along this road has a very African feel to it. You can eat rice and beans, fried plantains, meat dishes, and overfried fish. The best disco here is **Mambo**. **El Tiempo** has murals featuring motifs such as a melting clock and the grafitti in the men's room are something else! A third disco is **Disco Terraza Nuevo Mundo**, down the street from Codetel. **Disco Terraza Antony** has a "hotel" above it; it's more of a bar than anything else. The intimate **Rock Café** stays open until 4 AM or so and fills up after the disco closes. Prostitution is a growing industry here. Right across from El Tiempo, **Arco Iris Video** shows movies nightly for 40¢. Some 10 km towards Sánchez, **La Raquera** is hosted by an entertaining pistol-toting gentleman who resembles the Marlboro Man. At **Chichi** in the town of Sánchez itself, an old guy plays Latin classics.

SERVICES: There's no bank. You can change illegally, but you get less than you would at a bank. Hotels will only pay D$11.5 per $. A **Codetel** office (fax 240-6070; open daily 8-8) is on the main road as is **Las Terrenas Tourist Service** (tel. 240-6088, fax 240-6070). There's also a branch of the **Samaná Tourist Service** here. **Western Union** is also on the main road. Publishers of the mimeographed free publication *Las Terrenas News*, **Green Tours** is near the Tropic Banana. Car rentals ($60/day) are available near the beginning of the road to Portillo. Along the loop road, the **Ranchito** (tel. 240-6060) has horse rentals and a trip to the waterfall (advance reservations required). **Caribbean Rent-a-Motor** is on the main road.

DIVING: The growing popularity of Las Terrenas has spawned an increasing number of dive shops. **Divebold** is in front of Coco Loco. The **Stellina Dive Center** (tel. 240-6000, fax 240-6020) is a

German-operated dive operation in the Cacao Beach. German, Italian, Spanish, and English are spoken. In addition to two dive boats, they also have a glass-bottom boat. Call 01/531 18 09 or fax 01/431 02 57 in Zurich, Switzerland. Several **souvenir shops** are on the main road.

FROM LAS TERRENAS: Buses leave at around 5 and 7 AM (yawn!) to Santo Domingo and from 8 to Nagua. In the past, transportation to Limón has been scarce. You must hire a *motoconcho*. From there you can go on to Samaná. Otherwise, if you wish to head for Samaná, you must backtrack to Sánchez.

The Southeast

Sugarcane is synonymous with Eastern identity. Towns such as San Pedro de Macorís, Higüey, and La Romana host huge sugar processing plants that refine the nation's top export. But the region is not all fields of waving cane: some of the nation's top resorts are here as well. King of them all is Casa de Campo near La Romana. Although the inland portion of the SE is flat and dry, the beaches along the "Costa Caribe" here are splendid white sand stretches. And with some 9,000 beds available, there's never a shortage of accommodation!

EXPLORING: Buses run from Santo Domingo to San Pedro de Macorís, La Romana, and Higüey. Other locales such as Parque Nacional del Este and Parque Nacional Los Haitises are considerably more difficult to get to. Beaches are scattered along the Costa del Coco and the Costa Caribe. The most famous resorts are the Casa de Campo near La Romana, the hotels at Punta Cana just E of Higüey, and those at Juan Dolio and Guayacanes.

Parque Nacional Los Haitises

Located along the S shore of the Bahia de Samaná, Parque Nacional Los Haitises covers 78 sq. mi. (208 sq. km) and stretches 15 mi. W from Boca de Inferno and Bahía de San Lorenzo to the mouth of the Rio Barracote at the W end of Samaná Bay. Here, incredibly lush and verdant tropical limestone islands, up to 1,000 ft. high, appear like ships floating on the sea. Ordinarily this type of karst terrain accompanies semidesert vegetation, but rainfall of over 90 in. per year, combined with frequently overcast skies, have made them bloom, and tropical humid forest is the norm here. The most notable is Isla de Pájaros, one of many islands where birds nest. An additional attraction is a number of caves with pre-Columbian carvings and drawings.

FLORA AND FAUNA: Normally montane species such as begonias and mountain palms compete here with such lowland forest species as *copey*, *almacigo* (*gumbo limbo* or birch gum), and *balata*. Red and white mangroves line the reserve's shore. Crustaceans, mussels, and oysters residing on roots are visible at low tide. Seabirds found here include snowy egrets, roseate terns, frigate

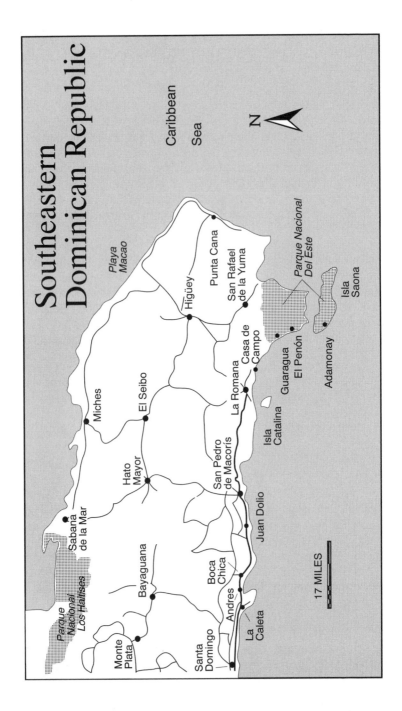

Southeastern
Dominican Republic

Caribbean

Sea

N

Playa
Macao

Punta Cana

Higüey

San Rafael
de la Yuma

Parque Nacional
Del Este

Isla
Saona

Casa de
Campo

La Romana

Guaragua

El Penón

Adamonay

Miches

El Seibo

Isla
Catalina

San Pedro
de Macorís

Hato
Mayor

Juan Dolio

Sabana
de la Mar

Bayaguana

Boca
Chica

Parque
Nacional
Los Haitises

Andres

Monte
Plata

Santa
Domingo

La
Caleta

17 MILES

least grebe, narrow billed-tody, white-cheeked pintail, and Ridgway's hawk. Farther up the river, northern jacana, the double-breasted cormorant, the great blue heron, and the coot may be found. Hutia and solenodons also reside here.

GETTING THERE: The park can only be visited by boat and by sea, a trip best undertaken in the morning. Travel agencies in Samaná offer tours, or you may charter MAMMA's deepsea fishing boat, but you must have the permission of the local Navy Office. For information about boat trips through the park contact Wolf Wirth (tel./fax 586-1201).

RESERVA CIENTÍFICA NATURAL LAGUNA REDONDA Y LAGUNA LIMÓN: These two muddy lagoons, Redonda and Limón, are found in the nation's NE some 17 and 27 km respectively from the village of Miches. The Laguna Redonda is connected to the sea by the Caño Celedonio. Limón can only be reached on foot or horse from the community of Los Guineos, 800 m to the S. The 22 species of birds found in the area include the great egret, black-crowned night heron, northern pintail, and the roseate spoonbill. **accommodation:** Swiss-run and adventure-oriented, **Hotel Punta El Rey** charges $40 pd including meals. For more information/reservations call the Hotel Palacio in Santo Domingo at 682-4730; fax 800-687-5535; or else write Apdo. 20541, Santo Domingo.

Higüey

Forty km NE of La Romana, Higüey is the capital of the province of La Altagracia. Founded in 1502 on the orders of Frey Nicolás de Ovando, the most notable features of Higüey are its churches. Using the town as a base, you might explore the palm- and sea grape-bordered beaches running along the coast from Bávaro 30 mi. to Laguna Nisibón. Watch out for the strong Atlantic currents if swimming here. **history:** The town was founded in 1494 by *conquistador* Juan de Esquivel, who later conquered Jamaica. It began to grow from 1502-1508 when Ponce de León became administrator.

SIGHTS: Most notable is the **Basilica de Nuestra Señora de la Merced** (Our Lady of Mercy). Located on the spot where Columbus's forces planted their cross while fending off an Indian attack, miracles are attributed to the soil here, which the Dominicans come to gather. According to legend, Columbus and his men, surprised by a Taino attack, were nearly done in, when lo and behold a vision of the Virgin Mary appeared on the cross, frightening the Indians and allowing the Spaniards to repel the attack. Inside the shrine are kept two splinters of wood believed to have come from that original cross; it's said Columbus cut wood for it from the **nispero** tree nearby. Replacing Nuestra Señora de la Merced (Our Lady of Mercy) as the nation's patron saint in 1922, La Altagracia (the Virgin of the Highest Grace) is credited with numerous miracle cures. In one, an aged and mysterious pilgrim (believed to have been one of the apostles) arrived in a small village in the E part of the country and begged food and shelter from a father with an ill daughter. Upon his departure, he gave a small picture of the Virgin Mary to the father. When the daughter gazed at the Virgin, she was cured instantaneously. The modern church – shaped like a pair of 200-ft.-high hands folded in prayer – was constructed on the site where the picture was first admired, and an annual pilgrimage is made here on Jan. 21 and Aug. 16. Set a little more than 5 km to the E, **La Otra Banda** is an attractive village with pastel colored houses.

PRACTICALITIES: Accommodations here include **Hotel Brisas del Este** (tel. 554-2312), Av. Mella; low budget **Hotel Ana** (tel. 554-3569), Av. Hijo 48; **Hotel Colón** (tel. 554-4283), C. Colón 46; **Hotel San Antonio** (tel. 554-2331), C. Colón 48; **Hotel Genesis** (tel. 554-2971), C. Colón 51; low budget **Hotel Presidente** (tel. 554-5990), C. Hnos. Trejos 136; low budget **Hotel San Juan Plaza** (tel. 554-3518), Altagracia 40; **Hotel Volcán** (tel. 554-3101); inexpensive **Hotel Restaurant Don Carlos** (tel. 554-2344/2713), C. Ponce de Leon; **Hotel Restaurante El Diamante** (tel. 554-2754, C. Santana 23; or more expensive (around $40) **Hotel El Naranjo** (tel. 554-2277), C. Altagracia. Eat at **Restaurant El Gran Gourmet**, C. Santana 117; **Restaurant La Fama**, Arz. Nouel 2; and **Restaurante El Español Original**, Carr. Mella at Km 1. **Codetel** is on Av. Bertillio.

Costa del Coco
(The Coconut Coast)

Stretching from Higüey up along the NE coast, this area offers over 40 km of white sand beaches edging crystal clear shallow water. Its beaches – Playa Macao, Playa Cortesito, Playa Bávaro, Punta Cana, and Punta Juanillo – have been groomed for the upscale tourist market, and there are now a number of resorts in the area.

Punta Cana

Just five min. by car from an international airport (a 30-min. flight from Santo Domingo; American Airlines also flies here in season), there are some beautiful beaches in this area. Set on 70 acres, 320-rm. all-inclusive luxurious **Club Méditerranée** (tel. 687-2767, 686-5500/5532; 567-5228/5229 in Santo Domingo) offers tennis, swimming, beach, nightly entertainment, and water sports. Charters bound here depart from the US and Canada. In the US call (800) 528-3100. Set on 100 acres, the **Punta Cana Yacht Club** (tel. 565-0011/3077, 686-0084) has villas and one-bedroom apartments as well as a golf course, four tennis courts, disco, and boutiques. The 340-room **Punta Cana Beach Resort** (tel. 221-CANA, 541-2714 in Santo Domingo, fax 687-8745) has restaurants, bars, discos, and a pool. Set on the E tip, the luxury-priced resort of **Bávaro Beach** and **Bávaro Gardens** (tel. 682-2161/2166, 686-5797) is the largest hotel: a total of 1,200 rooms faces a two-km beach. Facilities here include closed-circuit color TV, minimarket, clinic, pool, and other water sports. Others are the 126-room **Bávaro Golf** (tel. 686-5797) and the 168-room **Bávaro Casino** (686-5797). Comprising 700 suites, the **Melía Bávaro** (tel. 221-2311, fax 686-5427) opened in 1991. It has gardens, mangroves, two pools, four lighted tennis courts, water sports, five restaurants, and a disco. The **Caribbean Village Bávaro** at Cabeza de Toro will open in approximately Jan. 1995 and will have 450 rooms, a disco, two restaurants, a pool, and a beach club. At Playa de Arena Gorda, the 360-room **Hotel Riu Taino** (tel. 221-7515/2290, fax 685-9537) is a German-run luxurious resort; its sister is the 374-room **Hotel Riu Naiboa** (tel. 221-2290, fax 685-9537). Rooms have phones, satellite TVs, a/c, and terraces. From Punta Cana beaches run almost continuously for 20 mi. to Miches; the waves can be large with strong undertow. **Macao:** To get away from it all continue on to Macao which, save for a few *cabañas*, is relatively undeveloped. **Hacienda Barbara** (tel. 685-2594, 565-7176) is an exclusive family-style inn featuring tennis, pool, and beach. It borders a 1,000-acre coconut plantation. In the US call (516) 944-8060. The only low-priced place here is **Coco's Cabañas** which charges about $3, but bargaining is necessary to get this price. Bring your own water, and watch out for stingrays and the dangerous undertow. To get here, take a *camioneta* from Higüey.

The Rest of the South

The most populous as well as the most diverse region, the nation's S is sparsely populated outside of Santo Domingo. Although Santo

Domingo has become a center of finance and government, the area in the extreme SW near the Haitian border and Laguna Enriquillo is semi-desert terrain with few houses and minimal agriculture. Locals here survive on sugarcane and coffee.

The East

La Romana

Located 112 km from Santo Domingo, just under the E hook of the nation's S coast, this city – once noted only for its sugar production – is now better known as a vacation resort. Casa de Campo is a specially developed complex for upper-class tourists. Altos de Chavon, set up on a plateau above the Rio Chavon, is an artists' village (complete with museum) built in 16th C Spanish-style. This city of 102,000 also has the nation's largest sugar refinery; its name, meaning "the scales," came about because cane growers brought their crops here to be weighed and purchased.

ECONOMIC HISTORY: La Romana became a sugar town when the existing mill was built in 1917. The plant has grown over the years and now produces half a million tons per year – the bulk of the sugar exported annually. In the early 1960s, Gulf & Western entered the picture. Investment by this gigantic conglomerate grew to $200 million and included sugar, cement, cattle, factories, and the tourist complex Casa de Campo. In an attempt to make La Romana into the "Showcase of the East," Gulf & Western poured an estimated $20 million into the town. Although the corporation changed the face of the city, it employed administrators educated in the rough atmosphere of Batista's Cuba. Gulf & Western was charged with bribery and intimidation. The independent labor unions were destroyed and a company union substituted. The nearby free trade zone was also dominated by Gulf & Western.

ACCOMMODATIONS: In town there are the following places to stay. **Hotel Frano** (tel. 550-4744), Pd. Abréu 9, charges around $15 with a/c; the **Hotel Bolivar** (tel. 550-2626), Pd. Abréu 61; the **Hotel Condado** (tel. 556-3010), Altagracia 55; the **Hotel Persia** (tel. 550-0816), G. Luperón 45; **Hotel Jupiter** (tel. 556-5906), G. Luperón 122; the **Hotel Rendy** (tel. 556-

3540), Dr. T. Ferry 178; and the **Hotel Rincon Criollo,**(tel. 550-5525). There is also the **Hotel Adamay** (tel. 556-6102/6202), which is one km out of town enroute to San Pedro de Macorís and around priced $20. At Km. 4.5 on the way to San Pedro de Macorís, **Cabañas Tio Tom** (tel. 556-6212, fax 556-6201) has 72 comfortable rooms with a/c, a pool, and a disco. The stone and wood 58-rm. *bohio*-style **Dominicus Beach Village** (tel. 533-4897) has rooms with hammocks and raised platform beds, and cascade-style showers. It has a virtually private beach. Less than half an hour from Casa de Campo, **Apart-Hotel Casa de Campo** (tel. 566-7464, 567-2812) features swimming pool, bar, and restaurant.

SERVICES: Tricom is on C. Duarte and **Codetel** is in Parque Duarte. **Tropical Tours** (tel. 556-2636) is one local tour agency. **Banco Popular** is on C. Duarte and **Banco Nacional** borders Parque Duarte. **car rentals:** Contact Rentauto (tel. 556-4181), Honda (tel. 556-2609/3835), National (tel. 556-2512), or Nelly (tel. 556-2156).

Vicinity of La Romana

Casa de Campo

Spread out over 7,000 acres, this is the nation's preeminent tourist resort. It has been remodeled during 1994. Accommodation is available in more than a thousand hotel rooms and villas. There are 17 tennis courts , two 18-hole golf courses, a marina, and two conference rooms. Visit Playa Minitas for water sports such as windsurfing, snorkeling, and sailing as well as Hobie cats. Also available are deep-sea fishing, a sunset sail, river fishing, charter boating, tennis, golf, riding, polo, shooting. The Fitness Center provides racquetball, squash, aerobics and a fully-equipped gym with a Jacuzzi and sauna. Transportation is provided by shuttle bus, horse-drawn carriage, and golf cart. Rooms run from around $210 on up with an off-season low of about $100. A 10% service charge is added. Call (800) 223-6620 or (305) 856-5404 in the US or 682-2111 in the Dominican Republic.

Altos de Chavón

Designed in mock-Italian style and set on a hill 13 km (eight mi.) E of Casa de Campo, this $40 million creation – a cobblestone village which appears timeless – is like a theater set brought to life. Actually constructed in the 1960s, it has been artificially aged: stone-work and obelisks have been deliberately chipped. The "village" is wonderful to visit in the evening when lanterns illuminate the cobblestones. Silkscreen and photography are taught here, and paintings are exhibited. A free shuttle bus runs here from Casa de Campo every 15 min. **sights:** Named after Poland's patron saint in commemoration of the papal visit, the **Church of St. Stanislaus** overlooks the cliffs towering above the Río Chavon. Opened in 1981, the **Archaeological Museum** (open daily 9-9) exhibits indigenous artifacts collected by Dr. Samuel Pon. There are stone hatchets, clay pots, griddles used for baking *casabe* (cassava bread), heart-shaped vases, equipment used in ballgames, beads, and shells. Some of the most intriguing items are found in the Mythology and Art section. Taino religious worship centered around three *cemis* (idols) – one for crops, one to ensure painless childbirth, and one to bring sun or rain. Sex in Taino art was seen as being divine and mystical rather than crude and distasteful. The *cahoba*, the principal Taino religious ceremony involving inhalation of a hallucinogen, is spotlighted in one display. Note the *cemi* with a plate on its head for *cahoba* powder. The spatulas were used to cleanse the body prior to participation, and *dujos* are the special seats used in the ceremony. The **Chavón Art Galleries** exhibit works by artists from the Dominican Republic and around the world. The 5,000-seat **amphitheater** was inaugurated with a show by Frank Sinatra; Julio Iglesias, his Latin counterpart, has also appeared here.

ACCOMMODATION AND FOOD: The 10-rm. **La Posada Inn** has a pool. Two- and three-bedroom apartments are also available. There are five restaurants.

GETTING THERE: Buses and *publicos* run from Santo Domingo.

Boca de Yuma

Said to be the best point in all the Caribbean for blue marlin, this fishing village hosts a deep-sea fishing tournament in June. From here a road runs inland to Higüey. Some two km N of San Rafael de Yuma is the restored residence of Ponce de León, where he lived from 1505-1508, Also visit **Cueva de Berna** (Berna Cave) in the area.

Isla de Catalina

One of the nation's top dive spots, this island is accessible by boat from the La Romana marina. In recent years, it has become a target of cruise ships and some 200,000 tourists now arrive annually. If permission is obtained from the La Romana Naval Station in advance, one may camp here, but there are few facilities. Bring all of your own water and supplies. Offshore on the N side, there's a wall and reef.

Bayahibe

This fishing village is set on a small bay. Dive at the coral reef, which has a wide variety of sponges. Get here soon. The **Casa del Mar** tourism complex is slated for construction. **practicalities:** It can be reached either by taking a bus from Higüey and then a *motoconcho* or by taking a direct bus from La Romana. Accommodation here includes **Hotel Cabaña Milysade** and **Hotel Bayahibe**; both are priced at around $15. **Club Dominicus** (tel. 686-8720, fax 687-8583) is one km away. Set 10 km E of Bayahibe, the 129-rm. **Club Dominicus Beach** (tel. 686-5658) is an Italian-run tourist complex facing a beach. **food:** Eat at the **Bahía**, which has excellent lobster, or at the **Bayahibe** which has equally fine seafood.

Parque Nacional del Este

Set in the SE corner, this "National Park of the East" comprises portions of the mainland combined with oval-shaped Isla de Saona which is separated from the mainland by the Catuano canal. Some three to four ft. wide by 14 mi. long, the island has a few sandy beaches, tons of mosquitoes, and the two settlements of Adamanay (on the SW coast) and Punta Gorda (on the W coast) – but not much else. Adamanay was the settlement's original name; it was discovered by Michelle de Cuneo on Columbus's second voyage. Locals here survive through fishing and hunting pigeons and wild hogs. The park's beaches can only be reached by boat; Casa de Campo arranges tours. Bioluminescent Bahía de Catalina on the S coast displays orange and green whorls in its waters. Near Bayahibe in the Guaraguao area of the park, a number of caves have pre-Columbian indigenous carvings and drawings. **flora and fauna:** The area is comprised of tropical deciduous forest atop limestone. The endangered hutia and solenodon are also present. Manatees and bottlenose dolphins may be seen offshore. There are 112 species of birds. The endemic Antillean piculet is found in dry coastal areas, and the American oystercatcher lives around Punta Algibe on the mainland. Birds on Saona include the village weaver, the Hispaniolan lizard-cuckoo, the red-legged thrush, the black-crowned oriole, the black-crowned palm tanager, the palmchat, the limpkin, and the Antillean palm swift. Sea turtles and the rhinoceros iguana are also present.

PRACTICALITIES AND HIKING: A ranger cabin and office is at the park's W entrance near Bayahibe. A marked trail leads to a nearby cave that harbors bats and owls; rangers are available to guide visitors. Set near the town of Boca del Yuma, the E entrance has a ranger's cabin and a trail that runs parallel to the coast. Boats can dock at Adamanay on Saona. There are several trails on the island.

San Pedro de Macorís

Just 65 km E of Santo Domingo, this placid seaport (pop. 140,000) is set on the Río Higuamo surrounded by the sugar plantations which support it and by baseball fields which have fostered the sport; local youths regard baseball as the key to prosperity. The town supports the Universidad Central del Este (UCE) – whose medical school is reputed to be among the nation's best and has attracted many US students. It also supports a baseball stadium. One of the largest Industrial Free Zones is also located here. A nickname for locals is Serie 23 after the numeric code found on the *cedulas* (identification cards) belonging to inhabitants. **history:** The town was founded by a mixture of Italians, Germans, and Arabs in the 1870s. During the days of high sugar prices (up to 22¢ a pound) it was nicknamed "the Sultan of the East." In those prosperous days, Pan Am would fly its American Clipper hydroplanes from the US, landing in the Río Higuamo. These days the town has frequent electric blackouts. Never a favorite of Balaguer, as its inhabitants have consistently backed his opponents, it remains undeveloped in comparison to Santo Domingo and Santiago. Most streets remain unpaved, and the overall feeling is one of being in a country village. There isn't much here to attract the casual visitor.

SIGHTS: San Pedro's neoclassically-styled Church of St. Peter the Apostle serves as an orientation point; the bus terminal is right in front. The nicest place to walk is along the **Malecón**. Here, there are food stalls and you can watch the sea crash against the rocky crags.

A nearby sight is the **Cueva de las Maravillas** (Cave of the Marvels) which has a number of pre-Columbian paintings on its walls. Playa El Soco is suitable for swimming, and there's good fishing at the river by the small village of Cumayasa.

ACCOMMODATION: Inexpensive **Hotel Macorix-UCE** (tel. 529-3950,) has 28 a/c rooms, pool, disco, and tennis courts. Located on G. Deligne, in front of the Malecón and near the medical school, it provides special packages for students. Rates run around $17 s or d with fan and $25 s or d with a/c. Other hotels include **Hotel Datni** (tel. 529-4040), C. Toconal 6; **Hotel Macorís** (tel. 588-2530), C. Restauración 44; **Hotel Nuevo Central** (tel. 588-2304), C. San Francisco 49; **Hotel Olimpico** (tel. 588-3584); Av. Libertad (Carr. Nagua at Km 1); **Hotel del Jaya** (tel. 588-2705), San Francisco 40; and **Hotel Altagracia** (tel. 588-6470), Av. Libertad 132. **food:** One of the more attractive restaurants is **La Roco** which is on the Malecón right near UCE. The **Restaurant Club Nautico El Puerto**, on Av. Malecón at Enrique Rijo, specializes in seafood and flambé. The **De Marcos Cafeteria** is right under the Hotel Independencia. Others include **Restaurant Don Luis** and **Restaurant Osteria** on Av. 27 de Febrero; **Restaurant Don Ernesto** at Av. 27 de Febrero 155; **Restaurant Arias** at C. España 9; and **Restaurant Independencia** at Independencia 148.

ENTERTAINMENT: Seaview Disco is right on the Malecón.

INFORMATION: Call the **Ayuntamiento** at 529-3600 or the provincial government at 529-3309. **services:** The two **Codetel** offices are on Av. Independencia.

FESTIVALS AND EVENTS: *Guloyas* (Goliath), the local dance, was brought by the *Cocolocos*, immigrants from the Leeward and Windward islands. The dance known as *Momise* stems from the English mummer (masked dancing) tradition. Taking place on the June 29 *fiestas patronales* of San Pedro Apostol (St. Peter) as well as on other festive occasions, there are also three dance-dramas. Presenting a story similar to the St. George and the Dragon legend is *la danza del padre invierno* (the dance of father winter). There's also *la danza salvaje* (the wild dance), and *la danza de El Codril* which features a troupe of dancers linked arm-in-arm and divided into two rows. Costumes feature innumerable beads and mirrors. **baseball:** The town is known for its ballplayers, and the winter league games are still held here from Oct. to Jan. at Estadio Tetelo Vargas, with San Pedro favorites the Estrellas Orientales playing. Of the 300 or so Dominicans currently playing in the US major and minor leagues, more than half come from here. The Hiroshima Carp, a team from Japan's Central League, has been scouting in town, and its owner has announced plans to establish a $1.8 million baseball academy nearby.

The Costa Caribe

Boca Chica

About 30 km E of Santo Domingo and five min. from Las Americas International Airport, this is the capital's resort area; avoid coming here on weekends. Initially developing as a port in the 1930s because of its sugar mill, Boca Chica came into vogue in the 1960s before declining in the 1970s with the rise to preeminence of Puerto Plata. In recent years, however, its popularity appears to be reviving – with some even calling it "Playa St. Tropez." Europeans and French Canadians flock here. It has a spectacular beach and a shallow lagoon sheltered by reefs. At low tide you can walk out on to the reef or to the island of **La Matica** (The Little Tree). The larger **Los Piños** (The Pines) can be reached by swimming or by boat; it has its own private beach: La Escondida. Water sports available here include jet skiing, wind surfing, snorkeling, and scuba. Catamarans and pedal boats can also be rented. For deep-sea fishing contact **Club Andres** (tel. 685-4940).

ACCOMMODATION: The three-rm. **L'Horizon Hotel and Restaurant** (tel. 523-4375) is owned by Swiss expats. Also with only a few rooms, **Neptune's Club** (tel. 523-6703), secluded at the E end of the lagoon, offers a bar and restaurant. **Pensión Pequena Suiza** (tel. 523-4619), Av. Duarte 56, is another small hotel. **Don Juan Beach Resort** (tel. 523-4511, 687-9157; Apdo. 1348, Isabel la Catolica 162, Box 138, Santo Domingo) has 111 rooms. Facilities include restaurant, bar, pool, and water sports. In the US call (800) 922-4272 or (212) 432-1370. The all-inclusive **Boca Chica Beach Resort** (tel. 523-4521/4529, fax 523-4438), C. Juan Batista Vicini at 20 de Diciembre, features 209 apartments. In the US call (800) 828-8895. Also try 75-rm. **Sunset Beach Resort** (tel. 523-4580/4590, fax 523-4975) whose facilities includes a restaurant, solarium, and pool. In Santo Domingo call 523-4511 or fax 523-6422. The **Don Juan Beach Resort** (tel. 523-4511, fax 688-65271) charges from around $50 on up. Standard rooms have a/c, color TV, and phone; jr. suites and superior rooms are also available. In Santo Domingo call 687-9157. In the US, call (212) 432-1370, fax (212) 488-9580, or write One

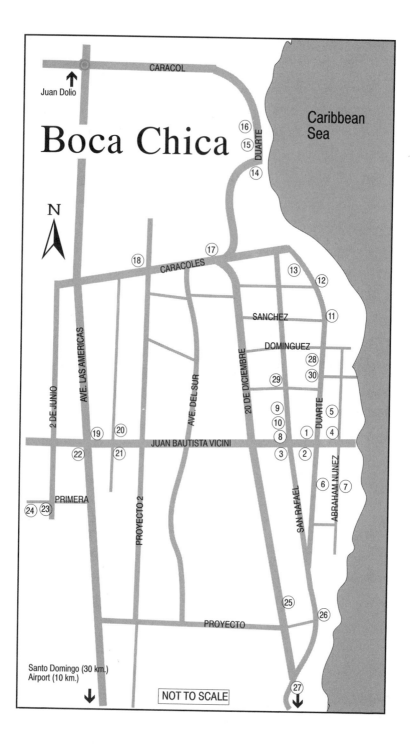

World Trade Center, Ste. 2747, NY, NY 10048. **El Cheveron** (tel. 523-4333), Av. Abraham Nuñez, charges from around $20. Run by AMHSA, the huge, all-inclusive and ultra-luxury priced **Hotel Hamaca Beach Resort** (tel. 523-4611, fax 532-6767; Los Piños 7, Santo Domingo), C. Duarte, is another option. In the US call (800) 472-3985 or in the DR (800) 955-0792. Others include **Hotel Ristorante Romagna Mia** (tel. 523-4647), C. Duarte 15; **Hotel Restaurant Macorís** (tel. 523-6242), C. Duarte 50; **Hotel Caney** (tel. 523-4314), C. Duarte 21; and **Hotel y Restaurant El Cheveron**, C. Duarte 54. The 23-cabaña **Hotel Fiordaliso** (tel. 523-4453) is on Autopista las Américas at Km 32. If you prefer to stay near the airport, there are a number of places, including the a/c **Tropicana Night Club Hotel-Villas** (tel. 596-8885/8835), Av. Las Américas

Boca Chica
1. Central Park/express bus stop for Santo Domingo
2. Post Office
3. Le Calypso Restaurant
4. Don Paco Guest House
5. McDeal Rent-a-Car
6. Western Union
7. Don Juan Beach Resort
8. Church
9. Police
10. Auberge La Fontaine de Soleil
11. Pequena Suiza Bar/Pensión
12. Portofino Bar & Restaurant
13. Codetel
14. Hamaca Resort
15. Mesón Isabela
16. Sunset Beach Resort
17. Pizzeria Dolce Vita
18. Taberna Alemana
19. Supermercado Santa Fe
20. Restaurant Terraza Quebec
21. Villa Sans Soucy
22. Don Juan Beach Resort
23. Alpha 3000 (auto rental)
24. Condominios Las Kasistas Del-Sol
25. Farmacia "Barbara María"
26. Boca Chica Resort & Beach Club
27. To Andrés (Boca Marina Yacht Club, DeMar Beach Club, Pop-eye Fisherman Club, Club Nautico)
28. Rte. 66 Restaurant

Km 8, which boasts 50 d rooms., 12 suites with marble floors, four apartments and pool, Jacuzzi, nightclub, and BBQ. **Mesón Isabela** (tel. 523-4224, fax 523-4136) is on C. Duarte 3. **Auberge La Fontaine de Soleil** (tel. 523-4679), C. Juan Batista Vicini 11, offers a pool and meals. **Villa Sans Soucy** (tel. 523-4461/4327, 800-463-0097, fax 523-4136) is at C. Juan Batista Vicini 48. It has a pool, bar, restaurant, and attractive rooms.

FOOD AND DINING: Supermercado Santa Fe is at C. Juan Batista Vicini 65. Local food is sold at *fritureras* on the beach including *yaniqueques* – johnny cakes. **Terraza Quebec**, C. Juan Batista Vicini 45, serves international dishes including seafood. On the same street, **Le Calypso** offers international specialties including lobster. At C. Caracol 15, **Dolce Vita** serves pizza and other Italian dishes. Try **L'Horizon** restaurant which has fondues or **Buxeda**, with excellent *centolla* (crab). **Portofino** is on C. Duarte. Popular watering hole **Route 66** (tel. 523-5744), C. Duarte 41, serves Indonesian specialties. **La Criolla Bar & Restaurant** offers Dominican food as well as entertainment.

ENTERTAINMENT: There are a large number of bars. Discos include **Golden Beach** and **Disco Elegancia Cumbre**. La Yola **Disco Club** is at Don Juan Beach Resort. The **El Guacamaya** is inside the Hotel Guamira, C. Abraham Nuñez 27.

SERVICES: Western Union is at C. Duarte 65. **Codetel** has its offices on C. J.B. Vicini. Established in 1967, the marina of the **Santo Domingo Club Naútico** is at the W end of the beach. It also offers water sports. For car rental contact **Alpha 3000** (tel. 523-6059) on C. Primera. **McDeal Rent-a-Car** (tel. 523-4414) is on C. Duarte near Juan Bautista Vicini. **diving:** Contact **Treasure Divers** (tel. 523-5320, fax 523-4444).

EVENTS: The town's *fiestas patronales* for San Rafael take place Oct. 24.

NEARBY BEACHES: Guayacanes and Embassy are popular.

FROM BOCA CHICA: Express buses to Santo Domingo leave regularly from the main square. To head E, walk up to the main highway and take a bus heading to the R.

Juan Dolio

Located E from Boca Chica, this resort development has plenty of hotels. It began developing as a tourist destination only in 1987 and a development association was formed in 1991. **practicalities:** The 152-unit **Punta Garza Bungalows** (tel. 529-8331, 526-3411) offers 46 rooms (in two-storey houses or cabañas) with kitchenettes and your choice of a/c or fan. Managed by AMHSA (tel. 562-7475, Los Piños 7, Santo Domingo), the all inclusive **Decámeron Beach Resort** (tel. 529-8531, 526-2307) has 280 rooms, pool, disco, tennis, children's playground, and water sports. In the US call (800) 223-9815. The **Ramada Guest House** (tel. 526-3310/2460) offers a bar, pool, and Jacuzzi. **Los Coquitos Beach Resort** (tel. 718-457-3211) has 80 one- and two-bedroom a/c apartments with color TV. Facilities include a restaurant, pool, and water sports. It's represented by **Prieto Tours** (tel. 586-3988). Both renting and selling one- and two-bedroom apartments, the 180-rm. **Metro Hotel** (tel. 526-1710/2811) is under the same management as the Embajador in Santo Domingo and Villas Doradas in Puerto Plata. Facilities include two restaurants, conference room, two swimming pools, Jacuzzi, lighted tennis courts, marina, and water sports. In the US call (800) 332-4872. or (212) 838-3322. The 56-rm. a/c **Playa Real** (tel. 526-1114) offers seaside swimming pool, coffeeshop, restaurant, tennis court, horseback riding, and a full range of water sports. Nearby, **Allen's** specializes in seafood; it's closed Mon. The 275-rm. a/c **Talanquera Hotel and Villas** (tel. 526-1510/1018) offers sauna, Jacuzzi, restaurants, disco, game room, horseback riding, tennis courts, all water sports, Olympic-sized pool, archery, and riflery. Condos and homesites are available. The **Hotel and Beach Resort Costa Linda** (tel. 526-3011/2011, fax 526-3601) has rooms from around $60 as well as more expensive cabinas. The expensive **Caribbean Village Costa Linda** (tel. 526-2161) has a pool. The 137-rm. **Marena Beach Resort** (tel. 526-2121, fax 526-1213, in Santo Domingo: 562-7475) is a "family-style" resort which has a pool and gardens. In the US call (800) 472-3985 and in the DR (800) 955-0792. Also try the 96-rm. **Hotel Embassy Beach Resort** at Playa Caribe (tel. 533-5401; José Contreras 98, Santo Domingo), the 77-room **Tropics** (tel. 526-2009), the 258-room **Villas Jubey Talanquera** (tel. 541-8431, 800-922-4272), **Sol y Mar** (tel. 529-8605), the **Hotel Ramada** (tel. 526-3310), and **Residencial Tamarindo** (tel. 526-1312). Finally, **Sotbe House Aparta Hotel** (tel. 526-3007) is at C. Central 66.

FOOD: There are a number of restaurants around. Try the **Oasis, BBQ, El Bambu, JR's,** and the **Quisqueya.**

SERVICES: In Juan Dolio, **Codetel's** office is at Centro Commercial Plaza Quisqueya. For diving information contact the **Neptuno Dive Center** (tel. 526-1473, fax 526-14410) and **Jerry's Dive Center** (tel. 526-1242). For tours contact **Venus Tours** (tel. 526-1197, fax 526-1340), C. Central 48. **car rentals:** Contact Budget (tel. 526-1907), General (tel. 529-8371), Honda (tel. 529-8221/4477), Metro (tel. 526-1706), or National (tel. 529-8656).

Parque Nacional Submarino La Caleta

La Caleta National Marine Park, is 22 km E of Santo Domingo and near the Santo Domingo airport. It was created in 1987 to protect a three mi. stretch of coast; the *Hickory* was sunk here, some ancient cannon and anchors were deposited next to it, and a reef has sprung up around them. The intention was to create an artificial reef to attract fish and so restock the waters emptied by local fishermen. Its crystal clear waters make it especially popular with underwater photographers. There's a small beach and Taino burial tombs; imitation carved stone Taino artifacts are on sale. A similar artificial reef has been created in Bahía de Ocoa, W of Santo Domingo. Displaying artifacts of the indigenous people, the museum of the same name is at the airport entrance. **diving:** To dive here contact **Actividades Marinas Del Caribe** (tel. 530-1837, unit 45; 541-1022). A one-day notice is necessary for reservations.

Spanish Vocabulary

Days of the Week

domingo	Sunday
lunes	Monday
martes	Tuesday
miercoles	Wednesday
jueves	Thursday
viernes	Friday
sabado	Saturday

Months of the Year

enero	January
febrero	February
marzo	March
abil	April
mayo	May
junio	June
julio	July
agosto	August
septiembre	September
octubre	October
noviembre	November
diciembre	December

Numbers

uno	one
due	two
tres	three
cuatro	four
cinco	five
seis	six
siete	seven
ocho	eight
nueve	nine
diez	ten
once	eleven
doce	twelve
trece	thirteen

catorce	fourteen
quince	fifteen
dieciseis	sixteen
diecisiete	seventeen
dieciocho	eighteen
dieci nueve	nineteen
veinte	twenty
veintiuno	twenty-one
veintidos	twenty-two
treinta	thirty
cuarenta	forty
cincuenta	fifty
sesenta	sixty
setenta	seventy
ochenta	eighty
noventa	ninety
cien	one hundred
cento uno	one hundred one
doscientos	two hundred
quinientos	five hundred
mil	one thousand
mil uno	one thousand one
dos mil	two thousand
un million	one million
mil milliones	one billion
primero	first
segundo	second
tercero	third
cuarto	fourth
quinto	fifth
sexto	sixth
septimo	seventh
octavo	eighth
noveno	ninth
decimo	tenth
undecimo	eleventh
duodecimo	twelfth
ultimo	last

Conversation

¿Como esta usted?	How are you?
Bien, gracias, y usted?	Well, thanks, and you?
Buenas dias.	Good morning.
Buenas tardes.	Good afternoon.
Buenas noches.	Good evening/night.
Hasta la vista.	See you again.
Hasta luego.	So long.
¡Buen suerte!	Good luck!
Adios.	Goodbye.
Mucho gusto de conocerle.	Glad to meet you.
Felicidades.	Congratulations.
Muchas felicidades.	Happy birthday.
Feliz Navidad.	Merry Christmas.
Feliz Año Nuevo.	Happy New Year.
Gracias.	Thank you.
Por favor.	Please.
De nada/con mucho gusto.	You're welcome.
Perdoneme.	Pardon me.
¿Como se llama esto?	What do you call this?
Lo siento.	I'm sorry.
Permitame.	Permit me.
Quisiera...	I would like...
Adelante.	Come in.
Permitame presentarle...	May I introduce...
¿Como se llamo usted?	What is your name?
Me llamo...	My name is...
No se.	I don't know.
Tengo sed.	I am thirsty.
Tengo hambre.	I am hungry.
Soy norteamericano/a	I am an American.
¿Donde puedo encontrar...?	Where can I find...?
¿Que es esto?	What is this?
¿Habla usted ingles?	Do you speak English?
Hablo/entiendo un poco español.	I speak/understand a little Spanish
¿Hay alguien aqui que hable ingles?	Is there anyone here who speaks English?
Le entiendo.	I understand you.
No entiendo.	I don't understand.
Hable mas despacio por favor.	Please speak more slowly.
Repita por favor.	Please repeat.

Telling Time

¿Que hora es?	What time is it?
Son las...	It's...
... cinco.	... five o'clock.
... ocho y diez.	... ten past eight.
... seis y cuaro.	... quarter past six.
... cinco y media.	... half past five.
...siete y menos cinco.	... five of seven.
antes de ayer.	the day before yesterday.
anoche.	yesterday evening.
esta mañana.	this morning.
a mediodia.	at noon.
en la noche.	in the evening.
de noche.	at night.
a medianoche.	at midnight.
mañana en la mañana.	tomorrow morning.
mañana en la noche.	tomorrow evening.
pasado mañana.	the day after tomorrow.

Directions

¿En que direccion queda...?	In which direction is...?
Lleveme a... por favor.	Take me to... please.
Llevame alla ... por favor.	Take me there please.
¿Que lugar es este?	What place is this?
¿Donde queda el pueblo?	Where is the town?
¿Cual es el mejor camino para...?	Which is the best road to...?
De vuelta a la derecha.	Turn to the right.
De vuelta a la isquierda.	Turn to the left.
Siga derecho.	Go this way.
En esta direccion.	In this direction.
¿A que distancia estamos	How far is it to...?
	de...?
¿Es este el camino a...?	Is this the road to...?
¿Es...	Is it...
... cerca?	...near?
...lejos?	...far?
...norte?	...north?
... sur?	... south?
... este?	... east?
... oeste?	... west?
Indiqueme por favor.	Please point.

Hagame favor de decirme donde esta...	Please direct me to...
... el telephono.	... the telephone.
... el excusado.	... the bathroom.
... el correo.	... the post office.
... el banco.	... the bank.
... la comisaria.	... the police station.

Accommodations

Estoy buscando un hotel....	I am looking for a hotel that's...
... bueno.	... good.
... barato.	... cheap.
... cercano.	... nearby.
... limpio.	... clean.

¿Dónde hay hotel, pensión, hospedaje?	Where is a hotel, pensión, hospedaje?
Hay habitaciones libres?	Do you have available rooms?
¿Dónde están los baños/ servicios?	Where are the bathrooms?

Quisiera un...	I would like a...
... cuarto sencillo.	... single room.
... cuarto con baño.	... room with a bath.
... cuarto doble.	... double room.

Puedo verlo?	May I see it?
Cuanto cuesta?	What's the cost?
Es demasiado caro!	It's too expensive!

Booklist

TRAVEL AND DESCRIPTION

Arciniegas, German. *Caribbean: Sea of the New World*. New York: Alfred A. Knopf, 1946.

Blume, Helmut. (trans. Johannes Maczewski and Ann Norton) *The Caribbean Islands*. London: Longman, 1976.

Bonsal, Stephen. *The American Mediterranean*. New York: Moffat, Yard and Co., 1912.

Hart, Jeremy C. and William T. Stone. *A Cruising Guide to the Caribbean and the Bahamas*. New York: Dodd, Mead and Company, 1982. Description of planning and plying for yachties. Includes nautical maps.

Morrison, Samuel E. *The Caribbean as Columbus Saw It*. Boston: Little and Co., 1964. Photographs and text by a leading American historian.

Radcliffe, Virginia. *The Caribbean Heritage*. New York: Walker & Co., 1976.

Sharpe, Kenneth Evan. *Peasant Politics: Struggle in a Dominican Village*. Baltimore: John Hopkins Press, 1977.

Ward, Fred. *Golden Islands of the Caribbean*. New York: Crown Publishers, 1967. A picture book for your coffee table. Beautiful historical plates.

Weil, Thomas E., et al. *Area Handbook for the Dominican Republic*. Washington, DC: Government Printing Office, 1973.

Wood, Peter. *Caribbean Isles*. New York: Time Life Books, 1975. Includes descriptions of such places as Pico Duarte in the Dominican Republic and the Blue Mountain region of Jamaica.

FLORA AND FAUNA

Humann, Paul. *Reef Fish Identification*. Jacksonville: New World Publications, 1989. This superb guide is filled with beautiful color photos of 268 fish. Information is included on identifying details, habitat and behavior, and on reaction to divers.

Humann, Paul. *Reef Creature Identification*. Jacksonville: New World Publications, 1992. The second in the series, this guide covers 320 denizens of the deep. Information is included on abundance and distribution, habitat and behavior, and identifying characteristics.

Humann, Paul. *Reef Coral Identification*. Jacksonville: New World Publications, 1993. Last in this indispensable series (which is now available boxed as "The Reef Set"), this book identifies 240 varieties of coral and marine plants. The different groups are also described in detail.

Hoppe, Jürgen. *The National Parks of the Dominican Republic*. Santo Domingo: Dirección Nacional de Parques, 1989. A photographic guide to the nation's parks.

Kaplan, Eugene. *A Field Guide to the Coral Reefs of the Caribbean and Florida*. Princeton, N.J.: Peterson's Guides, 1984.

de Oviedo, Gonzalo Fernandez. (trans. and ed. S.A. Stroudemire. *Natural History of the West Indies*. Chapel Hill: University of North Carolina Press, 1959.

Stockton de Nod, Annabelle. *Aves de la República Dominicana*. Santo Domingo, Museo de Historia Natural, 1978.

HISTORY

Bell, Ian. *The Dominican Republic: Politics and the Dominican Republic*. Boulder, CO: Westview Press, 1981. An important book for understanding the nation.

Calder, Bruce. *The Impact of Intervention: The Dominican Republic During the US Occupation of 1916-1924*. Austin, TX: The University of Texas, 1984. This fascinating study expores all facets of the US invasion and its aftermath.
Crassweller, Robert. *Trujillo, The Life and Times of a Caribbean Dictator*. New York: Macmillan, 1966.

Cripps, L.L. *The Spanish Caribbean: From Columbus to Castro*. Cambridge, Ma.: Schenkman, 1979. Concise history of the Spanish Caribbean from the point of view of a Marxist historian.

Deer, Noel. *The History of Sugar*. London: Chapman, 1950.

Hernan, Edward S. and Frank Brodhead. *Demonstration Elections: U.S.-Staged Elections in the Dominican Republic, Vietnam, and El Salvador*. Boston: South End Press, 1984.

Hovey, Graham and Gene Brown, eds. *Central America and the Caribbean*. New York: Arno Press, 1980. This volume of clippings from The New York Times, one of a series in its Great Contemporary Issues books, graphically displays Amnerican activities and attitudes toward the area. A goldmine of information.

Knight, Franklin W. *The Caribbean*. Oxford: Oxford University Press, 1978. Thematic, anti-imperialist view of Caribbean history.

Lowenthal, Abraham F. *The Dominican Intervention*. Cambridge, MA: Harvard U. Press, 1972.

Mannix, Daniel P. and Malcolm Cooley. *Black Cargoes*. New York: Viking Press, 1982. Details the saga of the slave trade.

Martin, John Bartlow. *Overtaken by Events: The Dominican Crisis from the Fall of Trujillo to the Civil War*. New York: Doubleday, 1966.

Rodman, Selden. *Quisqueya: A History of the Dominican Republic*. Seattle: University of Washington Press, 1964.

Ruck, Rob. *The Tropic of Baseball: Baseball in the Dominican Republic*. Meckler Press, 1991. Replete with anecdotes, this is a historical survey of the Dominican passion for its adopted national sport.

Sale, Kirkpatrick. *The Conquest of Paradise: Christopher Columbus and the Columbian Legacy*. New York: Knopf, 1991.

Slater, Jerome. *Intervention and Negotiation: The United States and the Dominican Republic*. New York: Harper and Row, 1970.

Szulc, Tad. *Dominican Diary*. New York: Delacorte Press, 1965. Welles, Sumner. *Naboth's Vinyard: The Dominican Republic, 1844-1924*. New York: Payson and Clarke, 1928.

Williams, Eric. *From Columbus to Castro: The History of the Caribbean*. New York: Random House, 1983. Definitive history of the Caribbean by the late Prime Minister of Trinidad and Tobago.

POLITICS AND ECONOMICS

Atkins, G. Pope. *Arms and Politics in the Dominican Republic.* Boulder, CO: Westview Press, 1980.

Atkins, G. Pope. and Larman Wilson. *The United States and the Trujillo Regime.* New Brunswick, NJ: Rutgers University Press, 1972.

Barry, Tom, Beth Wood, and Deb Freusch. *The Other Side of Paradise: Foreign Control in the Caribbean.* New York: Grove Press, 1984. A brilliantly and thoughtfully written analysis of Caribbean economics.

Black, Jan Knippers. *The Dominican Republic: Politics and Development in an Unsovereign State.* Boston: Allen & Unwin, 1986. A fine introduction to the nation covering history, government, and economy.

Blanshard, Paul. *Democracy and Empire in the Caribbean.* New York: The Macmillan Co., 1947.

Bosch, Juan. *The Unfinished Experiment: Democracy in the Dominican Republic.* New York: Praeger, 1963.

Diederich, Bernard. *Trujillo: The Death of the Goat.* Boston: Little, Brown, and Co., 1978.

Kryzanek, Michael J. and Howard J. Wiarda. *The Politics of External Influence in the Dominican Republic.* New York: Praeger, 1988. A sweeping, well-written overview of US intervention in the Dominican Republic along with history and recent economics.

Matthews, Thomas G. and F.M. Andic, eds. *Politics and Economics in the Caribbean.* Río Piedras: Institute of Caribbean Studies, University of Puerto Rico, 1971.

Mitchell, Sir Harold. *Caribbean Patterns.* New York: John Wiley and Son, 1972. Dated but still a masterpiece. The best reference guide for gaining an understanding of the history and current political status of nearly every island group in the Caribbean.

Roosevelt, Theodore. *Colonial Policies of the United States.* Garden City: Doubleday, Doran, and Co., 1937.

Wiarda, Howard. *The Dominican Republic: Nation in Transition.* New York: Praeger, 1968.

Wiarda, Howard. *Dictatorship and Development: The Methods of Control in Trujillo's Dominican Republic.* Gainesville: University of Florida Press, 1970. A brilliant treatise on the almost unbelievable methods and economic policies employed by the Trujillo regime.

Wiarda, Howard and Michael J. Kryzanek. *The Dominican Republic: A Caribbean Crucible.* Boulder, CO: Westview Press, 1982. Another fine introduction to the nation.

ART, ARCHITECTURE, AND ARCHAEOLOGY

Buissert, David. *Historic Architecture of the Caribbean.* London: Heinemann Educational Books, 1980.

Gosner, Pamela. *Caribbean Georgian.* Washington D.C.: Three Continents Press, 1982. A beautifully illustrated guide to the "Great and Small Houses of the West Indies."

MUSIC

Bergman, Billy. *Hot Sauces: Latin and Caribbean Pop.* New York: Quill, 1984. Includes a brief mention of *merengue.*

Dominican Republic Glossary

agregado – refers to the sugarcane workers who, up until the late 1940s, labored under the feudal system wherein wages were paid partially in goods and services received.

anatto – A small tree whose seeds, coated with orange red dye, are used to color cooking oil, commonly used in the preparation of Caribbean cuisines.

areytos – epic songs danced to by the Tainos.

asopao – a soupy rice dish containing beef, chicken, fish, or other seafood.

bacalao – dried salt cod, once served to slaves.

balneario – a government-administered beach area.

barrio – a city district.

bohio – Taino Indian name for thatched houses; now applied to the houses of country dwellers.

bola, bolita – the numbers racket.

bomba – Musical dialogue between dancer and drummer.

botanicas – stores on the Spanish speaking islands which sell spiritualist literature and paraphernalia.

calabash (calabaza) – small tree native to the Caribbean whose fruit, a gourd, has multiple uses when dried.

callaloo – Caribbean soup made with callaloo greens.

callejón – narrow side street; path through the cane fields.

campesino – peasant; lower-class rural dweller.

canita – the "little cane," bootleg rum (also called pitorro.)

carambola – see star apple.

Caribs – original people who colonized the islands of the Caribbean, giving the region its name.

carretera – a road or highway (abbreviated Carr. in the text)

caudillo – Spanish for military general.

cassava – staple crop indigenous to the Americas. Bitter and sweet are the two varieties. Bitter must be washed, grated, and baked in order to remove the poisonous prussic acid. A spongy cake is made from the bitter variety as is cassareep, a preservative which is the foundation of West Indian pepperpot stew.

cays – Indian-originated name which refers to islets in the Caribbean.

century plant – also known as karato, coratoe, and maypole. Flowers only once in its lifetime before it dies.

cerro – hill or mountain.

chorizo – Spanish sausage.

compadrazgo – the system of "co-parentage" which is used to strengthen social bonds.

conch – large edible mollusk usually pounded into salads or chowders.

cuerda – unit of land measure comprising 9/10ths of an acre.

cutlass – the Caribbean equivalent of the machete. Originally used by buccaneers and pirates.

duppy – ghost or spirit of the dead which is feared throughout the Caribbean. Derives from the African religious belief that a man has two souls. One ascends to heaven while the other stays around for a while or permanently. May be harnessed for good or evil through obeah. Some plants and birds are also associated with duppies.

escabeche – Spanish and Portuguese method of preparing seafood.

espiritismo – spiritualism.

fiestas patronales – patron saint festivals which take place on Catholic islands.

guava – indigenous Caribbean fruit, extremely rich in vitamin C, which is eaten raw or used in making jelly.

guayacan – the tree lignum vitae and its wood.

güiro – rasp-like musical instrument of Taino Indian origin which is scratched with a stick to produce a sound.

langosta – spiny lobster (really a crayfish) native to the region.

lechon asado – roast pig.

naranja – sour orange; its leaves are used as medicine in rural areas.

padrinos – godparents.

pasteles – steamed banana leaves stuffed with meat and other ingredients.

pastelitos – small meat-filled turnovers.

personalismo – describes the charisma of a Latin politician who appears and acts as a father figure.

pinoños – deep fried plantain rings stuffed with spiced ground beef and other fillings.

plebiscite – direct vote by the people on an issue.

plena – form of dance.

poinciana – beautiful tropical tree which blooms with clusters of red blossoms during the summer months. Originates in Madagascar.

público – shared taxi found on the Spanish speaking islands.

sancocho (sancoche) – stew made with a variety of meats and vegetables; found in the Spanish speaking islands.

santos – carved representations of Catholic saints.

sea grape – West Indian tree, commonly found along beaches, which produces green, fleshy, edible grapes.

sensitive plant – also known as mimosa, shame lady, and other names. It will snap shut at the slightest touch.

surrillos – fried cornmeal-and-cheese sticks.

tachuelo – a variety of tropical hardwood.

taro – tuber also known as sasheen, tannia, malanga, elephant's ear, and yautia.

trigueno – ("wheat colored"). Denotes a mulatto and differentiates brunettes from blondes.

velorio – Catholic wake.

zemi (cemi) – idol in which the personal spirit of each Arawak or Taino Indian lived. Usually carved from stone.

Index

Accommodations: 83-84
Acuario Nacional: 118
African influence: 48-49
Agriculture: 45-47
Agroindustries: 47
Aguas Blancas: 161
Airports: 101, 142
Alcázar de Colón: 108
Alcohol: 71-72
Altagracia Church, Higüey: 224
Altos de Chavón: 228-229
Amber: 91
American influence: 49
Anacaona: 21
Apart-hotels: 83
Art galleries: 139
Arts: 59-60
Ataranza, La: 110
Audencia , the: 21
Azua: 147-148
Bachata: 62
Báez, Buenaventura: 22-23
Balaguer, Joaquin: 29, 31-33, 34-36
Bambúla: 64
Baní: 147
Banica: 150
Barahona: 149-150
Bargaining: 92
Baseball: 76-77
Basilica de Nuestra Señora de la
  Merced: 223
Bayahibe: 230
Beaches: 74
Biblioteca Nacional: 116
Birds: 10-11
Black market: 89
Blanco, Jorge: 33-34
Boca Chica: 233-236
Boca de Yuma: 229
Bonao: 155
Bosch, Juan: 30, 35, 52
Botanical Gardens: 116
Bowling: 133
Broadcasting: 87
Bus routes: 80-81
Buses: 80-81
Buying land: 94

Cabarete: 198-201
Cabral, Donald Reid: 30, 36
Cacao: 47
Camping: 85
Caonabo: 21
Capilla de Nuestra Señora de Los
  Remedios: 110
Carnavál: 63
Casa de Bastidas: 109
Casa de Campo: 228
Casa del Cordón: 111
Catedral Primada de America:
  106-107
Catholicism: 30, 56-58
Cayo Levantado: 210
Centro de Los Heroes: 120
Chapel of the Remedies: 110
Christmas: 64-65
Cibao, the: 163-164
Ciénaga, La: 168, 169
Class structure: 50-51
Climate: 6
Coconut Coast: 224-225
Coffee: 46
Columbus Lighthouse: 118-119
Columbus, Bartolomew: 19
Columbus, Christopher: 18-19,
  118-120, 194
Compadrazgo: 53
Conduct: 93-96
Constanza: 159-161
Constitutionalists, the: 31
Coral reefs: 14-18
Cordillera Central: 155-164
Costa Caribe: 233-238
Costa del Coco: 224-225
Costambar: 179-180
Crafts: 59-60, 90-91
Credit cards: 90
Cueva del Paseo de los Indios: 117
Cultural differences: 93-94
Cultural Plaza, Santo Domingo:
  114-115
Customs: 92-93
Dance: 61
de Ovando, Nicolás: 19-20
Deep-sea fishing: 75

Dining: 72-73
Direccion Nac. de Parques: 138
Divorces: 89
Dominicans, the: 48-55
Driving: 82-83
Duarte, Juan Pablo: 22
Duty-free shopping: 91
Duty-free zones: 41-42, 43
Economy: 39
El Conde: 103
Elections: 38
Elias Piña: 151
Enriquillo: 21
Environmental conduct: 95-96
Epiphany: 62
Evangélicos: 58
Expenses: 77-78
Fanjul family: 42-43
Farming: 45-47
Faro a Colón: 118-119
Fauna; 9
Faxes: 87
Festivals: 61
Fiestas Patronales: 65-67
Fish: 12
Fishing: 44-45, 75
Flora: 8-9
Food: 67-73
Foreign investment: 41-42
Forestry: 44-45
Fortaleza de San Felipe: 175
Fortaleza Ozama: 108-109
Fruit: 70-71
Ga Ga: 63
Galeria de Arte Moderno: 115
Gambling: 133
Gazcue: 113
Geography: 1-6
Getting around: 80-83
Getting there: 78-79
Goat Island: 152-153
Golf: 76
Government: 37-38
Grí-Grí Lagoon: 202
Gulf & Western: 42
Guzmán, Antonio: 32
Haiti: 21-22
Haitian occupation: 22
Haitians, the: 23, 51-53
Health: 88, 89

Heureaux, Ulises: 23-24
Higüey: 223-224
History: 18-37
Holy Week: 63
Horseback riding: 76
Hospital-Iglesia de San Nicólas
   de Bari: 113
Hotels: 83-84
Humpback whales: 11
Hurricanes: 6-7
Hutia: 11
Iglesia de Carmen: 112
Indians, the: 18, 48
Information: 85
Isabel de Torres: 175
Isla Cabritos: 152-153
Jabaracoa: 157-159
Jaragua National Park: 153-154
Jardin Botánico Nacional: 117
Jellyfish: 13-14
Jimaní: 153
Johnson, Lyndon: 30-31
Juan Dolio: 237-238
Jutía: 11
Kennedy, John. F.: 30
La Caleta National Marine Park:
   236
La Isabela: 188-189
La Romana: 227-228
La Vega: 156-157
Laguna Enriquillo y Parque
   Nacional Isla Cabritos: 152-153
Lakes: 4
Land, the:1-6
Language: 58-59
Larimar: 91
Las Navidades: 64-65
Las Noches de Vela: 62
Las Terrenas: 214-220
Laundry: 86
Limón: 214
Livestock: 44
Los Haitises National Park:
   221-223
Lowlands: 1-4
Luperón: 181
Macao: 225
Majluta, Jacobo: 34-35
Manatees:10-11
Mangroves: 9

Manufacturing: 43-44
Marine life: 10-18
Measurements: 98-99
Media: 87
Merengue Festival: 63-64
Merengue: 60-61
Military, the: 55
Minerals: 40, 44
Mining: 44
Moca: 171
Monabao: 158, 164
Money: 89
Monte Cristi National Park:
190-191
Monte Cristi: 189-190
Motoconchas: 81-82
Motorbikes: 81-82
Mountains: 4-6
Museo de Amber: 175
Museo de Las Casas Reales: 110
Museo del Hombre Dominicano:
115
Museo Duartino: 108
Museo Maritimo: 110
Museo Nacional de Historia
Nacional: 116
Museo Nacional de Historia
y Geographica: 116
Museo Numismatico: 116
Museum of the Dominican Man:
115
Music: 60-61
Musical instruments: 60, 62
Nagua: 205
National Library: 116
National Pantheon: 110
National Park of the East: 230-2319
National parks and reserves: 99
National Theater: 116
Newspapers: 87
Organization of American States:
29
Package tours: 79
Palacio Nacional: 113
Palmar de Ocoa: 147
Panteón Nacional: 110
Parque Independencia: 103
Parque Los Tres Ojos de Agua: 117
Parque Mirador del Sur: 117

Parque Nacional Armando
Bermúdez: 162-163
Parque Nacional del Este: 230-231
Parque Nacional Jaragua: 153-154
Parque Nacional José le Carmen
Ramírez: 162-163
Parque Nacional Los Haitises:
221-223
Parque Nacional Monte Cristi:
190-191
Parque Nacional Sierra de
Bahoruco: 151
Parque Nacional Submarino La
Caleta: 238
Parque Zoológico Nacional: 117
Paseo de Los Indios: 117
Patron Saint Festivals: 65-67
Peña Gómez: 35, 36, 53
Photography: 99
Pico Duarte: 163-164
Playa Cofresí: 182-183
Playa Dorada: 173-178, 184-185
Playa Grande: 204
Playa Las Galeras: 214
Playa Rincón: 214
Plaza de la Cultura: 114-115
Political parties: 38-39
Political structure: 28-29, 37-38
Polo: 76
Population: 50
Portillo: 216-217
Postal service: 87
Públicos: 80-81
Puerto Plata: 173-187
Punta Cana: 225
Punta Rucia: 176, 182
Racial prejudice: 53
Rainfall: 6-8
Redonda and Limón Lagoons
Scientific Reserves: 223
Religion: 55-58
Renting a car: 82
Reptiles: 9
Reserva Cientifica Natural de Villa
Elisa: 191
Reserva Científica Natural Laguna
de Rincón: 151
Reserva Científica Natural Laguna
Redonda y Laguna Limón: 223

Reserva Científ. Valle Nuevo: 161
Restoration Day: 64
Río San Juan: 201-203
Rivers: 4
Roosevelt, Theodore: 24
Rosarios: 57
Royal Plain: 4
Ruinas de San Francisco: 111
Sailing: 74
Samaná Peninsula: 207-213
San Cristóbal: 145-147
San José de las Matas: 172
San José de Ocoa: 160
San Juan de la Maguana: 150
San Pedro de Macorís: 231-233
Sánchez: 214
Santa Bárbara de Samaná: 209-212
Santa Cerro: 156
Santana, Pedro: 22-23
Santiago de los Caballeros:
   165-171
Santo Domingo: 101-143
Santos: 57-58
Scuba: 75
Sea turtles: 11-12
Seafood: 69-70
Semana Santa: 63
Services: 85-88
Shopping: 90-91
Snorkeling: 74-75
Solenodon: 11
Sosúa: 191-199
Spain: 18-23, 49
Spanish influence: 49
Sponges: 13
Sporting events, Sto Domingo: 133
Sports: 74-77
Sugarcane: 26, 45-46
Surfing: 75

Swimming: 74
Taxes: 84
Taxis: 81-82, 103-104
Teatro Nacional: 116
Telephone service: 86-87
Tennis: 76
Theft: 94-95
Torre de Homenaje: 109
Tourism: 42, 43
Tourist cards: 85
Tours: 83
Traveling with children: 95
Trees: 8-9
Trujillo, Rafael: 24, 25-29, 37, 40,
   46, 50, 55-56, 145, 146, 151, 159,
   163, 168
Trujillo, Ramfis: 29, 30
Turtles: 11-12
Union International Airport: 174
Unions: 40
United States, the: 24-25
Universidad Autonomal Santo
   Domingo: 120
Valleys:1-2
Vega Real: 4
Vegetarian food: 73
Villa Elisa Natural Reserve: 191
Visas: 85
Voodoo: 58
Wages: 40
Waterfalls: 155, 158, 160, 161, 179,
   210, 211, 214, 218
Wessín y Wessín, Col. Elias: 30
Whales, humpback: 11
Whales: 207, 215
What to take: 97
Windsurfing: 75
Zoo: 117